GERMAN ARMY UNIFORMS OF WORLD WAR II

A PHOTOGRAPHIC GUIDE TO CLOTHING, INSIGNIA AND KIT

STEPHEN BULL

OSPREY
PUBLISHING

OSPREY PUBLISHING
Bloomsbury Publishing Plc

Kemp House, Chawley Park, Oxford OX2 9PH, UK
29 Earlsfort Terrace, Dublin 2, Ireland
1385 Broadway, 5th Floor, New York, NY 10018, USA
Email: info@ospreypublishing.com
www.ospreypublishing.com

OSPREY is a trademark of Osprey Publishing Ltd

First published in Great Britain in 2021

A catalogue record for this book is available from the British
Library.

Print ISBN: 978 1 4728 3806 3
ePub: 978 1 4728 3805 6
ePDF: 978 1 4728 3804 9
XML: 978 1 4728 3803 2

Index by Zoe Ross
Originated by PDQ Digital Media Solutions, Bungay, UK
Printed and bound in India by Replika Press Private Ltd.

22 23 24 25 26   10 9 8 7 6 5 4 3 2

Front cover: An NCO's *Feldbluse* (see page 20). This and back
cover images ©Stephen Bull.

Osprey Publishing supports the Woodland Trust, the UK's
leading woodland conservation charity.

To find out more about our authors and books visit www.
ospreypublishing.com. Here you will find extracts, author
interviews, details of forthcoming events and the option to
sign up for our newsletter.

ACKNOWLEDGEMENTS

Many institutions and individuals have helped to make this
book possible. Particular thanks are due to the Imperial War
Museum, London; the Bundesarchiv Koblenz; the Musée
Royal de l'Armée et d'Histoire Militaire, Brussels; the
Deutsches Historisches Museum, Berlin; the Sotamuseo,
Helsinki; the Muzeum II Wojny Światowej, Gdańsk; and the
Armémuseum, Stockholm. I should also like to thank
Europeana, the European Union digital library and platform
for cultural heritage. Personal thanks go to Mike Seed, Andrew
Taylor, Lisa Thomas and Martin Markelius.

AUTHOR'S NOTE

In describing German Army uniforms, weapons and
equipment of World War II, German, British and American
words and phrases in use prior to the end of the war in May
1945 have been preferred. Terms applied retrospectively have
been avoided wherever possible. The Select Bibliography at the
end of this volume is divided into primary sources and post-
war works. Evidence derived from German documents or
photographs dating from before May 1945 is given precedence.
Illustrations and photographs are drawn from the author's
collection unless otherwise specified.

IMAGES

All images are ©Stephen Bull unless otherwise acknowledged.

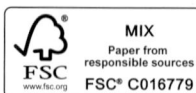

FSC
MIX
Paper from
responsible sources
www.fsc.org   FSC® C016779

CONTENTS

INTRODUCTION   6

CHAPTER 1: UNIFORM   15
Dienstrock, *Feldbluse* and *Waffenrock*
Officers' Dress
Markings and Orders of Dress
Quality and Change
The 1944 Uniform
Other Issue Clothing

CHAPTER 2: HEADGEAR   49
Peaked and Field Caps
Tropical Headgear
The Steel Helmet
Parade Helmets and the Panzer Beret

CHAPTER 3: PERSONAL EQUIPMENT   77
Rucksacks
Digging in and the Tent
Anti-gas Equipment
Food, Drink and *Brotbeutel*
Personal and Pocket Items

CHAPTER 4: SMALL ARMS   125
Rifles
Pistols
Submachine Guns
Automatic and Semi-automatic Rifles

Grenades
Edged Weapons

CHAPTER 5: SUPPORT AND SPECIAL WEAPONS 157
Machine Guns
Mortars
Anti-tank Weapons

CHAPTER 6: SPECIAL CLOTHING AND EQUIPMENT 185
Tanks and Motorized Uniforms
Tropical Uniform
Gebirgsjäger Uniform
Winter Clothing
Other Camouflage Clothing
Women's Uniforms

CHAPTER 7: HEER MEDALS AND AWARDS 219
Awards Sanctioned in 1939
Campaign Awards
Combat Badges
Senior Grades of the *Ritterkreuz* and the *Deutsches Kreuz*
Manufacture, Certification and Pricing

SELECT BIBLIOGRAPHY 247
INDEX 249

OPPOSITE The development of military uniform, 1670–1941, is depicted in this illustration from *Signal*, the international magazine arm of Wehrmacht (armed forces) propaganda. Smartness, historical continuity and the complementary influences of civil and military fashion are shown to culminate in the German uniform of World War II.

1670

1703

1680

1701

1760

1762

1790

1801

1812

1898

1917

1941

1853

1941

1868

INTRODUCTION

It is a remarkable fact that although the Third Reich was defeated as long ago as May 1945, its uniforms, weapons and equipment retain much fascination and emotive power. The subject of this book, the Heer (Army), was just one – though arguably the most important – of the German armed forces, collectively referred to, together with the Kriegsmarine (Navy) and Luftwaffe (Air Force), as the Wehrmacht (armed forces). Despite its exponential growth in the late 1930s, the Heer did not suddenly spring into existence after the Nationalsozialistiche Deutsche Arbeiterpartie (NSDAP: National Socialist German Workers' Party, commonly referred to as the Nazi Party) took power in 1933. As an arm of the German nation it drew on the traditions of the forces of the old German states, especially Prussia, the Imperial German Army (disbanded after World War I), and the Reichsheer (National Army) of the Weimar Republic (1918–33). Given the potential breadth of the subject, this book will focus on the individual: the uniform, weapons, equipment and other small items worn or carried by the German soldier. Vehicles and non-portable items are omitted, as are foreign Heer units and the small number of Heer parachutists raised in 1937 and incorporated into the Luftwaffe in 1939.

Even considering only portable items, it is obvious that Heer uniforms, weapons and equipment show huge variety and change over time; but arguably there are only three essential reasons for this: the impact of technology; increasing problems of supply; and the growing politicization of a force, which, though unarguably a bastion of conservatism, came under increasing pressure to reflect the totalitarian values of the Nazi state. Academic research has focused on this last reason with a variety of conclusions, but the crux of the matter is the dynamic relationship between Army and State. This was also true at the level of the individual soldier. In 1933, Heer recruits enlisted voluntarily into a very small, professional and essentially defensive army. By 1945, however, a young

Designed by the artist Paul Casberg (1883–1945), the first new Heer *Fahnen* ('colours' or unit flags) since before World War I were bestowed in March 1936. Dismounted battalion-sized formations acquired square *Fahnen*, while mounted, horse-drawn and motorized units received swallow-tailed *Standarten* (standards). *Fahnen* were made from appliquéd and embroidered heavy-duty silk, with the Heer stylized eagle and swastika at the centre of a cross. The ground was in the *Waffenfarbe* (arm-of-service colour) with additional swastikas at the corners. *Fahnen* were only paraded at specific events such as unit inspections, ceremonies where the *Führer* was present, major military funerals, national flag days and the swearing-in of recruits. Depicted (clockwise from left) are *Fahnen* and *Standarten* of the infantry, artillery, *Gebirgsjäger* (mountain troops) and cavalry.

conscript had lived much of his life under the Nazi regime, and was very likely to have been a member of the Hitlerjugend (Hitler Youth) or to have performed uniformed labour service. Peacetime soldiering had given way to a brutal total war in which active participation was enforced by the threat of capital punishment. The Nazi Party now monopolized most aspects of life in wartime Germany, and to a greater or lesser extent recruits reflected this, as did their uniforms. It is not insignificant that when the Volkssturm (a nationwide people's militia) was called out in October 1944, it was organized by the Nazi Party rather than the Heer.

The 'Nazification' of Heer flags, insignia and awards was no accident. As a frustrated fine artist who might have made a capable, if temperamental, graphic designer, Adolf Hitler saw both colour and symbolism as important to his movement and mobilization of the masses from the start. The red, white and black colours of Imperial Germany struck the appropriate patriotic chord. The eagle was a perennial national symbol with roots in the Middle Ages and the

When recruits took their oath of allegiance, a few were selected to place one hand on the flag, raising the other while repeating the words. From August 1934, with Hitler both chancellor and president, the oath of loyalty unto death was taken to him personally. *Fahnenträger* (flag-bearers) were senior NCOs who used a baldric to support the flag, their marks of office being an *Ärmelabzeichen* (arm badge) of crossed flags and a ceremonial *Ringkragen* (gorget). The basic colour party was three, the *Fahnenträger* being accompanied by two officers.

ABOVE After the Anschluss (annexation) of Austria in March 1938, Austrian troops were integrated into the Heer; 44. Infanterie-Division – redesignated 44. Reichsgrenadier-Division *Hoch-und Deutschmeister* in 1943 – retained some of the old traditions. The Austrian Imperial flag paraded here was kept by the division's Infanterie-Regiment 134. (ullstein bild/ Getty Images)

ABOVE RIGHT Werner Freiherr von Fritsch (1880–1939), Oberbefehlshaber des Heeres (Supreme Commander of the Army) 1933–38, had served on the General Staff of the Imperial German Army in World War I. Forced to resign on 4 February 1938, he proceeded to the front in Poland where he was killed on 22 September 1939 during the siege of Warsaw.

Holy Roman Empire, and in the versions used by the Heer in the 1930s was updated with an art deco twist. The swastika, a symbol of both the Freikorps (military volunteer units) and the Nazi Party itself, became the central motif of the new German national flag.

What is less obvious about the relationship between the Heer, its uniform and the Nazi Party is that the uniform trade itself had links to Nazism. Skilled craftsmen and small businessmen were more likely to be Nazi Party members than the average German; suppliers

A *Hornist* (bugler) during manoeuvres, *c*.1934. The old Reichswehr uniform is worn with braided *Schwalbennester* ('swallow nests') on the shoulders and a World War I *Stahlhelm* (steel helmet) with a manoeuvre band around the crown.

OVERLEAF, TOP
A Heer *Musikkorps* (military band) on parade in Cologne, *c*.1940. The *Musikmeister* (bandmaster) stands to the left: the *Musiker* (musicians) wear *Schwalbennester* on their *Feldanzug* (field uniform). Brass and drums were ideal for marching tunes.

BELOW RIGHT A *Ringkragen* worn by an *Unteroffizier* (corporal) of Zugwach-Abteilung 508. The *Ringkragen* was a badge of office, authority or special duty, being worn by *Fahnenträger*, *Feldgendarmerie* and *Feldjägerkorps* (military police), station and train guards. The basic format was a stamped steel plate with chain neck suspension and usually a backing of cloth or card. The *Fahnenträger's Ringkragen* had a Heer eagle and swastika, oak-leaf wreath and flags; police *Ringkrägen* featured a large eagle with outstretched wings, and both military-police and guard-detachment *Ringkrägen* had detail picked out in luminous paint.

BELOW Actor Fritz Genschow (1905–77) wearing the *Waffenrock* (dress uniform) for the 1939 film *Drei Unteroffiziere* ('Three NCOs'), shot using elements of what would later become the *Großdeutschland* Division and the Panzer-Lehr-Division. Genschow plays the part of Unteroffizier Fritz Kohlhammer, described as 'a daredevil with a weakness for beautiful women'. In one scene Kohlhammer gives up his uniform for his friend.

Standarten und Flaggen

Standarte des Führers und Reichskanzlers

Vorderseite   Standarte des Reichsmarschalls   Rückseite

Hoheitszeichen des Chefs des Oberkommandos der Wehrmacht

Desgleichen wenn Generalfeldmarschall

Flagge des Oberbefehlshabers des Heeres*)

Flagge des Oberbefehlshabers der Kriegsmarine, sofern er nicht Groß-admiral ist**)

*) Flagge wird z. Zt. neben der Flagge des Generalfeldmarschalls weiter geführt
**) Großadmiralsflagge: Unter dem Eisernen Kreuz zwei gekreuzte Großadmiral-stäbe, auf dem Eisernen Kreuz ein goldgelber, braun gezeichneter Wehrmachtadler

ABOVE LEFT Uniforms were integral to Prussian society, from the age of Frederick the Great (r. 1740–86) to Imperial Germany (1871–1918). In the Third Reich many organizations acquired new and distinctive attire. This postcard by the artist Gert Gagelmann is from the series *Frauen schaffen für Euch* ('Women Working for You').

ABOVE The flags of highest command, from a manual of 1942. From top: the *Führer Standarte*; both sides of the *Reichsmarschall Standarte;* the *Wimpeln* (pennants) of the Wehrmacht commanders: bottom left: *Oberbefehlshaber des Heeres*; bottom right: commander of the Kriegsmarine (Navy).

LEFT Following uniformed labour service and basic training, former members of the Hitlerjugend (Hitler Youth) are equipped during induction into Ersatz-Brigade *Großdeutschland*, January 1944. Kit is carried wrapped in a *Zeltbahn* (shelter-quarter): the *Feldbluse* (field blouse), foreground, bears the *Großdeutschland Ärmelstreifen* (cuff-title). (Bundesarchiv, Bild 183-J09127, Foto: Schwahn, Ernst)

The 14 *Waffenfarben* illustrated in *Die Wehrmacht* magazine soon proved inadequate in number for a growing Heer with increasing specialisms. *Kupferbraun* (copper-brown) was introduced for reconnaissance battalions and *Orangerot* (orange-red) for *Militärpolizei* in 1939; *Bordo* (Bordeaux red), used by smoke units, also covered gas formations and, later, rocket units. *Schützen* (motorized rifle) regiments took *Weissengrün* (grass green), a hue subsequently applied to *Panzergrenadier* units. *Heeresgeistliche* (Army chaplains) had violet, and *Hellgrau* (light grey) was assigned to propaganda companies from 1943.

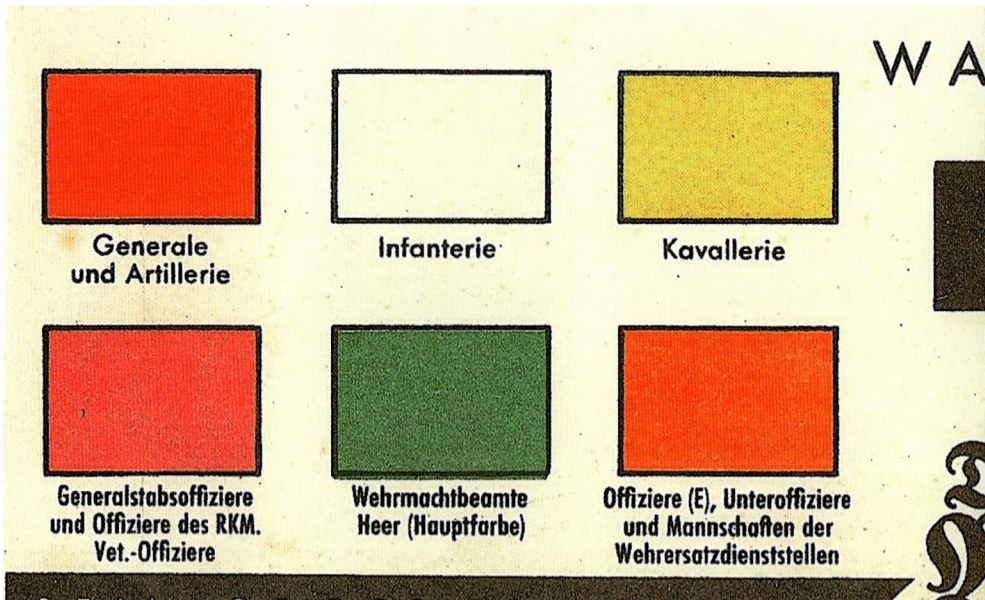

Generale und Artillerie

Infanterie

Kavallerie

Generalstabsoffiziere und Offiziere des RKM. Vet.-Offiziere

Wehrmachtbeamte Heer (Hauptfarbe)

Offiziere (E), Unteroffiziere und Mannschaften der Wehrersatzdienststellen

W A

FROHE WEIHNACHT

1939

1940

SO ÄNDERN SICH DIE ZEITEN

WH 11556

WH 11556

AUS DER HEIMAT

NACH

ENFARBEN

Nachrichtentruppe

Kraftfahr- und Fahrtruppen

Kraftfahr- kampftruppen

Nebeltruppen

Jäger und Neben- farbe für Apotheker

Sanitätsoffiziere und San.-Abteilungen

Besatztuch f. Schirmmützen, Rock-, Blusen- u. Mantelkrager Ärmelaufschläge am Rock

of Heer uniform also sold their wares to Nazi Party organizations and Jewish tailoring concerns were profitably 'Aryanized'. Otto Dietrich (1897–1952), publisher of the uniform trade journal *Uniformen-Markt*, was also Press Chief of the Nazi Party from February 1934 and Reich Press Chief of the Government from November 1937, and by 1941 ranked as an *SS-Obergruppenführer* (lieutenant general). World War II threw together industrial production, research and the Nazi state, which determined the allocation of resources and prices.

Virtually everything associated with the Heer has been reproduced or copied since 1945. These copies vary from the crude and readily apparent to the near-perfect. Though much has been manufactured purely for profit, there is also a wide range of material created for film and television use, for re-enactment groups and to fill gaps in exhibitions; in other instances, original pieces have been heavily restored or converted. Many items were also reused by other armies, either during World War II or after the end of hostilities.

OPPOSITE *'Frohe Weinacht'* ('Happy Christmas'), 1940. The lot of people in the German homeland had improved since the previous year with victory and a flow of luxury goods from France. The unhappy truth, however, was that the German war effort soon depended on conquered foes, plus the invention and production of cheaper substitute materials – for uniforms as much as anything else.

CHAPTER 1
UNIFORM

Detail of the NCO's *Feldbluse* shown on page 20.

DIENSTROCK, FELDBLUSE AND WAFFENROCK

German uniforms of the 19th century were a plethora of different hues and cuts, reflecting the fact that until 1871 Germany was not one nation but a collection of separate states with different styles of uniform distinguishing their respective troops. Though *Dunkelblau* (dark blue) dominated after the foundation of the German Empire, Bavaria, Saxony and Württemberg all maintained their own uniforms. Only a few years before World War I was it finally decided to adopt a less conspicuous field combat uniform in a colour described as *Feldgrau* (field grey).

After the war the new Reichswehr also used grey and in the 1920s introduced new uniform of updated cut and detail. The key garment was the *Dienstrock* (service jacket). Manufactured of new wool, it had a falling collar, pleated buttoned breast pockets, flapped and buttoned slash hip pockets, and buttoned *Schulterklappen* (shoulder straps). The *Dienstrock* was vat dyed using indigo, 'Helindon' brown and yellow, combined with white, to produce a greenish field grey. The front closure had eight buttons, reduced to six in 1928. The *Hose* (trousers) were of a different shade created with black and white dyes. Despite the greenish tone the *Dienstrock* was still described as being 'field grey' in colour, while the *Hose* were described as being *Steingrau* (stone grey). With new insignia, Reichswehr uniforms continued to be used well into World War II, with the

Photographed at Görlitz, Saxony, this infantryman wears the Reichswehr eight-button *Ausgehenanzug* ('walking-out dress') jacket with *Waffenfarbe* piping, first worn in the late 1920s but still evident during World War II. The *Stahlhelm* is a World War I type, updated with new insignia.

other ranks' issue *Dienstrock* and *Gebirgsjäger* (mountain troops) jacket now described as 'old types'. The same applied to the lightweight *Drillichanzug* (drill uniform), and no end date was set to the 'wearing out' process for these garments. The tailor-made Reichswehr officers' *Dienstrock* was updated with a dark-green collar, continuing in service as an 'old type' until at least 1942. Officers' Reichswehr *Waffenrock* (dress jacket) with *Waffenfarbe* (arm-of-service colour) piping, bright buttons and silver or aluminium insignia was likewise extended until 1941. The same date was applied to other ranks' Reichswehr *Ausgehenanzug* (walking-out dress), but old uniforms did not disappear entirely even then.

Work on what is now considered the classic Heer uniform of World War II, the *Feldanzug* (field uniform), commenced even before the Nazis came to power, and the new *Feldbluse* (field blouse) was introduced as early as May 1933. Originally, its falling collar and *Schulterklappen* were of the same field grey as the body of the garment, but the following year these were changed to a finer grey *Abzeichentuch* (badge cloth), and

A private-purchase, six-button *Dienstrock* tailored by Richard Ehmann of Stuttgart, 1934. The *Schulterklappen* denote a Heer official, technical service, equivalent rank of *Oberfeldwebel* (company sergeant major), and the breast eagle is embroidered. On the left breast are the ribbon of the *Ehrenkreuz des Weltkriegs 1914/1918* (Honour Cross of the World War 1914/1918) and a World War I *Verwundetenabzeichen* (Wound Badge) in black. The aluminium-*Schnur* (cord) dress aiguillette, attached by a button under the right *Schulterklappe* and the second button of the *Dienstrock* front, was worn on formal occasions.

ABOVE LEFT Prototype of the new *Feldanzug* (field uniform), 1933. The new *Feldbluse* collar is grey, and the uniform is worn with *Schnallenstiefel* (buckled boots). The *Stahlhelm* is an experimental model, and new personal equipment was also introduced before the outbreak of war. (Keystone/Archive Photos/Getty Images)

ABOVE RIGHT A soldier of Infanterie-Regiment 24 in *Feldbluse* with dark-bluish-green collar and pointed *Schulterklappen* without piping, manufactured *c*.1937. Mobilized in 1939 as part of 21. Infanterie-Division in East Prussia, Infanterie-Regiment 24 fought in Poland, France and the Soviet Union.

LEFT A soldier of Infanterie-Regiment 11 wearing the new *Feldbluse*, 1935. The collar and *Schulterklappen* are grey. The *Stahlhelm*, manufactured in the latter part of World War I, has new decals.

then, in September 1935, to a dark-bluish-green *Abzeichentuch*. As of 1936, 10 per cent *Zellwolle* ('cell wool' or rayon) was usual in *Feldbluse* cloth, with higher percentages allowed in caps and other garments. Switching to chrome dyes in uniform cloth production was considered, but following tests with wearability, abrasion, exposure to weather and colour fastness it was decided to stick with vat dyes produced by Farbwerke Hoechst of Frankfurt, part of the Interessengemeinschaft Farbenindustrie (commonly known as IG Farben) chemical and pharmaceutical conglomerate. A major reason for this decision was the need to avoid the use of imported materials.

The straight-legged, high-waisted *Hose* of the new ensemble were worn tucked into the top of mid-calf-length *Schnallenstiefel* (buckled boots) of a new pattern attempting to combine the advantages of laced footwear with the traditional German *Marschstiefel* (marching boot). The lower part of the boot was laced, the leg section enclosed by a leather flap fastened with buckles. The *Schnallenstiefel* were not a great success and by 1935 the traditional *Marschstiefel* was revived. It has variously been suggested that the *Schnallenstiefel* failed due to their impracticality, unpopularity or lack of durability, but they were also more expensive to produce. Whatever the truth, the *Schnallenstiefel* did not disappear entirely, but continued to be worn in training and replacement units.

The cut of the *Feldanzug*, as introduced in 1933 and subsequently updated in 1935, was distinctive, and for the time, fashionable. The *Feldbluse* was reasonably close-fitting, though large enough to wear over an issue pullover, and regulation fit allowed the hands to be brought together above the head without pinching at the shoulder. The falling collar fastened with hook and eye, and the front closure had five pebbled metal buttons. The *Feldbluse* was designed to be worn with a cloth *Kragenbinde* (collar liner), buttoned inside the *Feldbluse* neck. On the outside of the collar either side were sewn patches decorated with *Litzen* (bars), a traditional feature once restricted to specific regiments. The *Schulterklappen* were detachable and fastened to the *Feldbluse* with a button close to the collar; they showed an NCO's rank in braid and stars (NCOs also wore silver-coloured lace around the collar). Grades of *Gefreiter* (senior private, approximating to lance corporal in the British Army system) were indicated by stars and chevrons on the left upper sleeve. The sleeves left the hands fully exposed, and the *Feldbluse* was short, allowing wearers to sit without snagging the skirts. There were four large external patch pockets with pleats. The leather waist belt was worn over the *Feldbluse* and designed to rest on four hooks, at either side of the front and rear at about elbow level. The hooks appeared

The *Marschstiefel* ('marching boot') was used by the Prussian Army long before World War II. The boot originally measured 35cm or more in the leg, but orders of 1939 specified an economy of 3–5cm to be made during manufacture, so this pair, made in 1941, is only 32cm tall.

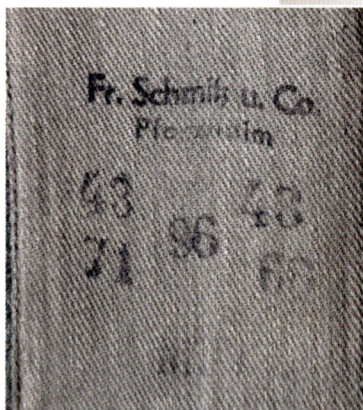

An NCO's *Feldbluse,* manufactured by Schmitz of Pforzheim and issued through the *Heeresbekleidungsamt* (Army clothing depot) in Munich. The *Schulterklappen* indicate a *Feldwebel* (staff sergeant) of Infanterie-Regiment 348, formed on 26 August 1939. The regiment participated in the French campaign of May–June 1940, and was rushed to the Eastern Front in the winter of 1941 where one of its *Kampfgruppen* (battle groups) survived being surrounded by Soviet forces. This *Feldbluse* has been slightly shortened during its service life to create a more fashionable impression. The marking gives the maker's name, sizing and *Heeresbekleidungsamt* stamp.

through one of three small reinforced holes set at slightly different heights, and were supported inside the garment on fabric straps allowing for adjustment. The waist belt was thus kept in position, and the weight of equipment was redistributed for comfort. Also inside the *Feldbluse* at the bottom of the right skirt was a small pocket for a field dressing.

While smart and reasonably practical, with its short fashioned *Feldbluse* the *Feladanzug* also tended to give a flattering illusion of height and longer legs. Yet despite claims to the contrary, it is highly unlikely that clothing designer Hugo Boss (1885–1948) was responsible for the design of the new Heer uniform, though his company was a supplier, and Boss himself was a member of the Nazi Party whose business profited from the manufacture of various uniforms for the regime. The Hugo Boss company workforce peaked at a little over 300 in 1944, by which time more than one-third were home workers and some forced labourers. Clearly the Hugo Boss works in Metzingen was by no means the largest, and the marks of

ABOVE Sanitätsfeldwebel (medical corps staff sergeant) Herman Metzger at Bad Cannstadt on the outskirts of Stuttgart, October 1940. He wears the *Feldbluse* with dark-bluish-green collar and round-ended, piped *Schulterklappen*. The medical corps' *Sonderabzeichen* (specialist badge), a yellow serpent entwined around the Rod of Asclepius, appears on his right forearm.

LEFT *Dienstgradabzeichen* (rank insignia), *c.*1939. Top row: officer *Schulterstücke* (shoulder boards). Middle row: NCO *Schulterklappen*. Bottom row: service grades applying to *Oberschütze* (senior private) and *Gefreiter* (lance corporal), as displayed on the left upper arm.

Schulterstücke für Offiziere

Generalfeldmarschall · Generaloberst · General der Infanterie usw · Generalleutnant · Generalmajor · Oberst · Oberstleutnant · Major · Hauptmann und Rittmeister · Oberleutnant · Leutnant

Schulterklappen für Unteroffiziere und Mannschaften

Stabsfeldwebel · Oberfeldwebel u. Oberfähnrich · Feldwebel (Pi.) · Sanitäts-Unterfeldwebel · Ufiz. (Stabsabt. Oberkdo.d.Hrs) · Unterführeranwärter · Waffenröcke der Mannschaft · Unterarzt · Unterveterinär

Dienstgradabzeichen der Mannschaften am linken Oberärmel

Oberschütze · Gefreiter · Obergefreiter unt. 6 Dienstj. / Obergefreiter über 6 Dienstj. 1 Winkel, 1 Stern · Stabsgefreiter

Uniform-finishing: seamstresses add detailing and hang *Feldblusen*. Advertisements in wartime trade journals suggest that many of the small sewing machines used were Adler or Singer models. Tasks were divided for efficiency, but production remained labour-intensive.

many contractors are found in uniforms. This is unsurprising, given the labour-intensive nature of production, and it is apparent that hundreds of companies supplied the uniforms required by millions of men. A specialist journal for the trade, *Uniformen-Markt*, was established in 1934, and despite mergers and a change of title to *Deutsche Uniformen-Zeitschrift*, publication continued until early 1945. Through its pages, outfitters and manufacturers nationwide were kept abreast of myriad regulations and changes to uniform and accoutrements across the spectrum of the Wehrmacht and other organizations. At the same time, suppliers of cloth, sewing machines, badges, medals and accoutrements were able to advertise their wares to tailors and outfitters.

It would be wrong to say that even the other ranks' *Feldanzug* was 'mass produced', its manufacture being more accurately described as batch production with a great deal of individual finishing. For issue garments the cloth was laid out in multiple layers forming a thick block on the cutting table, after which the tailor pinned on paper patterns and chalked the outlines. He then cut a number of identical cloth panels with a mechanical blade, the German word *Schneider* translating both as 'tailor' and 'cutter'. Pieces were then sewn together and linings, collars and detailing were added by seamstresses working at sewing machines. *Feldblusen* were supplied complete with *Schulterklappen* from the contractor, though various mismatches are evidence of changes of unit, promotions and refurbishments. (The workers' genders mentioned above are deliberate as, initially at least, tailors were usually male, seamstresses female. As the war progressed and labour became scarce, however, the regime increasingly resorted to the use of conscripted labourers of both sexes.)

The *Waffenrock* (left and right) compared to the *Feldbluse* (centre). Distinguished by the *Blitzabzeichen* (lightning-bolt badge), the signaller to the left wears the *Dienstgradabzeichen* of a *Gefreiter* on a grey backing. The man to the right has his rank badge on dark-bluish-green *Abzeichentuch* (badge cloth) and *Schulterklappe* numerals.

According to 1934 regulations, *Feldblusen* were graded in four conditions. Grade I was pristine, held in company store; Grade II was issued, but perfect for parade and 'walking out'; Grade III was for use as *Dienstanzug* (service dress); and Grade IV covered everyday garments. Details varied, but the principle of the condition scale endured. Photographs of barrack lockers show that soldiers usually held several jackets: one for general use, another possibly of a dress or old pattern, a drill or fatigue type, and possibly a fourth purchased privately. Naturally, not all these were taken on active service, and war reduced supply, but *Soldbuch* (pay book) records suggest that possession of more than one issue *Feldbluse* was perfectly normal. We know that NCO Franz Wirtz, for example, was issued with two *Feldblusen* and a *Drilljacke* (drill or fatigue jacket) in 1940: a 1944 re-issue consisted of one *Feldbluse* and one *Drilljacke*. Richard Prechel, a *Gefreiter*, also had two *Feldblusen* plus a *Drilljacke* for the majority of his service. Schütze (private) Felix Mohr was less fortunate, being initially issued only one *Feldbluse*, but a *Drilljacke* was provided a few months later.

Also introduced in 1935 was the new *Waffenrock*, of traditional cut in fine-quality field-grey cloth and worn on formal guard duties as well as for parades and 'walking out'. The garment had eight bright buttons to the front closure, a dark-bluish-green stand-and-fall collar and buttoned *Schulterklappen*, but lacked any pockets to the front. The slightly overlapped rear skirt was slashed to the waist, ornamented with three buttons either side and contained two concealed triangular pockets. The cuffs were decorated with dark-bluish-green cloth and two bright-aluminium *Borte* patches and buttons; unlike the *Feldanzug*, the *Waffenrock* was piped in the *Waffenfarbe*. Private-purchase *Waffenröcke* might boast not only a better quality of finish, but taller and fashionably pointed collars. Though manufacture of the *Waffenrock* ceased after the outbreak of World War II, it continued to be worn by some units on appropriate occasions. A *Großdeutschland*-variant *Waffenrock* of 1939 did not see full distribution due to the war.

The new *Großdeutschland*-variant *Waffenrock* of March 1939 was distinguished by elongated double *Litzen* on the collar, matt-white metal buttons, three horizontal lace bands on the French-style cuffs, 'GD'-monogrammed *Schulterklappen* and a regimental *Ärmelstreifen* in Gothic script. NCOs were entitled to rank lace at the cuffs as well as on the collar on this uniform. (New York Times Co./Getty Images)

The two main models of other ranks' *Mäntel*. At right is the type in production until 1940, with a collar of dark-bluish-green *Abzeichentuch*. The *Mantel* worn by the *Gebirgsjäger* (left) was made much later. As of 1940, the *Mantel* collar was of ordinary field-grey cloth, and from 1942 larger, being 12cm wide at the front and giving better protection when pulled up. Both men wear waist belts over the *Mantel* and removable *Schulterklappe* slides.

The issue *Mantel* (greatcoat), worn over basic uniform, was double-breasted, mid-calf length, the same colour cloth as the *Feldbluse* and lined in grey. There were six buttons down each side at the front, two hip pockets, one inside pocket and buttoned *Schulterklappen*. As with the *Feldbluse*, the *Mantel's* collar had a hook-and-eye fastener and was initially field grey, but changed to dark-bluish-green in the mid-1930s only to change back to field grey during World War II. Raised in bad weather, the collar could be secured with a cloth bridle and a button. On first issue, the large pleat down the back of the *Mantel* was sewn shut, giving a neat fit for parade, but as *Mäntel* began to degrade pleats were opened, giving a looser fit, and the garment was now used for field and general service. Initially, *Mäntel* were made with hooks at the bottom, allowing them to be turned up at the front for easier riding or marching, a feature deleted during the war. Private-purchase *Mäntel* were of better quality but omitted the back pleat, and might feature bright buttons and different linings. Slashes and short cloth straps fixed internally allowed officers and senior NCOs to carry sabres and daggers more conveniently. General officers wore the *Mantel* collar open, exposing a distinctive red lining.

OFFICERS' DRESS

Officers were entitled to a clothing allowance, and usually purchased bespoke uniform from tailors fitted in the manner of a quality civilian suit. Materials to make officers' uniform *Feldblusen* were available both through the trade and via the Heereskleiderkasse (Army clothing outlet) in Berlin. According to the price list of May 1939, one metre of *Feldbluse* cloth of the type used in ordinary soldiers' uniform could be had for RM 10,50, while an 'elegant' gaberdine for summer wear was RM 11,25. The very best quality worsteds for the *Waffenrock* and the *Geschmückte Feldbluse* (decorated field blouse) were anything up to RM 20 per metre. Officers' *Umhänge* (cloaks) and *Mäntel* could also be made to measure.

Other items supplied by the Heereskleiderkasse included caps, trousers, badges, *Schulterstücke* (shoulder boards), collars, buttons, gloves, belts, sabres, daggers, vests, handkerchiefs, socks and shoes. Shirts were provided in no fewer than six white varieties, plus ten different sports shirts and a 'riding shirt'(*Reithemd*). A 'service shirt' (*Diensthemd*) for Panzer troops in 'grey-black' poplin, with two collars, was available for RM 8,50. A simple nightshirt was stocked, but at the luxury end of the nightwear range the best-quality officers' pyjamas started at RM 9,50. *Unterhose* (underpants) alone formed a bewildering range of nine different types in five different sizes and five different lengths and the choices included designs for riding. Clearly, being a well-turned-out German officer at the outbreak of the war was an expensive business, so it was fortunate that the Heereskleiderkasse could extend credit of up to RM 500, with aspirant officers being allowed RM 150.

Because they were cut for the individual, officers' uniforms were more labour-intensive to produce than other ranks' attire. Moreover, officers were entitled to specific embellishments and variations, and more were added by individual choice. The basic

Franz Blume, Landshut
Zivil- u. Uniformschneiderei
Militäreffekten
Rosengasse

TOP The reverse of a small hand-mirror promoting uniform tailor and outfitter Franz Blume of Landshut. Many businesses supplied bespoke uniforms, mainly to officers and senior NCOs.

LEFT The officers' *Feldbluse*, here worn by a Heer *Beamte* (official) ranking as *Leutnant* (2nd lieutenant), December 1941. *Beamten* carried out various specialist tasks both at home and in occupied countries. Their uniforms were similar to those of officers of equivalent rank, with these distinctive collar *Litzen* – similar to those used by *Sonderführer* (special leaders) – being introduced in 1940.

BOTTOM LEFT The officers' *Feldbluse*, worn with breeches and boots, leather leggings, or trousers and shoes. Three of the group have the old pattern field caps (peaked cap) without a cap cord.

ABOVE The *Geschmückte Feldbluse* ('decorated field blouse'), featuring *Waffenfarbe* trimming around the cuffs and collar and down the front, was an optional *Feldbluse* chosen by many officers for formal wear.

ABOVE CENTRE Tiger tank ace and *Ritterkreuz* (Knight's Cross) recipient Leutnant Otto Carius (1922–2015) is pictured wearing the summer *Weisser Rock* (white tunic). Carius was initially refused entry to the Heer due to his puny stature before being admitted to the infantry. Ultimately, he was credited with the destruction of over 150 enemy armoured vehicles.

ABOVE RIGHT Oberleutnant Kurt Liebeneiner of Grenadier-Ersatz-Bataillon 414 is pictured here with his wife. His *Dolch* (officer's dagger) is in his left hand.

officers' *Feldbluse* had a white button-in collar and embroidered insignia. There were *Schulterstücke* instead of *Schulterklappen*, showing rank by a system of plain or twisted metallic cords and stars. As with the other ranks' *Feldbluse*, the collar of the officers' garment changed to dark-bluish-green *Abzeichentuch* in 1935. To cut more of a dash, some officers and NCOs made unofficial changes, including more pointed collars, shortening the *Feldbluse* still further and making alterations to pockets. The variant *Geschmückte Feldbluse*, approved in 1937, was something of a contradiction because it was a 'field' jacket not intended for combat; nevertheless, it was very popular for formal wear. The key differences compared to the ordinary *Feldbluse* were *Waffenfarbe* piping, and collar *Litzen* in bright aluminium.

Like the men, officers wore the *Waffenrock* on formal occasions. The officers' version was individually tailored and worn with a dress brocade belt (*Feldbinde*) featuring a circular buckle with the *Hoheitsabzeichen* (National Emblem) of an eagle atop an oak-leaf wreath within which was a swastika. *Weisser Röcke* (white tunics) were permitted for officers in summer in training areas and when other ranks wore fatigue dress, and a new version was introduced in 1937. Worn between 1 April and 30 September only, it was also authorized as mess dress, for parties, sports and similar events. It was made of linen or cotton fabric and had eight buttons, a stand-and-fall collar and four outside pockets. It was unlined and buttons and other fittings were removable as white was easily soiled and the jacket washable.

Just how much clothing a German officer might actually possess is difficult to ascertain, and a question to which regulations and catalogues can give only partial answers. It is possible to cite at least one concrete example, however. On 18 July 1944, Oberleutnant Kurt Liebeneiner was at Le Hom, Normandy, 20km from Villers-Bocage. He escaped the battlefield, but his kit was 'lost to enemy action'. At the first opportunity, Liebeneiner typed a *Verlustmeldung* (loss report) in an effort to obtain reimbursement of expenses: these were reckoned at RM 838,50 for new replacement, or RM 624,50 for second-hand.

The *Verlustmeldung* comprised: three caps; two uniform jackets with matching trousers; a third pair of trousers for wear with *Marschstiefel*; breeches described as '*Feldgrau* with leather trimming'; two pairs of braces; a *Mantel*; raincoat; leather jacket; two black neck-ties; seven shirts (two of which were of *Trikot*); 11 shirt collars; six pairs of socks with two pairs of 'sock suspenders'; four pairs of underpants; marching boots and a boot pull; shoes; leather gloves; sports shirt and shorts; two pairs of pyjamas; slippers; 14 pocket handkerchiefs; wash and grooming kit; three hand-towels; map case; briefcase and trunk. Extensive as this list is, it cannot have been Liebeneiner's entire wardrobe. Photographs show him with a *Dolch* (officer's dagger) and a *Stahlhelm;* and some equipment items were almost certainly issued, while items not required on campaign were most likely left at his home or home station. Lastly, it seems improbable that he departed Normandy without at least the clothes on his back, which, by process of elimination, included a waist belt and weapon. The most expensive items in Liebeneiner's list were his *Marschstiefel*, assessed at RM 140 new, and a *Feldbluse* at RM 100: by contrast, a handkerchief was just RM 0,75 new. The officers' caps cost from RM 15 to RM 17 each. It is unknown whether compensation was forthcoming, but Liebeneiner was in the Eifel region of Germany in September 1944, and still alive in February 1945.

MARKINGS AND ORDERS OF DRESS

Initially, issue uniforms contained the maker's name or mark, and location. From this it may be determined that uniform was made all over Germany and Austria. Berlin, Hamburg, Munich, Stuttgart and other major cities were home to numerous suppliers, but there were also many contractors in rural areas. For example, Otto Aulbach, of the tiny but ancient town of Heimbuchenthal, and the Süweda company were but two of several based in the Aschaffenburg area of north-western Bavaria, a district well known for tailoring men's suits. 'Lago', a stamp encountered quite frequently, was not one specific uniform maker but signified clothing manufactured by a co-operative of companies. Massive demand was also satisfied by establishing factories in occupied countries. A particularly large concern was the E. Reitz Uniformwerke in the Merksem district of Antwerp, Belgium, set up by the German industrialist Erich Reitz from Wuppertal in December 1940. This company moved its wares to depots via the canal system and boasted its own factory guards.

By the middle of the war it was decided that the names and locations of manufacturers should be omitted from clothing stamps on grounds of security. It remained desirable, however, that officials should be able to determine who supplied material, so each company was now allotted a nine-digit *Reichsbetriebsnummer* ('RB', code number) derived from existing Reichsministerium für Rüstung und Kriegsproduktion (Ministry for Equipment and War Production) file numbers, location, name and type of business. Usually, the first digit gave the type of business, for example '0' for industry generally or '1' for a craft concern. The next four digits were for the location of the business, with '0496' being Hamburg, '0556' Aachen and '1325' Posen, to mention just three. Finally came four digits for the company itself. Interestingly, manufacturers still included their name 'in clear' on a small detachable paper label when clothing was delivered to the assigned *Heeresbekleidungsamt* (Army clothing depot), to be removed when the item was deemed satisfactory and marked by the depot. The *Heeresbekleidungsämter* were identified by a letter stamp followed by the last two digits of the date. Before 1939 there were five depots – Berlin, Königsberg, Erfurt, Munich and Hanover – but the number grew with the addition of Frankfurt, Stettin, Breslau, Cologne, Koblenz and others in occupied countries. A garment marked 'E 37' was thus delivered to the Erfurt depot in 1937, and 'M 43' denoted Munich in 1943.

Issue uniform was meticulously sized, being stamped internally with measurements in centimetres. *Feldblusen* usually carried five measurements arranged so the central figure represented the chest; top left the length of back; bottom left the overall length; top right the collar size and bottom right the arm length. *Waffenröcke* were measured slightly differently, with length of back given first on the left. *Hosen* received four measurements, with top left being inside leg;

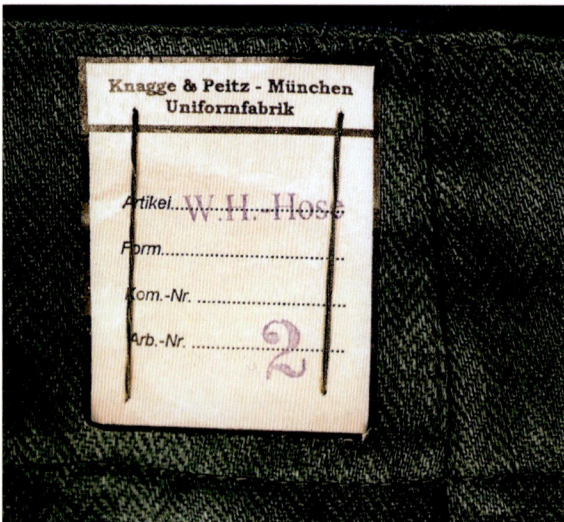

Manufacturer's temporary label on an unissued pair of green *Drillichhose* (drill trousers), 1944 or 1945. This label was to be removed when *Heeresbekleidungsamt* stamps and *Reichsbetriebsnummern* ('RB' code numbers) were applied to uniforms. 'Knagge & Peitz' of Munich was both a clothing works and a department store. Note the 'herringbone' pattern in the cloth, typical of these *Drillich* garments.

bottom left the overall length; top right, waist; and bottom right, hips. Privately purchased bespoke uniform required no such markings.

To understand the appearance of the German soldier requires not just an appreciation of individual garments, but knowledge of the various 'orders of dress' regulating what was worn, for what purpose and on which occasion. As illustrated in the 1940 edition of Wilhelm Reibert's *Der Dienstunterricht im Heere* ('Service Instruction in the Army') manual, there were seven orders of dress for other ranks:

Field dress: Complete field uniform with steel helmet; *Gefectsgepäck*; belt equipment; rifle and bayonet; ammunition pouches.

Service dress: Field uniform with belt, bayonet and field cap.

Guard dress: Field uniform with steel helmet; rifle; belt; bayonet; ammunition pouches and *Tornister*. Marksman's lanyard, if awarded.

Parade dress: Parade uniform (*Waffenrock*) with lanyard; steel helmet; *Tornister* (complete with *Zeltbahn* and *Mantel* attached); rifle, bayonet and ammunition pouches.

Reporting dress: Field uniform with belt and bayonet, lanyard if awarded; *Schirmmütze*.

Walking-out dress: Parade uniform (*Waffenrock*) with bayonet; lanyard, if awarded. laced boots or shoes rather than marching boots; *Schirmmütze*.

Sports dress: Singlet, shorts and running shoes.

Though *Waffenrock* manufacture was discontinued in March 1940, those who had them continued to wear them in appropriate orders of dress. When no longer fit for parade use, old *Waffenröcke* were supposed to be modified to resemble *Feldanzug* for general duty until worn out, or, more commonly, passed to the Ersatzheer (Replacement Army). This left the best *Feldanzug* doing duty for parade and walking-out attire.

Officers' orders of dress were described in the approved *Taschenkalendar* (pocket calendar). According to the 1942 edition, cultural events, parades, memorial parades and the presence of the *Führer* or a foreign dignitary warranted the wearing of the officers' *Feldbluse* (or an old-style *Rock*), steel helmet, long boots, grey gloves and sabre or pistol. When attending church, sabre or dagger and peaked cap were used, but not a pistol. Officers at social events wore shoes, gloves, sabre or dagger and peaked cap. On service it was expected that both officers and senior NCOs would adopt the same order of dress as the men, altering equipment according to duty, with officers wearing 'dismounted' breeches rather than trousers. Officers and senior NCOs in *Dienstanzug* wore the *Schirmmütze* when the men were in field caps or helmets;

TOP RIGHT Officers'
Schulterstücke. Left to right:
Leutnant of a transport unit;
Leutnant of an engineer unit,
numbered '3'; *Oberleutnant* Machine
Gun battalion; *Hauptmann* (captain)
of an artillery-observation unit,
numbered '6'; *Oberstleutnant*
(lieutenant-colonel), Panzer-
Regiment 7.

RIGHT More officers'
Schulterstücke. Left to right: Heer
Beamte equivalent rank of *Leutnant;*
Oberleutnant (lieutenant) of a gas,
smoke or rocket unit numbered
'101'; *Oberleutnant* of an armoured
Panzerjäger unit; *Stabsarzt* (senior
Heer doctor); *Oberstleutnant* of the
military school, Dresden.

generals could still wear an old-style *Rock*. In order not to appear conspicuous
in action, however, officers in the front line frequently abandoned distinctions,
adopting, for example, other ranks' belt, trousers and *Bluse* similar to those of
the men.

Heeresgeistliche (Army chaplains) ranked as officers and wore either the
vestments of their denomination or uniform, according to duty. Their field-grey
Dienstanzug, introduced in 1935, was similar to that of other officers, but lacked
Schulterstücke and was distinguished by violet *Waffenfarbe*. A neck cross was

Officers gather for parade, *c*.1940. Best *Feldanzug* is worn with brocade belts (*Feldbinden*) and decorations: a leather sabre belt with cross-strap is worn by the figure on the left.

worn during services. There was also a distinctive knee-length field-grey frock coat of 'Lutheran' inspiration. Described as the *Langer Feldgrauer Rock (Überrock)* in *Uniformen-Markt* in 1937, the coat had eight buttons, deep cuffs and a standing collar and bore the *Hoheitsabzeichen* on the right breast. *Heeresgeistliche* carried no arms until an order of 1941 instructed them to wear pistols in occupied countries.

QUALITY AND CHANGE

The *Feldbluse* underwent numerous changes during the war, but while these alterations may help with the dating or history of a specific garment, until 1944 none of them constituted a new model. Proof of this statement is provided by the *Taschenkalender*, which continued to refer simply to the *Feldbluse*, while noting certain significant changes. Modifications were the result of three factors: the need to make uniform manufacture cost-effective in the face of material shortages; practicality; and the dictates of fashion. As early as 1935, approximately 5 per cent rayon fibre was included in the cloth. In 1939, the introduction of new leather carrying straps to be worn over the *Feldbluse* and attached externally to the leather waist belt began to make the internal fabric strap arrangement redundant. As a result, the integral support system was gradually phased out. By 1943, internal fabric straps had ceased to be included; but belt hooks remained, and in the later versions of the *Feldbluse* these were held by short strong tabs sewn directly onto the inside of the *Feldbluse* around elbow level.

An *Unteroffizier Feldbluse* manufactured by the Württemberg 'Lago' (co-operative) for the *Heeresbekleidungsamt* in Frankfurt, 1941. The *Feldbluse* and collar are of the same dark-field-grey material, and the *Schulterklappen* and collar are braided. As with the majority of combat uniforms, no unit numerals are shown. The detail shows the interior of the right skirt and the small field-dressing pocket: two dressings, one large, one small, was the usual issue. Also visible are details of the lining and the slit and holes for the initial internal equipment-suspension system.

As originally conceived, the *Feldbluse* had had a grey collar, and this was of a different shade to the grey trousers. It therefore took no great leap of the imagination to see that making the whole *Feldanzug* out of one type of cloth would save both time and materials. Accordingly, an order of May 1940 changed the collar of newly made garments to the same material as the rest of the *Feldbluse*, and *Hosen* were altered to the same colour, which was now a slightly darker field grey than previously. Nevertheless, *Feldblusen* with and without the dark-bluish-green collar remained acceptable. Perhaps predictably, some – particularly NCOs – decided that green befitted their station or appearance better than hum-drum grey and had collars in the dark-bluish-green *Abzeichentuch* retrofitted to new *Feldblusen*.

It was also realized that savings could be made by using sulphur dyes, and companies were now allowed their own preference when colouring rayon. A three-month test also revealed, however, that the mix of wool, recycled wool and rayon now being used was less resistant to weathering than pure virgin wool had been. Diversity of appearance was further compounded by the reuse of many Austrian *Feldanzüge* after the annexation of Austria in March 1938. These were rebadged, though they remained identifiable due to their shade, differently shaped pocket flaps or other details. Some of the ex-Austrian *Feladanzüge* remained in use after the outbreak of war. After the success of early campaigns, large stocks of uniform, and especially cloth, were also acquired from other countries. The result was the entry of additional non-standard materials into the supply chain.

Even before the outbreak of war, Heer troops in formation might be ordered to open their collars, but in combat this became commonplace. By September 1940, this practice was recognized in regulation when it was officially declared that by order of a superior, detachments on active service, plus troops in transit, and at the front, could wear the *Feldbluse* open at the neck. Additionally, individuals travelling by train in summer could make this decision on their own initiative. There was more to this than simple practicality, however. *Feldblusen* buttoned to the neck were commonly regarded as old-fashioned and redolent of working-class status and manual labour: open collars with neat shirt and tie symbolized smartness, modernity, rank and individuality. Moreover, Heer soldiers of the dashing Panzer arm already wore a short, double-breasted *Jacke* with an open neck. So, whenever possible, soldiers unbuttoned the top of the *Feldbluse*, and when officialdom accepted that uniform could be open at the

An Eastern Front veteran sports a raffish polka-dot scarf and collar pressed open. His *Feldbluse* is of a simplified form with the collar of the same material as the rest of the garment, which has a six-button closure, while the breast pockets lack pleats. Medal ribbons denote the *Winterschlacht im Osten 1941/42* (Winter Battle in the East 1941/42) and *Eisernes Kreuz 2. Klasse* (Iron Cross 2nd Class).

Uniformen und Abzeichen des Heeres

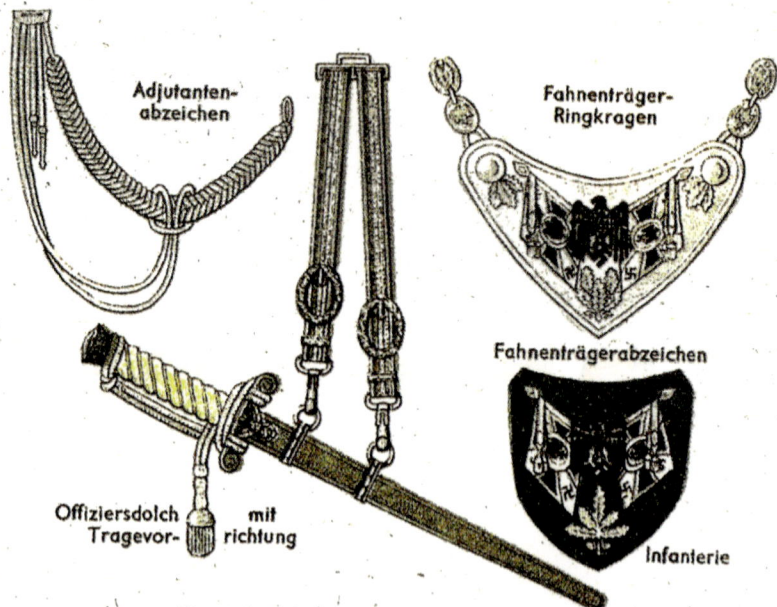

Adjutanten-abzeichen

Fahnenträger-Ringkragen

Fahnenträgerabzeichen

Offiziersdolch mit Tragevor- richtung

Infanterie

Abzeichen besonderer Dienststellungen

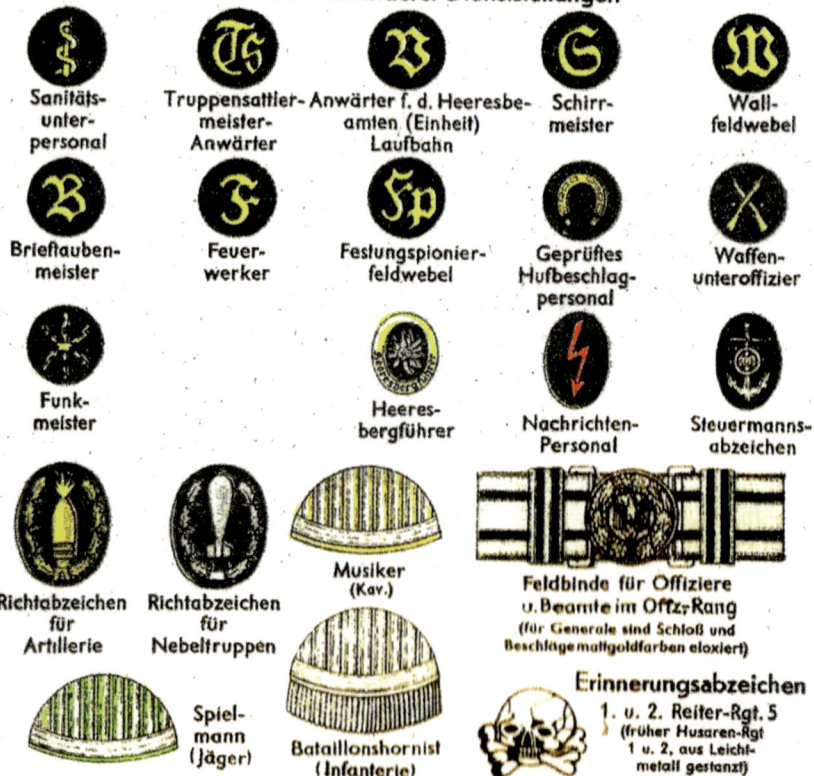

Sanitäts-unter-personal

Truppensattler-meister-Anwärter

Anwärter f. d. Heeresbe-amten (Einheit) Laufbahn

Schirr-meister

Wall-feldwebel

Brieftauben-meister

Feuer-werker

Festungspionier-feldwebel

Geprüftes Hufbeschlag-personal

Waffen-unteroffizier

Funk-meister

Heeres-bergführer

Nachrichten-Personal

Steuermanns-abzeichen

Richtabzeichen für Artillerie

Richtabzeichen für Nebeltruppen

Musiker (Kav.)

Feldbinde für Offiziere u. Beamte im Offz.-Rang
(für Generale sind Schloß und Beschläge mattgoldfarben eloxiert)

Spiel-mann (Jäger)

Bataillonshornist (Infanterie)

Erinnerungsabzeichen
1. u. 2. Reiter-Rgt. 5
(früher Husaren-Rgt 1 u. 2, aus Leicht-metall gestanzt)

ABOVE An *Unteroffizier* in *Feldbluse, c.*1940, with the collar made of the same material as the *Feldbluse*. The Gothic-script 'F' badge of the *Feuerwerker* (equivalent to the Ammunition Technician/Technical Officer qualification in the Royal Army Ordnance Corps) on the right forearm denotes an artificer with responsibility for explosives and pyrotechnics.

RIGHT Manual illustration showing the officers' dagger and brocade belt (*Feldbinde*), the standard-bearer's *Ringkragen* and arm badge, trade badges, and the musician's shoulder 'wings' (*Schwalbennester*). The trade badges are (from top left): (staff) medic; (TS) troop saddler; (B) aspirant official; (S) equipment administration; (W) fortress maintenance; (B) messenger pigeon handler; (F) ordnance technician; (FP) fortress works personnel; (horseshoe) farrier; (crossed rifles) armourer; (lightning bolts) signals instructor; (Edelweiss) mountain leader; (single bolt) signaller; (anchor) boat pilot; (shell) gunnery proficiency; (mortar bomb) smoke or chemical troops proficiency.

TOP FAR LEFT The Gothic-script 'S' denoting an NCO *Schirrmeister* (equipment administration specialist).

TOP LEFT The Gothic-script 'GU' *Dienststellungsabzeichen* ('service position insignia' or trade badge) for a gas-defence NCO.

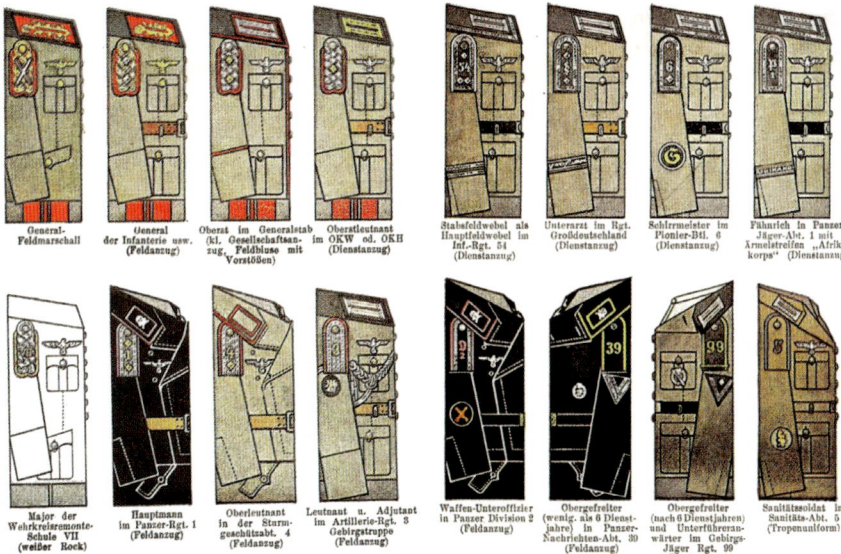

FAR LEFT Eight illustrations from the 1943 *Taschenbuch* (pocket book), depicting officers' uniforms. Top row, left to right: *Generalfeldmarschall* (field marshal); *General der Infanterie* (lieutenant-general); *Oberst* (colonel) of the General Staff; *Oberstleutnant* (lieutenant-colonel) of the OKW or OKH. Bottom row, left to right: *Major* of Wehrkreisremonte-Schule VII (Remount School VII), white summer uniform; *Hauptmann* (captain), Panzer-Regiment 1; *Oberleutnant*, Sturmgeschütz-Abteilung 4; *Leutnant* and adjutant, Gebirgs-Artillerie-Regiment 3.

LEFT Eight more illustrations from the 1943 *Taschenbuch*, depicting uniforms. Top, left to right: *Stabsfeldwebel* serving as *Hauptfeldwebel*, Infanterie-Regiment 54; junior doctor, Regiment *Großdeutschland*; master saddler, Pionier-Bataillon 6; *Fähnrich*, Panzerjäger-Abteilung 1, with AFRIKAKORPS armband. Bottom row, left to right: *Unteroffizier* armourer, 2. Panzer-Division; *Obergefreiter*, Panzer-Nachrichten-Abteilung 39; NCO aspirant *Obergefreiter* (up to six years' service), Gebirgsjäger-Regiment 99; Medic, Sanitäts-Abteilung 5, tropical dress.

collar, individualism took another swipe at authority by displaying non-regulation shirts, perhaps a tie, and even pressing collars open semi-permanently. Manual illustrations began to show the correct position for open collars, and fashion was further reinforced by the appearance of open-necked tropical uniforms. It was but a small step for Heer officers in Europe to begin wearing purpose-made open-necked uniform, about 1942, and for this to be designed into all ranks' uniforms in 1944.

Initially, *Feldbluse* cloth had been of good quality, but as time went on new wool became increasingly difficult to obtain. Three solutions were found: more recycled wool, increased rayon content, and less cloth being used for each garment. Contrary to common misconception, the bulk of the fibre initially used for rayon was not from German forests, but 60 per cent sourced in neutral Sweden. Only with considerable research and development was it found possible to substitute German beech, pine and straw pulps for Swedish

ABOVE At left, the woven *Stabsgefreiter Ärmelabzeichen* for the *Feldanzug*. This insignia, consisting of two chevrons and a pip, was introduced as early as 1928. *Stabsgefreiter* approximates to 'Senior Staff Private', the highest of three '*Gefreiter*' grades, under the level of full NCO. Despite a period when no new promotions to this rank were allowed, the *Stabsgefreiter* rank existed throughout the war. At right, the arm rank pip for an *Oberschütze* for wear on a *Drillichanzug*.

RIGHT The *Feldanzug* (left) compared to the *Waffenrock* (right), *c*.1944. *Waffenröcke* were handed over to the Ersatzheer after manufacture was discontinued.

spruce wood, but even then some raw material still came from Sweden. From the outset, research in this area was strategic in conception and only made possible by the Nazi planned economy.

Rayon manufacturers were organized in collaborative combines or 'rings', the two biggest being led by Vereinigte Glanzstoff-Fabriken and IG Farben. Total production rose from less than 40,000 tonnes in 1934 to more than 400,000 in 1943, and in the process two fully synthetic fibres were also developed – a much-celebrated achievement. Considerable effort was devoted to giving rayon characteristics that were as similar as possible to those of wool. According to the American investigators charged in 1945 with examining the firms involved, industry managers had led the authorities to expect that the new products could entirely replicate the qualities of natural fibre. As far as laundering and resistance to abrasion were concerned, they were broadly correct. Exposure to water and the Russian climate quickly revealed shortcomings, however, and manufacturers were put 'under duress' in an effort to ensure their boasts were made good.

As early as 1939, *Uniformen-Markt* specified the standard composition of *Feldbluse* cloth as 20 per cent rayon, but by the latter part of the war it was anything up to 65 per cent. As new wool became scarce, the remainder of the

ABOVE Interior detail of a *Feldbluse* manufactured in 1943, showing one of the short tabs for a belt hook which replaced the earlier, more elaborate arrangements.

LEFT An other ranks' six-buttoned *Feldbluse* with grass-green *Panzergrenadier Waffenfarbe* on the *Schulterklappen*, and insignia in subdued tones, marked at the *Heeresbekleidungsamt* in Berlin, 1943. While a reduction in the quality of materials and a lack of pocket pleats is apparent, the standard of tailoring remains good.

Detailing of the new *Hose* of 1943, made of coarse field-grey cloth and showing stamped metal buttons and provision for both waist belt and braces.

NCO *Schulterklappen*. Left to right: *Unteroffizier*, artillery headquarters; *Unteroffizier*, artillery unit with unit slide '680'; *Feldwebel*, Panzer-Regiment 4; officer aspirant, military police.

material was now recycled wool (known in English as 'shoddy'). Both recycled wool and rayon had an impact on the *Feldbluse*. Rayon makes very good artificial silk, so it was particularly useful for replacing natural-fibre linings and threads. It is also comfortable and absorbent, but its thermal quality is poorer than wool, and it has relatively poor wet tensile strength. It was apparently to help the *Feldbluse* maintain its shape and not to gape that a six-button front closure was introduced in mid-1941.

The increasing amount of recycled wool naturally affected texture, and dying recycled wool consistently was tricky. The drive to reduce both the amount of cloth used and production time led to the formal elimination of pocket pleats in 1942, and straight edges to pocket flaps became standard not long afterwards. Even so, despite a decline in the quality of materials used, tailoring and quality control remained good, and where unsatisfactory garments were delivered, *Heeresbekleidungsämter* were entitled to return them to the makers.

In some instances, wool was eliminated from uniform altogether when private-purchase garments were created with warm weather in mind. Garments

TOP LEFT NCO *Schulterklappen*. Left to right: *Unteroffizier*, Infanterie-Regiment 5 (with old-style braid, mid-1930s); *Feldwebel* 11th company Infantry Regiment Nr 20 c.1938–40; a recruiting *Feldwebel* of Wehrkreis XVIII, c.1938–40; *Oberfeldwebel* Infantry regiment Nr 7, c.1939–44. The dates given here indicate the approximate date of manufacture, photographic evidence showing that obsolete types of *Schulterklappe* continued to be worn for some time, sometimes years, when older patterns of clothing were retained or privately purchased.

LEFT *Schulterklappen* of private soldiers and *Gefreiter*. Left to right: the basic *Schulterklappe* for the *Feldbluse* without unit designation, c.1936–38; an artillery unit numbered '50', c.1936–38; Aufklärungs-Abteilung 6, c.1939–40; infantry *Schulterklappe* with the slide of Landesschützen-Bataillon 881, c.1941–42.

cut to the same, or similar, patterns as the *Feldbluse* are found in 'moleskin' (a woven cotton fabric with a short, soft pile), unlined 'drill' materials such as cotton canvas, and ribbed cottons. These lightweight garments appear to have been ordered primarily by officers and NCOs, and worn mainly in occupied countries or on campaign. This was not a new development; canvas versions of the *Dienstrock* had been made in the Reichsheer years, and private-purchase lightweight jackets were also worn in World War I.

Repairs to uniform were undertaken in three different ways. Soldiers used personal sewing kits for small jobs, with more difficult work such as alterations being undertaken by unit tailors. It was also possible to take uniform to the civilian trade, particularly where private-purchase items were involved: charges for such work were officially regulated by the amount of time taken and the location.

THE 1944 UNIFORM

A good deal of misinformation has been published regarding both the 1944 uniform and the *Einheitstuch* ('universal cloth') from which it was eventually made; but in point of fact neither the uniform, nor the apparently mystifying brownish cloth, were any sort of accident. Though the war ended before the plan could be brought to fruition, the intention was to rationalize all uniform for the forces, including that of the Heer, Kriegsmarine, Luftwaffe and Waffen-SS, and at the same time improve camouflage. Experiments with new uniform in 1943 led to field trials of a radical new design.

The new uniform reduced demands on materials and labour with an outfit resembling British 'battle dress'. The Feldbluse 44 had two large external unpleated patch pockets at the breast, and, while fairly generously cut around the chest, had a much more fitted broad waistband. *Schulterklappen* were secured in the usual way, folded around a bar of cloth and fastened with a button, and it would appear that straps of various pre-existing types were sometimes incorporated into the new garment. There were six front buttons of the customary painted pebbled type, two of these being located on the waistband. The top button and collar were almost always open, with photographs showing the *Feldbluse* worn over a shirt, shirt and tie, or round-necked sweater. Internally, the garment was partially lined and had two inside pockets and a pair of tabs for belt hooks, though it lacked a dedicated field-dressing pocket. The insignia worn universally were collar *Litzen*, usually of subdued grey, and a breast eagle. Again, time and energy were saved as other ranks almost always wore a machine-woven eagle on a triangular backing which was easy to sew onto the jacket by machine with three straight runs of stitching.

ABOVE The triangular woven breast eagle as used on the 1944 uniform. Though woven insignia are sometimes described as 'BeVo', that was actually the brand name of one major supplier, Bandfabrik Ewald Vorsteher in Wuppertal, first established in 1896.

LEFT An other ranks' *Feldbluse* issued by the *Heeresbekleidungsamt* in Munich to a *Panzergrenadier* unit in 1944. This early example of the Feldbluse 44 is in field grey rather than the brownish shade of the final *Einheitstuch* ('universal cloth'), and has the simplified breast insignia. The shortness of the new *Feldbluse* is apparent in comparison to the arm length.

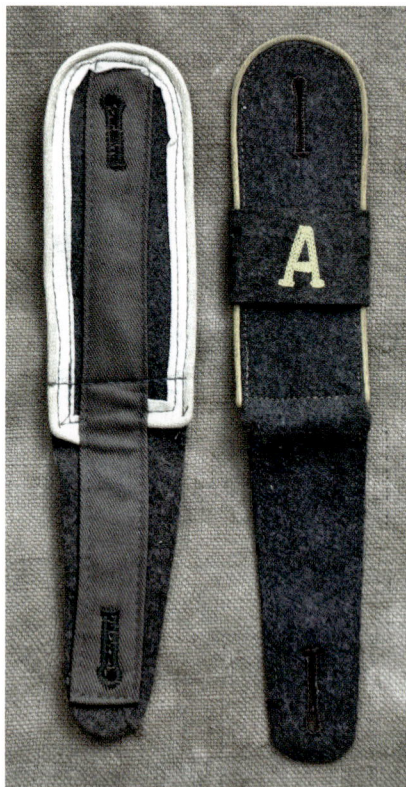

ABOVE Construction details of other ranks' *Schulterklappen*, c.1943–45. At left, the underside of an infantryman's *Schulterklappe*, showing the white rayon *Waffenfarbe* folded and sewn around the edge. At right, a signaller's *Schulterklappe* with lemon-yellow *Waffenfarbe*. The slide with a yellow 'A' denotes a *Nachrichten-Aufklärungs-Ersatz Abteilung* (signals intelligence replacement detachment).

ABOVE RIGHT German prisoners of war taken at the crossing of the Rhine, March 1945. Several wear the 1944 uniform with its distinctive short Feldbluse 44.

The trousers worn with the Feldbluse 44 were straight-legged, with artificial-cotton cords at the ankles allowing them to be worn conveniently with *Gamaschen* (gaiters). There were flapped hip and rear pockets as well as a watch pocket, but this last was probably not much used as such because troops possessing timepieces now mainly had wristwatches. The trousers had belt loops and were often paired with a basic issue waist belt. These varied and in one version had leather ends on an artificial-cotton strap: this was comfortable and flexible, but more importantly saved a little on materials. Other waist belts were entirely of fabric or linen. Alternatively, the trousers could be held up with braces.

The reason for changing the colour of the 1944 uniform was camouflage. Existing field-grey uniform suffered in comparison to Soviet uniform, being more visible in the early morning and late evening. At the same time it was realized that the indigo dye in field grey was particularly apparent under the infrared light being developed for battlefield use. The problem therefore was to create a field grey without using indigo, but as effective as Soviet uniform. Extensive experimentation with vanadium sulphate, lamp black and other substances failed to find a way to replicate traditional *Feldgrau* in such a manner as to meet the new requirements, so a Farbwerke Hoechst formulation for a browner shade of cloth

Kragen- und Ärmelpatten mit Stickerei und Abzeichen

Generale

Offiziere des OKW. und OKH. (Generalstabs-offiziere weißes Aluminium-gespinst)

Uffz. u. Mannsch. (Pion.)

Übrige Offiziere (Nachrichten-Abt.)

Sanitäts-Offiziere

Wehrmachtbeamte im Generalsrang — hier OKW. und OKH. —

Höhere Wehrmachtbeamte (Wehrkreis-verwaltung)

Wehrmachtbeamte im Offizierrang (Amtsrat)

Schützenabzeichen(fürArt.) — hier 12. Stufe 5.-8.Stufe: Plakette, Schieber,Granaten aluminium-farben

Wehrmacht-beamte im Offizierrang (Zahlmeister)

Wehrmacht-beamte ohne Offizierrang (Assistent)

Kragenpatten zur Feldbluse

Offz. OKW. und OKH. (Generalstabsoffz. weißes Aluminiumgespinst)

Übrige Offiziere (Nebel-Tr.)

Veterinär-Offiziere

Einheitsdoppellitze f. Uffz. u. Mannsch. siehe HVBl. 40 (B) Seite 190 Nr. 314

Schieß-aus-zeichnungen usw.

Richtabz. für Art.

für Nebeltr.

Plakette zur 9.—12. Stufe

Plakette zur 1.—4. Stufe

ABOVE *Reithose* (riding breeches), worn by a junior NCO as part of wedding ensemble. *Reithose* were used by mounted personnel of all branches, early examples being of stone-grey cloth, but after 1940 of the same field-grey material as the *Feldbluse*. They were reinforced with either leather or cloth trimming and could be worn by all officers, 'dismounted' officers' *Reithose* lacking the reinforcement.

LEFT Collar patches and cuff decoration details for Generals, NCOs, Wehrmacht *Beamte* (forces officials), staff officers and specialists. In the bottom row are the marksmanship awards.

was accepted. This was: 25 parts tan rayon, ten parts green rayon, 30 parts 'brown green' waste wool and reworked wool, 27 parts 'gold' wool and eight parts white wool. It was later discovered that this did not work properly either, so a simplified formula was used, the colour combination reportedly being 30 parts yellow, 20 'olive grey', 40 'field green' and eight white. As the December 1944 edition of *Deutsche Uniformen-Zeitschrift* explained, the shade was designated Feldgrau 44.

The new uniform was widely issued, and given to *Panzergrenadiere* first. Officers also used the new pattern, and private-purchase examples were made, with tailored *Feldblusen* featuring officer-grade insignia and minor embellishments such as concealed buttons. However, the 1944 uniform never replaced all the earlier garments, which continued to be used. Due to its developmental history, and the using up of materials, the new uniform was produced in a wide variety of shades. These included various leftovers of cloth, existing field grey of different hues and the two types of the new grey-brown *Einheitstuch*.

OTHER ISSUE CLOTHING

Items of clothing issued to Heer other ranks were noted on a printed form in the *Soldbuch*. The record was updated periodically as new items were issued, and from alterations and extensions to the basic form pasted into the *Soldbuch*, it is possible to see how distributions changed over time. The items mentioned below represent the majority of the types of clothing issued to other ranks on a regular basis.

RIGHT These troops in training wear early-type off-white *Drillichhose* with *Feldanzug* and gasmasks, *c.*1940. (FPG/Hulton Archive/Getty Images)

BELOW General der Artillerie Werner Freiherr von Fritsch (right) presents prizes at the Heer point-to-point competition, Karlshorst, 1935. The officer on the left wears the Reichsheer *Weisser Rock* with new breast eagle. The other two competitors wear *Reitjacken* ('riding jackets'), without eagles but with small standing collars. Sashes and armbands in regimental colours are also worn: coloured *Reitjacken* were announced in 1939. (ullstein bild/Getty Images)

BELOW RIGHT A kitchen orderly in *Drillichjacke* enjoys the benefits of his position.

As the *Feldanzug* was made from wool or wool mixtures it was suitable for temperate climates but not easily cleaned. Accordingly, a suit specifically designed for drill and work was provided. Traditionally, this suit of *Drillichjacke* and *Drillichhose* was of off-white linen or cotton: easily soiled, but with buttons that could be removed during washing. The *Drillichanzug* introduced in 1933 was of cotton herringbone twill with five buttons to the *Drillichjacke*. At least initially, it was intended to be worn with a *Kragenbinde*: some examples had two pockets, many had none. The *Drillichhose* were cut much like those of the *Feldanzug*, and photographs show them being worn with the *Feldbluse* to create a type of summer uniform. Regulations refer to the *Drillichanzug* suit as *Rohgrau* (raw grey), but as early as 1938 experiments were conducted with a less conspicuous and darker grey, and in 1940 the colour was changed to reed green. This had interesting consequences because the *Drillichanzug* was now practical for wear in combat zones, particularly in warm weather, and though regulations had previously precluded the addition of *Schulterklappen* and the *Hoheitsabzeichen*, both of these began to be used unofficially. One or two sets of *Drillichanzug* were issued to other ranks during the war.

Two or three issue shirts were usual, the type prescribed by 1933 regulations being of off-white 'tricot' warp-knitted fabric, collarless, with three buttons. Its half-front opening entailed pulling it on and off over the head, and the lack of a collar necessitated the use of the *Kragenbinde*, with the uniform jacket. Soldiers generally received two such *Kragenbinden*, these being green or field-grey faced and white inside. The 1941 regulations refer to the *Kragenbinde* as being of field-grey cotton *Zanella* or twill. The inconvenience of the *Kragenbinde*, plus the conspicuousness of the white shirt and the fact that it looked like underwear, proved very disadvantageous, particularly in warm weather. As a stop-gap shirts were dyed green, and not long after the outbreak of war a new type was devised. This was of a machine-knitted cotton rayon mix: it still pulled over the head, but was reed green in colour and had an attached collar.

By 1942, shirts were being manufactured with flapped and buttoned breast pockets and were sometimes worn with *Dienstgradabzeichen* (rank insignia) and *Schulterklappen*. An order of 1943 confirmed this configuration, and the wearing of grey-green shirts as outerwear. There were three sizes of shirt, and both *Hoheitsabzeichen* and *Litzen* are sometimes evident in photographs. Also shown are non-regulation shirts, which were quite widely worn and sometimes tolerated by officialdom, particularly in combat zones. Such garments might approximate to issue shirts, or be very different: white shirts with collars, foreign patterns, coloured and even checked types. Stinginess of official issue was one explanation of this phenomenon: a hint of individuality in a sea of grey was another.

Initially, the soldier received one example of what the *Soldbuch* called an *Unterjacke* (under jacket), but is more accurately translated as 'cardigan'. The *Unterjacke für Hoch Gebirgstruppen* was intended specifically for mountain troops operating at high altitudes. It was of pure, knot-free, green-grey worsted wool, V-necked with five buttons, and with pockets. Other troops were initially provided with a simpler six-button cardigan without pockets. By the outbreak of war, however, the general-issue item was the Schlupfjacke 36 (Smock model 1936) – actually a simple grey pullover – by regulation 90 per cent wool and 10 per cent rayon, of material which had to be 'spun in Germany'. At first, this *Schlupfjacke* had a V-neck ornamented by a green stripe, but gradually both these features disappeared and the rayon content increased. An official *Rollkragenpullover* (turtleneck pullover) in grey appeared in 1944.

The *Kopfschütze* (literally 'head protection') was a simple but useful piece of clothing. It consisted of a tube of field-grey knitted woollen textile about 40–42cm in length with hems at both ends. Though it could be used in a number of ways, the basic method was to put it on over the head and down to the neck. Here it became a basic scarf; pulled up, it was a form of balaclava. *Soldbuch* records suggest an issue of one per man, though this varied in practice. Again, wool gradually gave way to rayon as the war progressed.

The issue socks and gloves were both of a similar grey woollen knit, with from two to four pairs of socks and a single pair of gloves per man. Woollen gloves were issued personally, but at the front they were also kept at unit stores, being distributed in cold weather and collected again later. Both gloves and socks were sized by means of a series of rings around the open ends. These rings were green initially and white later: the greater the number of rings the larger the size, with four for the biggest and one for the smallest. White suede gloves were an option for 'walking out', but not usually issue items. Variant socks introduced in 1944 were the so-called *Finnensocken* (literally 'Finnish socks');

TOP LEFT Two photographs of Pionier Walter Gelhard at Bad Hönningen on the Rhine, illustrating differences between the *Waffenrock* (left) and the *Feldanzug* (right). The *Waffenrock* was usually worn with the *Schirmmütze*, while the *Feldanzug* was accompanied on service by the *Feldmütze*. The *Schulterklappen* of the *Waffenrock* are sewn into the shoulders of the uniform and embroidered with the numerals of the unit. Those of the *Feldanzug* are folded and buttoned around a bar of material, and are plain and easily removable. The collar *Litzen* and breast eagle are brilliant white on the *Waffenrock*, slightly less conspicuous on the *Feldanzug*. The *Waffenrock* is closed by eight gleaming, usually aluminium, closely placed buttons, the *Feldbluse* having five less obvious fastenings. As the vestige of a chevron appears in the corner of the *Feldbluse* portrait, it may be conjectured that the *Waffenrock* photograph was taken soon after recruitment, but the *Feldanzug* photograph is a later image, taken after Gelhard's promotion to *Gefreiter*. Walter was the brother of Ernst Gelhard, whose *Eisernes Kreuz* appears later in this volume.

LEFT Men of a veteran *Panzerjäger* unit, depicted *c*.1941. The *Feldblusen* are of several slightly differing patterns, with both dark-bluish-green and field-grey collars, and with five or six buttons. *Verwundetenabzeichen* and an *Eisernes Kreuz* ribbon are apparent.

these lacked a defined heel and so reduced complexity of manufacture. Ideally, the soldier rotated this sock each time it was put on, so reducing wear in any spot. Another curiosity were the issue *Fußlappen* (foot wrappings), of which each soldier equipped with *Marschstiefel* received one pair. These white flannel squares wrapped around the foot, and could be quite effective if the soldier was able to avoid creating uncomfortable ridges or bunching underfoot.

According to *Soldbuch* records, troops received issue *Unterhose*, often two pairs. Regulations from the first half of the war speak of both *Trikotunterhose*, of 'smooth American cotton' and *Körperunterhose* of white twill. As with other items of dress, however, increasing amounts of rayon were used and, like shirts, underwear was soon produced in a less conspicuous grey. Both long and short underwear was used, the former being primarily for winter and the latter for summer. While pyjamas sometimes feature in hospital and barrack photographs, regulation nightwear for other ranks was a white-cotton nightshirt. Curiously, some printings of the *Soldbuch* include space to note an issue nightshirt, and some do not.

CHAPTER 2

HEADGEAR

MG 34 machine-gunners of the Deutsches Afrikakorps wearing the *Tropenhelm* (see page 60). The example on the right appears almost white due to sun bleaching. (ullstein bild/ Getty Images)

PEAKED AND FIELD CAPS

The 1930s and 1940s were an era of hats: worn to church on Sunday, to work during the week, and donned as both weather and sun protection. Headgear was doffed in greeting, or respect. Many felt improperly dressed without headwear; and street photography of German civilians at the end of the 1930s shows not only a majority wearing hats, but different types and styles of headgear marking trades and status. The Heer took all of this to a different level. Military headgear was an integral part of uniform and displayed insignia of state and branch of service. Historically, salutes developed as a substitute for a respectful removal or touching of the hat: and so it was that the Reichsheer did not salute without headgear. Though military headgear often evolved into something ceremonial or symbolic, the root of virtually all development was practical function: protection against either the elements or the enemy. Heer headgear of the Nazi period incorporated both traditional features and new innovations in military fashion.

At the outbreak of World War I, all ranks wore a peaked *Dienstmütze* (service cap) with the coloured *Waffenrock*. A flat-topped peakless forage cap of a type previously used by the Prussian Army served as a *Feldmütze* (field cap) for other ranks on active duty in *Feldanzug*. Being soft, light and flexible, and adorned only with small national and state *Kokarden* (cockades) and coloured band and welts for branch of service, the *Feldmütze* was practical to stow, serving whenever helmets and shakos were not required. As the *Waffenrock* was eclipsed, however, the visorless cap became the mark of the ordinary front-line soldier, though certain second-line and transport troops still used peaked caps. Only in 1917 was a field-grey *Einheitsmütze* (universal cap) with a peak introduced for general use, and in hindsight this was an important development. In the aftermath of World War I, the new German state force also opted for a soft peaked cap in field grey, and also sported a stiffened cap for formal wear, the eagle of the German Republic being adopted in place of the national red, white and black cockade.

With the advent of the National Socialist regime, further changes were made to what was now referred to as the *Schirmmütze* – the peaked or 'visored' cap. In 1933, Reich President Paul von Hindenburg agreed to the reinstatement of the old *Reichskokarde* (national cockade), and in the following year plans were drawn up to put the *Hoheitsabzeichen* of eagle and swastika on the *Schirmmütze*, a change formally introduced in 1935, the same year in which the band was changed in colour from grey to dark-bluish-green *Abzeichentuch*. So it was that, by the mid-1930s, all ranks of the Heer were wearing the *Schirmmütze*, the standard arrangement of insignia being the eagle on the crown front, over the *Kokarde* enclosed by an oak-leaf wreath on the band. *Waffenfarbe* piping surrounded the crown and upper and lower edges of the band, general officers'

LEFT An artillery officer's *Schirmmütze* with silver cords and red piping. (© IWM UNI 22)

BELOW FAR LEFT A *Gefreiter* of Landesschützen-Bataillon 740, wearing the other ranks' *Schirmmütze* with metal insignia and white *Waffenfarbe* piping. His unit, indicated by the *Schulterklappe* slide 'L740', was raised in May 1940 and used mainly for guarding prisoners of war.

BELOW CENTRE LEFT A saddle-shaped *Schirmmütze;* the slight tilt to the side can sometimes be seen in photographs, but was contrary to regulation.

LEFT Front view of the officers' *Schirmmütze* showing stamped metallic oak-leaf *Kokarde*, cap cords and eagle.

Schirmmützen having piping of gold metallic cord. The chin strap, which was very rarely used as such, rested on top of the visor and was of black patent leather or vulcanized fibre for other ranks, and a silver-plated or aluminium cord was used for company and field officers. A gold-coloured version of the cord was worn by generals. A circular wire stiffener maintained the shape of the *Schirmmütze*, which was initially described as *Tellerform* (plate like), but after the mid-1930s the front of the crown was raised higher than the back, resulting in a distinctive saddle shape.

Such were the basics, but in practice there were significant variations, many of which came about through dictates of comfort or fashion, economies in materials or influence of tradition. One of the most obvious points to observe

The 'old pattern' officers'
Feldmütze worn by a *Leutnant*,
1939. This soft cap with woven
insignia remained popular long
after it ceased to be current
regulation.

The 'old pattern' officers'
Feldmütze worn by a *Leutnant*,
1939. This soft cap with woven
insignia remained popular long
after it ceased to be current
regulation.

was that officers' caps were usually bespoke, and often made of finer materials. Embroidered wreaths were frequently used on officers' caps, and sometimes even on other ranks' caps because they were also allowed to wear a privately purchased cap when 'walking out'. Interior linings were light-brown cotton when provided from store, but varied from light reddish-brown to yellowish-tan when tailor made, and private-purchase caps are usually also indicated as such by the manufacturer's name and other details on a label beneath a celluloid diamond-shaped shield under the crown.

Issue headgear had an official 'wearing-out period', and being subject to slower deterioration than trousers or combat gear could last a considerable time. So it was that flat *Tellerform* caps and technically obsolete peaked caps continued to be worn during World War II. The most popular of these was the so-called 'old pattern' officers' *Feldmütze*, introduced in 1934. This approximated to the *Schirmmütze* in general form, but lacked internal stiffening and had a flexible peak. No chin strap was worn with the old-pattern *Feldmütze*, and the oak-leaf wreath and *Kokarde* insignia were woven. The old-type cap had an official 'wearing-out' period set to end in 1942, but war and the demand for a practical, flexible soft peaked cap saw this stricture not only widely disregarded, but unofficial modifications of *Schirmmützen* to replicate the desirable characteristics of the old cap. Stiffeners, chin straps and buttons were therefore sometimes removed contrary to regulation. Other affectations included private-purchase caps with exaggerated saddles, and wearing the cap aslant on the head.

There were also official modifications to the *Schirmmütze* over time: later in the war, for example, officers' cap cords were made in grey rayon. Certain *Traditionabzeichen* ('tradition' badges), worn in addition to basic insignia, were also accepted. These included a small Prussian-style *Totenkopf* (Death's head comprising a skull and crossbones) awarded to various units between 1938 and 1944 in commemoration of their lineage from the Guard Hussar units of the Imperial German Army; a Brunswick-style *Totenkopf* introduced for descendants of former Brunswick units over the same period; and a small Prussian-style *Dragoneradler* (dragoon eagle) granted to various mounted units between 1937

ABOVE A 1938-dated infantry other ranks' *Schirmmütze*, with white *Waffenfarbe* piping and a *Totenkopf* (Death's head) *Traditionabzeichen* commemorating Brunswick antecedents.

FAR LEFT The *Dragoneradler*, or *Schwedter Adler*, *Traditionabzeichen*, photographed at Steglitz in 1940. Worn below the *Hoheitsabzeichen*, this small Prussian-style 'dragoon eagle' was commemorative of the former 1. Brandenburgisches Dragoner-Regiment 2 and originally worn by two squadrons of Kavallerie-Regiment 6, and, from 1937, by Kradschützen-Bataillon 3. In 1943 it was also granted to Kavallerie-Regiment *Mitte* on the Eastern Front. In 1944 it was allowed to the entirety of 3. Kavallerie-Brigade.

LEFT An infantryman presenting a more fashionable image by wearing the *Schirmmütze* without a stiffener.

and 1945. *Gebirgsjäger* were entitled to a small Edelweiss badge on the *Schirmmütze* from 1939 onward. Not a *Traditionabzeichen*, but worn in the same way, was the small Gothic cross of *Heeresgeistliche*. All of these emblems were placed between the eagle and *Kokarde* on headgear, except when these were made in one piece, in which case *Hoheitsabzeichen* were worn above the tradition badges.

The survival of some of the earlier soft peaked caps highlights the main shortcoming of the *Schirmmütze*, namely that while smart and practical for certain orders of dress, it was really too delicate for active service. An attempt to address this shortcoming was made in 1934 with the introduction of the soft fore-and-aft-folding *Feldmütze* of the same material as the *Feldanzug*. The original inspiration was Austro-Hungarian, and fore-and-aft field or 'side' caps were already worn by various armies of the 19th century. The new *Feldmütze* was described as *Bootsform* (boat shaped) and tapered toward the rear. It had a flap which could be lowered to cover the ears in bad weather and two small front buttons, and was lined in field-grey cloth. Initially, an inverted *Soutache* (cord chevron) of coloured wool worn at the front apex of the cap denoted arm of service, and within the *Soutache* was a *Kokarde*. This arrangement was soon replaced by the *Hoheitsabzeichen* eagle-and-swastika device at the top with *Soutache* and *Kokarde* below, and the cap assumed a sharper appearance in keeping with the style of the period by deletion of the front buttons. According to regulation, the *Feldmütze* was worn so that the rear of the head was covered, with the *Kokarde* at the centre line of the face, and tilted slightly so the cap edge lay 3cm above the left ear and 1cm above the right, and 1cm above the right eyebrow.

As of late 1942, troops of *Jäger* divisions were permitted to wear an *Eichenlaubabzeichen* (oak-leaf badge) on the left side of both the *Feldmütze* and the *Bergmütze* (mountain cap). In 1944 a similar badge with a ski across oak leaves was granted to personnel of 1. Skijäger-Brigade. It is also worth noting that a number of other semi-official or unofficial badges were applied to the side of various examples of the *Feldmütze* and *Bergmütze* during the war. Many were specific to unit and included the *Sardinienschild* (Sardinia shield) peculiar to 90. Panzergrenadier-Division, the 1. Panzer-Division oak leaf, the whippet of 116. Panzer-Division and the little sword sported by 290. Infanterie-Division. A chamois (goat-antelope) badge was used by 5. Gebirgs-Division, and eagle badges by leaders of some of the *Hochgebirgs* (high mountain) formations.

In 1938, an officers' version of the fore-and-aft-folding *Feldmütze* was introduced. This differed most obviously from the other ranks' model in that it was piped with aluminium cord (gold-coloured for generals), but it was also made of better materials and shaped to a more flattering cut with a narrower top.

Photographs suggest that other ranks also attempted to make the *Feldmütze* appear more up to date by wearing the top partially folded and canting it more to the side, particularly during the war years. That this more elegant version of the *Feldmütze* had been a less-than-practical triumph of form over function was cruelly demonstrated in the Soviet Union during the winter of 1941/42, when its inability to protect the wearer from anything stronger than a cool breeze became apparent. With little else available to cover their heads, soldiers wound scarves

LEFT An other ranks' *Feldmütze*, photographed in July 1942. Owing to its shape, later incarnations of the *Feldmütze* were nicknamed the *Schiffchen* ('little ship'). The inverted cord *Soutache* is in *Waffenfarbe*. The wearer has tilted this *Feldmütze* much further than the regulation angle.

BELOW LEFT The other ranks' *Feldmütze*, *c*.1943. Note that there is no *Soutache* in *Waffenfarbe*. This man wears both shirt and *Feldbluse* with *Litzen*.

BELOW The black Panzer variant of the *Feldmütze* with the *Soutache* in *Waffenfarbe*.

A Heer *Nachrichtenhelferin* (female signals auxiliary) pictured wearing a *Feldmütze* at Koblenz. The women's cap was of a distinctive stone grey with yellow piping and had a cloth *Blitzabzeichen* on the left side. Senior auxiliaries had piping running around the badge as well the flap and crown in yellow and black, silver or gold according to rank.

around capped heads or combined inadequate *Feldmützen* with *Kopfschützen* ('toques', tubular 'head-overs' of knitted material). The *Feldmütze* was also crammed under helmets and occasionally worn with improvised felt or fabric face masks in an often vain attempt to keep 'General Winter' at bay. Front-line efforts at protection were soon supplemented with captured Soviet headgear, both military and civilian, charitable collections from Germany and production of various *Pelzmützen* (fur and sheepskin caps). These last naturally varied considerably in type and design, but many incorporated field-grey fabric of the type used in uniforms, a lined or quilted interior, and flaps to protect the neck and sides of the face. Some were badged, but many were not.

In a belated but predictable volte-face, the standard other ranks' field cap was now redesigned, and the replacement – the new *Feldmütze* announced in the summer of 1942 – was in the shape of the *Bergmütze*, but without a visor. The new *Feldmütze* reintroduced the pair of vertically arranged front buttons deleted only a few years earlier (these could now be unfastened to drop a deep flap to protect the neck and sides of the face and refastened in front of the chin) and usually bore woven insignia, but did not have a *Soutache*, something already deleted from the original *Feldmütze*. Though the new headgear was initially announced as being intended for other ranks, officers could also wear the new type *Feldmütze* with appropriate silver piping. The fact that the redesigned *Feldmütze* was based on the *Bergmütze* was interesting and would set a precedent for future development.

It was also during 1942, in preparation for the coming winter, that manufacture of a *Kopfhaube* (literally a 'head cowl' or hood) took place on a large scale. This form of textile balaklava of grey or green wool came down round the shoulders and closed in front of the neck with a fabric tape. Many troops in the East received a *Kopfhaube*, and those that did not were supposed to be given two *Kopfschützen*. According to instructions for the *Kopfschutz*, a pair of these knitted tubular 'head-overs' could be worn together by pulling one over the head and down to the neck, and the other on to the head and over

One of the more common types of *Pelzmütze* used on the Eastern Front, with field-grey cloth shell and artificial-silk padded liner. The flaps are covered in what appears to be rabbit fur and may be pulled down to fasten under the chin. The soldier depicted wears the flaps in the raised position and appears to be wearing his zipped tracksuit underneath his *Feldbluse* for additional warmth.

TOP FAR LEFT A *Ritterkreuz* recipient blowing a signal whistle and wearing another of the more common types of *Pelzmütze*, featuring flaps with tapes fastening under the chin. Officers could obtain their own binoculars and though specialists used more powerful varieties, the standard type for infantry-squad leaders was the 6×30 *Dienstglas*, also intended to equip other arms of service.

TOP LEFT A young official in Finland, *c.*1942, wearing a tall, local-type white *Pelzmütze*. While unusual, this cap was not unique as other men, apparently in the same unit, were pictured in similar headgear.

ABOVE This issue-type *Pelzmütze* with field-grey cloth body, fur flaps, eagle badge, *Kokarde* and *Soutache* was worn reasonably frequently in the East.

FAR LEFT An astrakhan-style fleece cap of the Caucasus type with regulation eagle badge, sometimes worn in the East.

LEFT A much-decorated Heer *Major* wearing what may well be a unique deerskin winter cap with the animal skin mounted on what appears to be a regulation officers' field-grey *Feldmütze* with badges.

ABOVE AUF WACHT ('On watch'), a contemporary postcard showing a sentry wearing a *Kopfschutz* under the other ranks' *Feldmütze*, and a *Wachtmantel*.

ABOVE RIGHT The *Bergmütze* worn with snow goggles by a *Gebirgsjäger* manning an MG 13 light machine gun, just prior to World War II.

the ears. The lower one could then be pulled back up as far as the top of the head so as to leave only the eyes and middle of the face exposed.

Gebirgsjäger wore distinctive headgear; with the re-formation of the *Gebirgsjäger* in the 1930s, the cap chosen was modelled on an Austrian original, but was also very much a sleeker version of the mountain headgear worn in World War I. The new *Bergmütze* was of field-grey material, and high at the front. The peak was calculated to shade the eyes when the wearer's hands were occupied during climbing or shooting. Two buttons released a fold-down flap to cover the lower head. These buttons changed in type over time, but as of the mid-1930s were of a *Steinnussbraun* (stone nut brown) natural material; the eagle and swastika and *Kokarde* were introduced under the Nazi regime. Stiffening to the front of the *Bergmütze* was deleted in 1936, and as of May 1939 the practice of wearing an Edelweiss badge on the wearer's left-hand side of the *Bergmütze* was formalized. As with other field caps, the officers' variant *Bergmütze* incorporated silver or aluminium piping, officially noted from 1942, and officers usually ordered their headgear privately. As *Gebirgsjäger* were frequently deployed at altitude and in snowy conditions, the *Bergmütze* was also worn with a white camouflage cover, and occasional – presumably unofficial – white versions of the cap are also encountered.

FAR LEFT The *Einheitsfeldmütze* ('universal' field cap) worn by a veteran of the Eastern Front, *c.*1943–44.

CENTRE LEFT Panzer commander Oberstleutnant Franz Bäke (1898–1978) wears the officers' black Panzer variant of the *Einheitsfeldmütze*. The highly decorated Bäke fought in both world wars and won not only the *Ritterkreuz mit Eichenlaub und Schwerten*, but both classes of the *Eisernes Kreuz* and three *Panzervernichtungsabzeichen*. At the end of World War II he commanded Panzer-Division *Feldherrnhalle 2* as a *Generalmajor*. After being released from US captivity in 1947, he resumed his civilian career as a dentist in Hagen.

LEFT The Panzer troops' version of the *Einheitsfeldmütze* was of the same design as the ordinary type, but in black cloth.

TOP LEFT The interior of the same Panzer *Einheitsfeldmütze*, showing the grey lining, the size (55) and date (1944), and the 'RB' code number, denoting the (unknown) manufacturer.

The *Bergmütze* proved popular and practical, and, as noted above, inspired the redesigned *Feldmütze*. Almost immediately, a much more important and logical step was taken when in mid-1943 an *Einheitsfeldmütze* (literally 'universal field cap') was introduced to replace all field caps for all ranks. The *Einheitsfeldmütze* betrayed its lineage very clearly, having the same double-button arrangement as the *Feldmütze* and *Bergmütze* plus a pronounced peak, and was made of field-grey uniform cloth. It was also similar in outline to the *Tropen Feldmütze* (tropical field cap). Like the earlier field caps, it was also produced in black for armoured troops and a silver- or aluminium-piped version for officers.

In the winter months of the last two years of war, some privately purchased and unofficial versions of the *Einheitsfeldmütze* incorporating wool and fur panels were also in evidence. Despite its relatively late appearance, the new 'universal' cap was made in huge numbers, and was the dominant form of soft headgear when the war ended even though many other types of cap were still in use. Interestingly, camouflage caps approximating to the *Einheitsfeldmütze* design, made from official materials, also appear in period photographs. These are not, however, issue items, having been privately made. That the *Einheitsfeldmütze* of 1943 was a great success and formed a model for various pieces of post-war military headgear is not in doubt. One is, however, left wondering whether a huge amount of time and effort might have been saved by retaining the universal cap of 1917, rebadging and producing it in new materials or with flaps as required.

TROPICAL HEADGEAR

As Germany had been stripped of its colonies after World War I, there was little use for tropical military equipment of any kind in the interwar period. A good deal of material was disposed of as a consequence, and the original 'brown shirts' of the Nazi Party, for example, have been attributed to surplus stocks of tropical kit found in Austria. The entry of the Heer into areas with warm climates during World War II therefore presented no small problem.

Some Heer troops in North Africa adopted captured French, Dutch or British tropical helmets, but a German type was also issued. The new *Tropenhelm* was of the classic 'pith' or sun-helmet type, being made of light pressed cork covered in six panels of olive or khaki cloth. A grey leather band protected the bottom rim, and a felt ring, leather sweatband and red lining completed the interior. The button atop the *Tropenhelm* concealed a vent. A second, simplified, version of the *Tropenhelm* existed in which the helmet body was of olive pressed felt with an olive leather band around the rim. Limited use was also made of a third type of *Tropenhelm*, in white, for parades only.

In truth, the *Tropenhelm* was not a particularly imaginative answer to the need for tropical headgear. Derived from 19th-century technology, it offered no ballistic protection whatsoever and – balanced against the resources required for production – its level of climatic protection was modest. Arguably, it said more about Germany's aspirations to rejoin the Imperial club, and it was certainly distinctively German, having small metal shields on either side of similar design to the insignia found on the *Stahlhelm*: the Heer eagle and swastika on the left, and the red, white and black national colours on the right. These detachable emblems proved useful as they could also be used to rebadge captured helmets. The white parade *Tropenhelm* lacked side shields, having a large white-metal *Hoheitsabzeichen* to the front instead. The marginal utility of the *Tropenhelm* was tacitly acknowledged at the end of 1941 and it was gradually abandoned thereafter.

The *Tropen Feldmütze* (tropical field cap) was much more successful, and while there were peakless types based on the folding *Feldmütze*, it was the peaked version

which proved practical and popular, becoming forever associated with the Deutsches Afrikakorps. Formally introduced in 1941, it was of similar outline to the *Bergmütze*, though with a longer peak. Made in olive cotton drill, it was lined in red, and though an external seam lent the impression of a fold or flap, there was none present. Initially, the *Tropen Feldmütze* included a Russia-braid *Soutache* in *Waffenfarbe*, but this was deleted on later examples. The eagle and *Kokarde* were generally of woven manufacture on a mustard-colour backing. Officers' *Tropen Feldmützen* retained the usual aluminium piping around the crown. Well worn under the blazing sun, the *Tropen Feldmütze* faded to almost any shade between olive-brown and off-white. Like other tropical items, the cap was worn in various warm theatres and its manufacture continued until 1944.

THE STEEL HELMET

The German *Stahlhelm* (steel helmet) worn in World War I was developed in 1915 and widely issued from 1916. It was designed to address the problem of head injuries sustained by soldiers in trenches, and specifically to prevent wounding by often small and low-velocity shell fragments, and indeed anything else thrown around in battle. Developmental work included testing trial *Stahlhelme* on an artillery range. As finalized, the first *Stahlhelm* was not bullet-proof, but was fitted with two prominent side lugs onto which a brow plate could be fitted for a measure of bullet protection to the front upper head. The liner system was primitive but clever, consisting of three pads, and increasing or decreasing the amount of wadding combined with different-sized helmet shells enabled a good fit to be obtained for virtually any head. The 1916 *Stahlhelm* was bulky but effective, and soon popular, being preferred to leather helmets or soft caps on the battlefield.

For more than a decade after the end of World War I, there was no need to make significant changes to the *Stahlhelm* design, though a state emblem in the shape of a *Wappenschild* (coloured shield) was often applied to the side. In 1931,

BELOW A soldier in Reichsheer cap altering *Stahlhelm* decals, *c.*1933. Note how the unit abbreviation and name of each soldier is painted in white on the inner skirt of the headgear. (Prisma/UIG/Getty Images)

ABOVE RIGHT Staff officers examine documents during manoeuvres, *c.*1939. The helmet worn in the centre is a 1918 *Stahlhelm* with cut-outs over the ears to improve the hearing of the wearer and an identifying manoeuvre band around the crown. (ullstein bild/Getty Images)

TOP LEFT A World War I *Stahlhelm* with Innenaustattung 31 and Nazi-period decals as re-used during World War II.

ABOVE A soldier wearing a 1917 or 1918-manufactured *Stahlhelm* early in World War II.

LEFT Front and side views of an *Unteroffizier* of a *Landesschützen-Bataillon* wearing a 1916-type *Stahlhelm* without decals.

however, a modern liner system, the Innenaustattung 31, was devised and subsequently retrofitted to helmets in service. This liner consisted of a pair of metal bands to hold a ring of perforated leather tongues inside the shell. A drawstring linked the tips of the tongues and could be tightened to secure a good fit. Like the earlier liner system the Innenaustattung 31 served to keep the wearer's head cushioned and clear of the helmet shell, thus reducing the shock of impacts or the danger caused by damage to the steel outer surface. Despite the change of political regime there was no change to the basic helmet, but as of 1933 it was ordered that a new *Wappenschild* should be applied in the national colours of red, white and black. The following year, instructions introduced a new Heer eagle-and-swastika decal to be worn on the left side, and it appears

ABOVE A left-side view of a Stahlhelm 35. The air vent over the Heer insignia has a separate bushing in the hole and the edge of the helmet is rolled over for a smooth finish.

ABOVE RIGHT A Thale-manufactured Stahlhelm 35 as worn in c.1939–40, with the very prominent shield in national colours on the wearer's right-hand side.

RIGHT A right-side view of a Stahlhelm 35. From this angle we see the national shield, featuring diagonal stripes of black, white and red.

that many helmets were now also repainted field grey. Despite the introduction of a new model of *Stahlhelm* from 1935, massive demand ensured that the old combination of World War I helmet with new liner and insignia continued to be worn throughout World War II, usually in second-line units. Indeed, new insignia were also applied to old Austrian helmet shells, and to variants of the original 1916 *Stahlhelm* including the 1918 type with cut-outs over the ears, originally designed to improve the hearing of the wearer.

Nevertheless, it was recognized that at some point an entirely new helmet would be required, and with redesign, the bulk, weight and thermal properties should be reconsidered. So it was that in 1932, a radical new type of helmet was put forward for testing. At first glance, the experimental piece looked broadly similar to the old, but it was made out of vulcanized fibre and, including liner, weighed a mere 450g. Though this fibre helmet reached troop trials, it was perhaps too far ahead of its time, so in the event the new helmet eventually accepted for service was effectively a sleeker, more compact version of the steel World War I model with an Innenausstattung 31 liner. Following further trials focused on the effects of weapons fitted with optical devices, hearing when wearing the new helmet and practical field tests with troops, the Stahlhelm 35 was announced as such by Generalmajor Werner Freiherr von Fritsch, *Oberbefehlshaber des Heeres* (Commander-in-Chief of the Army), in June 1935.

As notifications remarked, the Stahlhelm 35 offered improvements over the World War I helmets, being less bulky and lacking the prominent side lugs of its predecessors. The helmet shell was a steel pressing to which separately manufactured parts, liners, rivets and straps were fitted after initial painting. It was produced in six helmet-shell sizes (60cm, 62cm, 64cm, 66cm, 68cm and 70cm) with 11 possible liner fittings accommodating head sizes from 53cm to 63cm. The Stahlhelm 35 steel was 1.1–1.2mm thick, and the helmet shell weighed approximately 1kg, variations depending on size. As was reported in 1943, the ballistic testing process involved sample helmets being evaluated by shooting at them, originally using 11mm lead bullets, but after February 1943 with a bench-rested P 08 semi-automatic pistol at a 5m range using a sintered-iron bullet and a reduced propellant charge of 220mg. Shots were aimed at the helmet's front above the visor, the rear, and to the side of the liner rivet. Some of the sample helmets were also shot in the sides and vertically from the top. A shallow dent was acceptable, but any penetration, cracking or fragmentation was deemed to be a failure. Despite this test, the Stahlhelm 35 was definitely not bullet-proof against full-load rifle and machine-gun bullets at anything but extreme range or very shallow angles, and it was regularly penetrated in battle.

Officially, a properly fitted helmet rested 2cm above the wearer's eyebrows and the gap between scalp and helmet was also 2cm. On the Eastern Front, however, it was soon discovered that the gap between metal and head – so vital to protection – was a menace in sub-zero temperatures. Official advice was that the helmet be lined, for example with the crown of an old felt hat, a handkerchief or crumpled paper, the soldier being careful not to touch the bare metal of a frozen helmet. The chin strap was to be worn slightly loose so that blood circulation was not impaired. Regulations stated that simple repairs to helmet fittings could be undertaken by a unit armourer, and for remedial work to leather, a saddler might be employed. Misuse of the helmet, for example as an improvised cooking pot, was strictly forbidden because heat had a detrimental effect on its ballistic resistance. Badges other than approved side decals were likewise forbidden.

Though there were detailed changes to the original specifications, these did not constitute new 'models', and until 1945 the *Stahlhelm* was described as the '35' in official documentation, distinguishing it from old types which should theoretically have been superseded, but in practice were still in use. Despite the designation, few helmets of the new type were actually issued in 1935, but large orders began to arrive in 1936. Some early delays in production were attributable to problems with rivets and fulfilling a large export order from China, but the key factor was the burgeoning size of the Heer, so that as late as April 1937, OKH (Oberkommando des Heeres) still required 2.2 million new helmets.

ABOVE Detail of the Innenaustattung 31 liner, showing the eight perforated leather tongues joined by a drawstring. The '57' denotes the head size in centimetres.

ABOVE RIGHT A Stahlhelm 35, code letters 'SE', manufactured by Sächsische Emaillier-und Stanzwerke AG, one of the first firms to begin production of the new helmet.

RIGHT This Heer medic's Stahlhelm 35 is code-marked 'EF', indicating it was manufactured by Emaillierwerke of Fulda. This large-size example (66cm shell circumference) has the sharp edge to the rim associated with late production.

BELOW Stahlhelm 35 interior, showing the eight perforated leather tongues of the liner, the drawstring in the crown and the black leather chin strap.

Total production of German *Stahlhelme* from 1935 to 1945 was huge and has been estimated as high as 25 million items: by far the largest single user was the Heer, but a proportion served the other armed forces and the Schutzstaffel (SS), and, despite an order to the contrary in 1941, a few were used by other organizations. Though ceremonial and lightweight *Stahlhelme*, liners, chin straps and accessories were manufactured by other concerns, there were just five major manufacturers of the helmet shell: Eisenhüttenwerke of Thale, Emaillierwerke of Fulda, Vereinigte Deutsche Nickelwerke of Schwerte, F.W. Quist of Esslingen and Sächsische Emaillier-und Stanzwerke of Lauter.

Excepting camouflage measures, almost all changes to the wartime *Stahlhelm* are explicable in terms of expediency, simplification and cost cutting. In March 1940, OKH announced the deletion of the separate bushings to the helmet air vents which were now merely an embossed part of the shell; and it was also about this time that the national decal was omitted from the right-hand side. Tri-coloured shield badges on the side of the helmet were conspicuous in battle, so many were painted over or removed altogether. Leather liners declined in quality and were now often made from pig hide. The use of zinc in liner rings increased and that of aluminium decreased due to the latter being needed elsewhere in war production. In 1942, the inward crimping of the helmet rim was abandoned, leaving a relatively sharp edge. At the same time the helmet shell's thickness was increased very slightly, apparently more to make the manufacturing processes easier than to improve protection. Application of the Heer's eagle insignia was discontinued in 1943.

None of this constituted the introduction of a new model: using up old materials was permitted, and there were instances where regulations were ignored, and old helmets were also refurbished. Moreover, even the change to the vent bushings was not an innovation of 1940 at all. The idea was patented as early as October 1938 on the grounds of both savings and the potential danger that the bushings might become flying fragments when helmets were damaged in combat, and Eisenhüttenwerke Thale may have implemented the change before the formal notice to do so was issued.

BOTTOM LEFT This Stahlhelm 35 features blotches of tan-coloured paint and a 1940-dated *Brotbeutel* (bread bag) strap rigged to take foliage for additional camouflage.

BELOW Helmet rim details showing (left) the turned-over, smooth edge of early-production helmets, and (right) the unfinished or 'raw' edge of late-production examples.

BOTTOM Stahlhelm 35 inner shell marking 'ET64', denoting the manufacturer (Eisenhüttenwerke Thale AG) and the shell circumference (64cm).

The Stahlhelm 35 colour also changed over time. Early issues were finished in a smooth field-grey paint of a noticeably greenish hue. Some Heer soldiers accentuated the smartness of the finish by polishing or even varnishing it to a parade-ground shine, though this was officially frowned upon as ruining the original surface and compromising camouflage. The campaign against gloss went further in March 1940 with official orders for helmets to be painted in a roughened 'slate grey'; pending arrival of official textured paint, troops were to smear them with earth or clay in an attempt to reduce shine. The colour slate

RIGHT The Stahlhelm 35 worn by this crewman of a 5cm light mortar has an arrangement of straps to help retain camouflage in place.

BELOW Members of an infantry squad with an MG 08/15 light machine gun wear natural helmet camouflage retained by elasticated bands and straps, *c.*1939.

LEFT An MG 34 machine-gunner wearing a mosquito net over his *Stahlhelm*.

BELOW How the *Stahlhelm* could disappear in battle: an observer uses a helmet band packed with local vegetation. This photograph was taken by a *Propagandakompanie* in April 1940.

BOTTOM A machine-gunner with a helmet net and foliage concealing his *Stahlhelm*. (Bundesarchiv, Bild 146-1991-024-10A, Foto: Bauer)

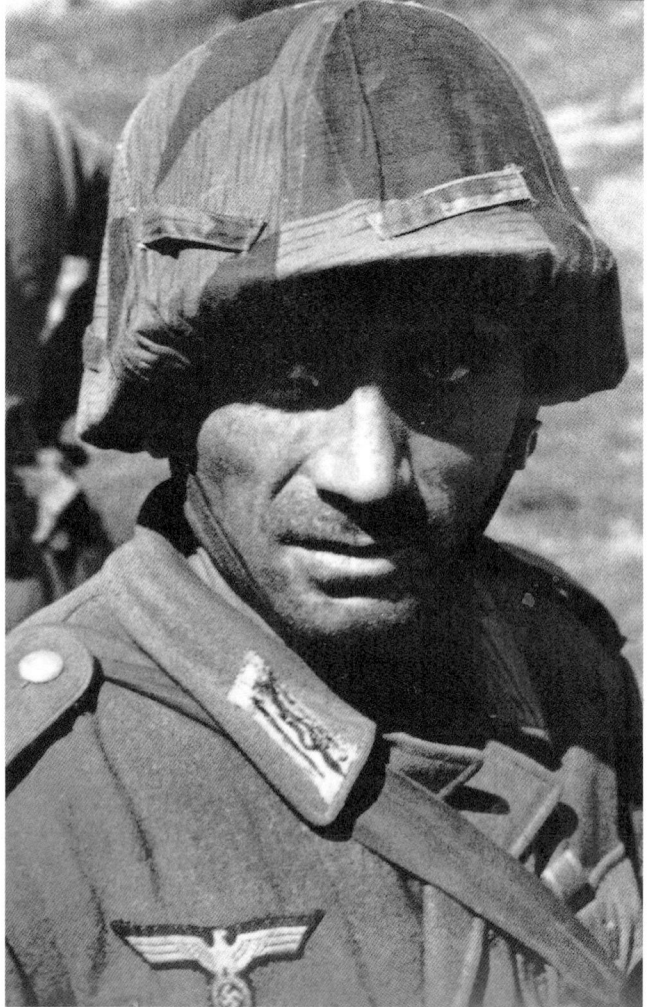

ABOVE Armed with a *Panzerfaust* anti-tank weapon, this *Unteroffizier*, photographed in June 1944, wears a *Panzervernichtungsabzeichen* and an improvised helmet cover made from sacking and chicken wire.

ABOVE RIGHT An issue-type camouflage helmet cover in use. Note the fabric loops for holding additional foliage.

grey appears to have been liberally interpreted, with helmets now in anything from a medium grey to almost black tinged with green. Those helmets painted in factories or completely refurbished received a thorough job inside and out, but those repainted hastily by units in the field often retained the old smooth interior. The texturing could be coarse or subtle. Later helmets were again painted in various shades of field grey, this time with a dull finish. Colours varied more dramatically with the requirements of theatre and terrain. Whitewash or white paint was partially or completely applied over the existing colour in snowy conditions, and a yellowish-sand colour was used in North Africa, Italy and other warm areas. Red-brown, sand and green were all found in the camouflage palette for equipment and vehicles, and particularly later in the war all these colours were applied to helmets. Sometimes, colour was applied randomly with grey patches still visible underneath; at other times, soldiers used their artistry and imagination to create swirls, flecks and geometric designs, copying patterns from shelter-quarters or mimicking specific environments.

Camouflage is most effective when it disguises or conceals the outline of a helmet, and during World War II there were many different attempts to achieve this, both by creating shadows and by hiding the shape entirely. A very basic technique used a *Helmband* (helmet band) into which was pushed local vegetation: some *Helmbanden* were rubber or elasticated, but equipment and bag straps and other improvisations were commonplace. Wire, particularly chicken wire, could be effective. A helmet net for the *Stahlhelm* was patented in 1938, and during the war helmet nets existed in both official and unofficial forms. Instructions for an issue type introduced in 1942 describe a helmet net with hooks at the rim and a drawstring to tighten around the helmet. Some helmet nets were significantly larger than the helmet itself, allowing both a portion to hang in front of the face and the use of plenty of vegetation or straw. Out of combat zones, helmet nets could be stowed inside the helmet under the liner.

Camouflage helmet cover worn with oak leaves attached to a band, by a soldier armed with a P 08 semi-automatic pistol and equipped with a *Klappspaten* (folding spade).

Reversible helmet covers with sprung hooks were patented in February 1937, the patent being issued jointly in the names of Johann Schick, director of the German camouflage research unit, and Reichführer-SS Heinrich Himmler. Nevertheless, as in World War I, Heer *Stahlhelme* were worn with both official issue and improvised helmet covers, basic types of which were made locally from sacking, or from white cloth for snowy conditions. Moreover, Heer camouflage helmet covers were usually secured with drawstrings or bands, rather than hooks. Official issue of a *Zeltbahn*-pattern-printed camouflage-material helmet cover appears to have started in 1941: this was reversible to white and was attached with a drawstring. Worn *Zeltbahnen* and other camouflage materials were also cut up to create helmet covers. In North Africa, tan-coloured fabric helmet covers were sometimes used. Occasionally, helmet covers were teamed with face veils or hanging strips of camouflage material.

Stahlhelme worn with mosquito nets in the down position on the Eastern Front in the summer of 1942.

Interestingly, the Stahlhelm 35 was being re-evaluated almost as soon as it was issued. In 1936, Dresden-based inventors Bath and Wagawa registered patents for new chin straps, as well as a peakless model of the helmet for use in conjunction with gas masks. In 1937 and 1938, helmet hanging straps were devised by both Josef Welte and Franz Schmidt. It was also realized that the somewhat slab-sided Stahlhelm 35 offered too many surfaces for perpendicular bullet strikes, and Professor Hugo Leven patented an extraordinarily tall curvaceous helmet, which – happily – was never manufactured. Also in 1938, the inventor Amelie Banfield von dem Knesebeck produced designs for several different face visors with slots, or that slid down to cover the face much like the helmet used by a medieval knight. Such fanciful ideas had little practical impact, however, but with the advent of war, official interest in improvements was triggered.

As early as the end of 1939, after the conclusion of the Polish campaign, Professor Fry and Dr Hänsel of the Chemisch-Technischen Reichsanstalt vom Institut für Wehrtechnische Werkstoffkunde Berlin (Chemical-Technical Reichs Institute for Defence Technology and Materials Research Berlin) gathered German, French and British helmets for evaluation. All were penetrated by small-calibre rifle bullets. Further interest concentrated on reported shortcomings of the Stahlhelm 35: these included its near-vertical sides and the angle between its sides and skirt, both of which were potential areas of ballistic weakness, plus the continuing complaints about difficulties of both operating equipment and hearing while wearing the Stahlhelm 35. Progress appears to have been limited for some time, however, but given increasing worries about head wounds, prototypes of new *Stahlhelme* were eventually brought forward. By 1944, laboratory and factory work had produced several experimental models, all of which were smoother in outline, simpler and more conical or domed than the Stahlhelm 35, lending both ballistic and manufacturing advantages as they required only three steps in the stamping process rather than the then-current four. New *Stahlhelme* were tested at Infanterie-Schule Döberitz in combination with a wide variety of weapons and equipment. Further trials were planned with Ersatz-Brigade *Großdeutschland* and a cavalry regiment, but the progress of the war overtook the process and no new *Stahlhelm* model was adopted before May 1945.

ABOVE MG 34 machine-gunners wearing a *Helmband*, *c.*1939. Note the remote trigger used in conjunction with the sustained-fire mounting.

LEFT A Stahlhelm 35 made by the F.W. Quist company of Esslingen with a Helmband 36 around the crown. The manoeuvre band in red and yellow was reversible to distinguish different participating forces in exercises.

ABOVE A Panzer crewman wearing the *Schutzmütze*. The black-cloth outer cover concealed a shock-absorbing sponge-rubber inner to protect the tank crewman's head against knocks sustained while operating within an armoured vehicle.

ABOVE RIGHT A veteran *Feldwebel* wearing a lightweight parade helmet with distinctive large air vents. He may be using the lightweight helmet due to a head injury which has disfigured the right-hand side of his face, here turned away from the camera.

PARADE HELMETS AND THE PANZER BERET

Parade helmets were privately purchased lightweight versions of *Stahlhelme* obtained mainly by officers and NCOs for ceremonial functions. They looked smart, were more comfortable to wear than full-weight headgear, and had the less obvious benefit that the purchaser was spared the tedious business of making an issue combat *Stahlhelm* spotless for every formal occasion. Parade helmets could be had direct from manufacturers, or bought over the counter in retail outfitters. At a glance, the various types look similar to the Stahlhelm 35, or its predecessors, but closer examination betrays important differences. World War I-type *Stahlhelme* were produced in both aluminium and vulcanized fibre, and from the mid-1930s could be encountered with the standard Heer decal arrangement. In another variant, the outline of the World War I *Stahlhelm* was but loosely interpreted, having a relatively wide skirt. Copies of the Stahlhelm 35 began soon after the model was settled upon, and again *Vulkanfiber* and aluminium were the main materials.

Perhaps the best-known brand of fibre helmet was the *Erel*, advertising for which claimed that its manufacturer, Robert Lubstein of Berlin, was the largest producer of both fibre helmets and shakos. The *Erel* fibre helmet was described as being 'extra light', and in at least one version the visor was downwardly inclined: this may have helped keep the glare of the sun out of the wearer's eyes, but it also had the side-effect of the wearer tending to keep his head more upright, thus encouraging soldierly bearing. In addition to their materials and outline, parade helmets also differed from standard *Stahlhelme* in terms of details such as rivet and air-vent types and positions. It is also worth noting that some very small helmets were not intended for service use at all, as toy manufacturers also took advantage of young popular interest in the *Stahlhelm*.

Another unusual headgear was the *Schutzmütze* (literally 'protective cap'), better known in English as the Panzer beret. Neither term fully describes this headgear as it was actually both a protective helmet and a beret. The inner was a thick cap of firm, shock-absorbing sponge rubber with a black oil-cloth liner over which fitted a large black 'beret' of woven wool. Initially, the only insignia was a woven *Reichskokarde* with oak-leaf wreath, but the eagle and swastika was also specified from 1935. During the war, a field-grey version of the beret was issued for assault-gun crews, though it was never universally used. There was even a variant for winter use in which the cover over the basic rubber cap was of field-grey cloth and fur. Like many tank-crew helmets, the *Schutzmütze* was not so much a form of protection against the enemy as an attempt to minimize the many knocks to the head that tank crewmen suffered while crawling through and bouncing about within an armoured vehicle. First produced in 1934 and widely worn in the early campaigns of World War II, the *Schutzmütze* was discontinued in 1941, but it had an official 2½-year 'wearing out' period and a few could still be seen in service long afterwards.

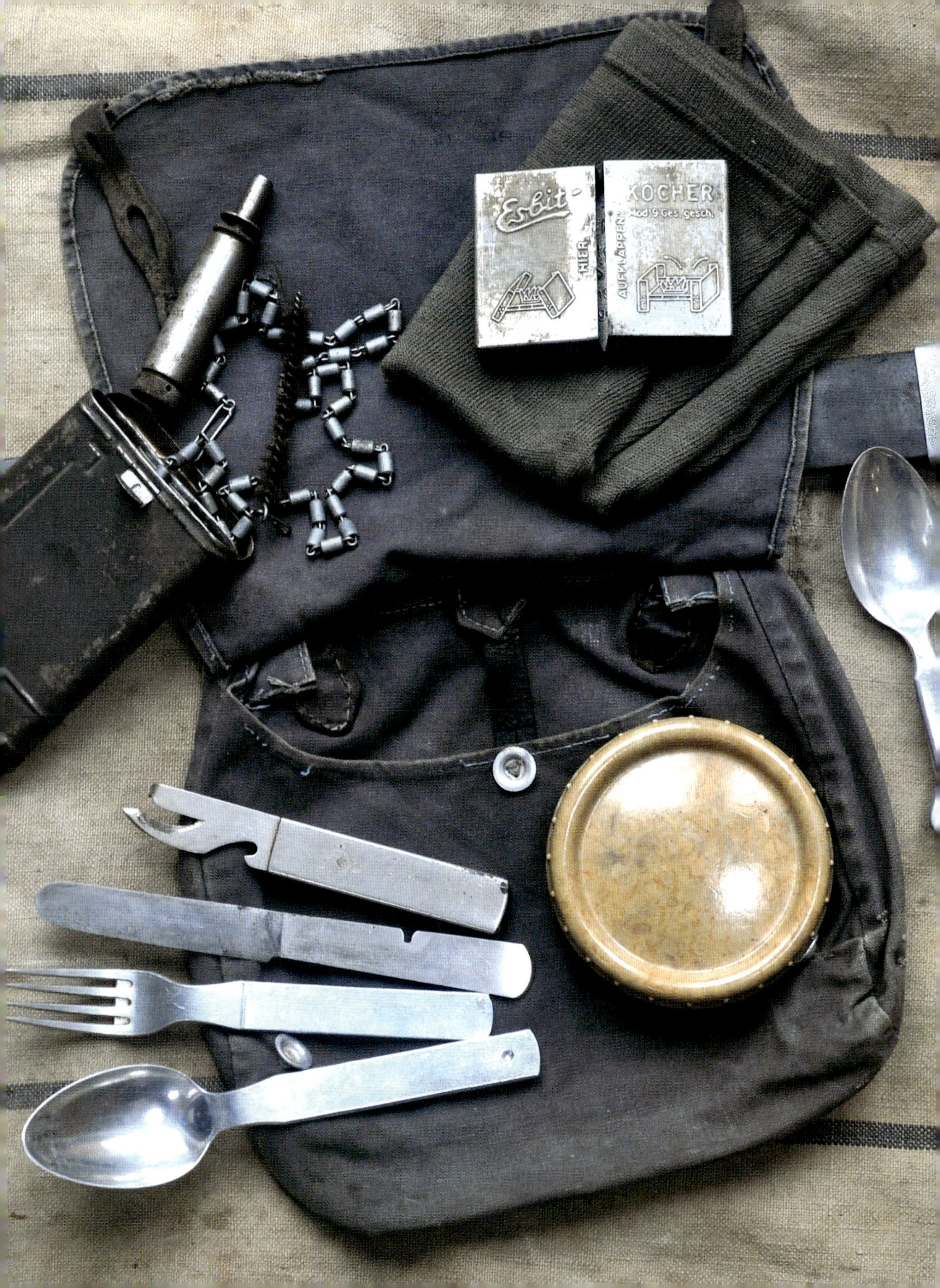
Esbit-
KOCHER
Mod 9 Ges. gesch.
HIER

CHAPTER 3
PERSONAL EQUIPMENT

A *Brotbeutel* with typical contents, laid out on a 1938-dated Heer food sack. The cutlery (left) is an issue clip-together four-piece set; part of a private-purchase hinged lightweight spoon-and-fork is shown to the right. The yellow-brown Bakelite *Fettbüchse*, for fat or spreads, is marked with the 'OX' mark of Karl Friedrich Seiter of Bollwerk. The rifle-cleaning kit (top left) contains brushes, tools, oil bottle, 'pull throughs' and lubricant and is marked 'cmr 43', indicating Hauswirtschaftsmaschinen GmbH (HAWIG) of Berlin, 1943. Top right: the Esbit Kocher Modell 9 is by the Schumm company of Stuttgart, *c.*1940–43. The cooker rests on a knitted *Kopfschutz* manufactured in 1944.

A soldier's personal equipment serves to ease the burden of the many things taken to war, both in combat and in movement from place to place. Its key functions are to spread weight comfortably and adaptably. It must be tough and durable, and able to absorb as far as possible the impacts of climate and heavy usage. Ideally, personal equipment is also smart and inexpensive, though these qualities may stand at odds with practicality. While some solutions are better than others, none is perfect in a long war as new weapons are introduced, technology moves on and shortages are felt. Change is therefore inevitable, and this was very much the case with the Heer in World War II.

German infantry had entered World War I wearing equipment designed at the end of the previous century. Its basis was a leather waist belt on which hung vital items including *Patronentaschen* (ammunition pouches), bayonet, *Brotbeutel* (bread bag), digging implement and *Feldflasche* ('field flask', i.e. water bottle). Introduced in 1895, the Tornister 95, a framed backpack, retained a hairy cowhide exterior, and three separate short straps allowed a soldier's *Mantel* and *Zeltbahn* to be mounted over the top and down the sides. This was quickly found to be imperfect because carrying out an assault while wearing a heavy pack was difficult, but attacking with nothing except what could be accommodated on a waist belt often left the soldier cold and wet after an initial clash of arms. Orders soon allowed main packs to be dumped prior to the start of an attack, which led to the *Sturmgepäck* (assault kit) being officially sanctioned. The *Sturmgepäck* was cobbled together from straps, *Zeltbahn* or *Mantel*, *Kochgeschirr* (mess tin) and other necessaries. Sandbags, grenade bags and other carriers appeared. The *Tornister* survived, but manufacture was simplified, with greater use of canvas. Cavalry equipment of World War I was distinctively different because much of the weight was on the horse rather than the rider. The mounted man carried a lighter burden, mainly on his waist belt supported by straps over the shoulders.

Not much was likely to be achieved in the 1920s in terms of equipment design, given that Germany now had a very small army and was a country on its knees economically. It is surprising, however, that more dramatic progress was not made by the mid-1930s. As it was, the basic leather *Gewehrpatronentaschen* (rifle-ammunition pouches) remained little changed except that the smaller 60-round capacity (in two triple pockets worn either side of the belt) was made standard for infantry as well as cavalry. The other ranks' leather waistbelt acquired a Heer eagle-and-swastika clasp in 1936. Introduced in 1931, the canvas Brotbeutel 31 was similar in general form to its World War I equivalent.

The same year also saw the appearance of a *Bekleidungssack* (clothing bag) in field-grey canvas, described by regulation as being made of lightweight waterproof cotton of the type used for the *Brotbeutel*. Soft and flexible, about

OPPOSITE A Bekleidungssack 31 with typical contents as used by an NCO during training, *c.*1944. The items shown are a late-type shirt with attached collar and 'U.S.' (*Unteroffizier-Schule*) *Schulterklappen*, a *Kragenbinde* for a uniform jacket, *Gamaschen* (gaiters), torch and a copy of *Darüber lache ich heute noch* ('I still laugh about it today'), a 1944 officially produced piece of humour for the troops.

The Tornister 34 with integral carry straps and unshaven-hide flap over a closure panel was a modest improvement on its World War I predecessor. Nevertheless, its capacity and versatility were limited, particularly if the *Kochgeschirr* (mess tin) was carried inside.

the size and shape of a briefcase, the *Bekleidungssack* was not really intended for field use but was extra capacity for transport or leave. It was a fairly general issue item, and indeed during the war some troops in rear-area units, not having a pack, were given two. The *Taschenkalender* of 1941 lists the contents of a dismounted soldier's *Bekleidungssack* as being his *Drillichanzug*, one pair each of underpants and socks, a *Halsbinde* (neck band) and 'other commodities'. Additionally, mounted troops were supposed to cram in a pair of *Schnürschuhe* (ankle boots). This was an extremely optimistic wish list for what was a small space, and while bulging *Bekleidungssacke* can be seen in photographs, it is very unlikely that they contained the regulation load.

Though it lacked a wooden frame, the Tornister 34, introduced in 1934, bore distinct similarities to its predecessors. It had an unshaven-hide flap closed by two buckles and over-the-shoulder straps linking to the *Patronentaschen* at the front, with secondary straps passing under the arms to connect to the bottom of the pack. The pack body was of double water-repellent canvas. Under the outer vertical flap were two further thin canvas flaps closing horizontally with buckles. These were opened to provide access to the main void in which was a small pouch designed to hold the *Kochgeschirr* as well as a relatively modest space for the other contents. By regulation, the items stowed here were shoes or ankle boots, socks, tent rope, cleaning materials and a canned-meat ration. Under the outer flap was a pouch intended for shaving and sewing kit, towel and underwear. The Tornister 34 was made in three sizes. Several editions of the *Taschenkalender* describe a method for strapping a spade to the pack, though during the war, digging implements were usually suspended from the belt.

When shelter-section and *Mantel* or blanket were carried these were wrapped neatly, bound with three *Mantel* straps and placed around the top and sides of the pack. When correctly fastened, it was not necessary to unbuckle all the carrying straps to remove the rolled *Mantel* and shelter-section as they were connected by tabs passing through leather loops on the pack. Nevertheless, preparing and fitting neatly required time and practice. That this was the case is attested by the existence of the *Mantelroll*, a stuffed-cloth roll made from worn-out *Mäntel* with no function other than to appear like a neatly packed *Mantel* and blanket. With a *Mantelroll* the soldier escaped the chore of packing and unpacking for the parade ground and saved crumpling his coat. It appears that this device was not general issue, however; it was was kept only in barracks and saw little use during wartime.

Despite other developments, we can be certain from surviving examples that production of the Tornister 34 continued well into World War II. Most late-production examples had a canvas back-flap edged with leather reinforcement, and one of the companies still manufacturing the design in 1940 was C. Pose Wehrausrustungen of Berlin. It is also interesting to note that soldier slang referred to the hairy and potentially burdensome backpack as

Barrack equipment parade, *c.*1938. The troops' Tornister 34 backpacks are laid out in front of them on stools together with their *Kochgeschirre*, *Brotbeutel* and other items.

RIGHT Interior detail of a Tornister 34 manufactured by Otto Sindel of Berlin, 1937. The *Kochgeschirr* has its own pouch, sewn permanently to the inside-top of the main compartment.

BELOW Textbook *Tornister* packing from the Reibert manual. Laundry and a hand towel are inside the closure flap; laced shoes, cleaning kit and iron rations are packed tightly around the *Kochgeschirr* in its fabric pouch. A *Mantel* is rolled around the outside and secured with straps.

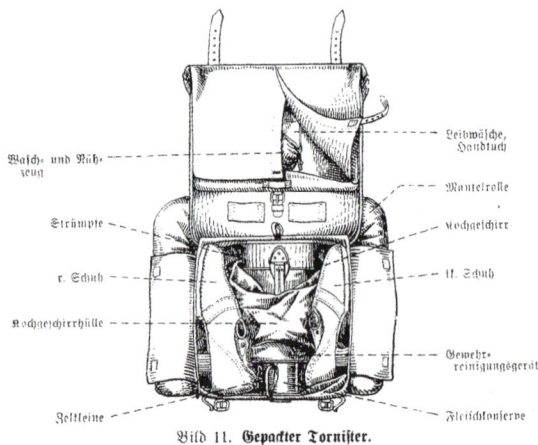

Bild 11. Gepackter Tornister.

OPPOSITE The support straps and *Gefechtsgepäck* with mess tin and small bag fitted.

an *Affe*, from its resemblance to an ape or monkey. One is therefore left wondering whether the phrase 'to have a monkey on your back' is not an English expression as is commonly assumed, but a literal translation of German soldiers' historic grumbles regarding weight of equipment.

Only on the eve of World War II were significant advances made in personal equipment. As of April 1939 a new system was introduced which attempted to build upon the old *Sturmgepäck* idea, combined with a revised backpack, the Tornister 39. Crucial to this was the introduction of new support straps for the infantry, the *Koppeltragegestell mit Hilfestragerriemen* (belt supports with auxiliary straps). Like earlier types they were made of leather, formed a Y-shape and came up either side of the front of the soldier's body to pass over the shoulders and join on the back, and down to connect with the waist belt at the rear. When no *Patronentaschen* were worn, short leather loops with rings could be slipped on to the waist belt at the front to ensure that there was somewhere for support straps to connect. Unlike earlier types of support straps, the new version was fitted with a metal ring behind each shoulder, and auxiliary straps either side. This was an innovative departure as now the soldier could wear the straps as a form of support for belt equipment, as previously, or different equipment could be suspended from the back rings and secured by the auxiliary straps as necessary. After the beginning of the war, support straps were made in webbing as well as in leather.

In guard or parade order, or when moving from station to station, the *Koppeltragegestell* rings supported the new Tornister 39. The Tornister 39 was similar to the Tornister 34 but obviously required no integral shoulder straps, having instead only fittings to hook to the support and auxiliary straps. The Tornister 39 also lacked an integral pouch for the *Kochgeschirr*, and had a small external vertical strap on the lower part of the flap. As with uniform, early *Tornister* were marked with the maker's name, location and date of production, while later examples carried an 'RB' code number. *Tornister* manufacture continued until at least 1944, and similar packs were used by organizations other than the Heer with many different markings applied, so it is unsurprising that variations are encountered. As in World War I the cowhide was sometimes deleted, though this does not seem to have occurred across all production at any specific date. Hides with plain red-brown hair are common, but other hues are found, and the colour of the canvas also varies, as does the detail of stitching and fittings. While the Tornister 39 was produced in vast numbers, the Tornister 34 was clearly durable and the two types co-existed.

For action, the new *Gefechtsgepäck* (combat pack) took the place of the *Tornister* on the support straps. Despite its name, this was simply a truncated triangle of reinforced webbing with straps and buckle attachments, mounted on the soldier's back, apex upward.

Various methods of loading the *Gefechtsgepäck* were used, but the basic essentials of keeping dry, warm and fed, with weapon(s) working, remained the primary objectives. The *Kochgeschirr* was usually strapped to the upper part, and the small issue canvas *Beutel* (bag), buttoned to the lower part; the *Zeltbahn* could then be folded and strapped over the *Beutel*. Manual illustrations show a sweater, rations, tent rope and rifle-cleaning kit as the basic contents of the *Gefechtsgepäck* of an infantryman serving in a rifle company. This may have been what was intended to be carried, but the *Gefechtsgepäck* bag was tiny, and much depended on the soldier's duties and whether he also wore a *Brotbeutel*. Another novel feature was that on the march, the little *Gefechtsgepäck* frame could be fastened onto the outer flap of the back of the *Tornister*. Photographic evidence

Typical contents of the Tornister 39. In the main compartment, ankle boots and *Kochgeschirr* occupy the major space, but these are filled with smaller items such as food and brushes. The flap holds spare underwear and a linen towel (dated 1938); the shaving kit is hidden at the bottom of this pack. Initially, undergarments and towels were white or off-white, but green later became common, being less likely to give away positions when washing was hung out to dry. The socks are marked with three rings, indicating that they are large sized. The orange tin, dated 1942, contains *Lederfett* (leather grease or dubbin) for the waterproofing and preserving of boots and other leather kit. *Feldpost* letters, a little *Liederbuch* (songbook) and a family photograph complete the load.

FAR LEFT Ungainly but authorized method for carrying the Tornister 39 and *Gefechtsgepäck* together. The *Gefechtsgepäck* frame is attached ready-loaded to the Tornister 39. The muzzle-down attitude of the Kar 98k rifle was permitted when marching in rain as a means to prevent rusting of the bore.

LEFT A recruit using a *Tornister* to carry the *Gefechtsgepäck*.

BELOW The Heer eagle-and-swastika belt-buckle of 1936. The biblical motto GOTT MIT UNS ('GOD WITH US') was used by the Prussian Army from the beginning of the 18th century and subsequently adopted by the Imperial German Army.

shows that this was definitely done, but the arrangement was probably too ungainly to permit much vigorous activity with a full load.

Glimpses can be gained of the soldier's equipment through manuals, memoirs and photographs, but the picture is fleshed out with other sources such as the *Soldbuch*. Franz Wirtz, mobilized as an

ordinary soldier with Landesschützen-Bataillon 470 in Westphalia in July 1940, was probably typical in being initially issued with the following equipment: Tornister 34; *Kochgeschirr*; *Zeltbahn* (without tent poles or pegs); belt-buckle and belt leather; *Seitengewehrtasche* (bayonet frog); *Brotbeutel* (without strap); *Feldflasche*; field cutlery; hand towel; *Fettbüchse*; gas mask; two field dressings; and identity tag.

RUCKSACKS

Rucksacks have a long history as a convenient way to carry items in mountainous terrain and military expedients consisting of sacks or cloth bundles secured to the back are also of some antiquity. The word *Rucksack* is German, translating literally as 'back bag'. Framed rucksacks were in use in Norway by the

Gebirgsjäger enter Salzburg on the annexation of Austria, March 1938. Each man carries full equipment including a bulging *Rucksack 31*, *Brotbeutel* and gas-mask canister. (FPG/Hulton Archive/Getty Images)

OPPOSITE One of several slightly varying models of the *Rucksack für Artillerie*. This type was suspended from the standard support-strap rings by hooks and had a pair of additional buckled straps to the rear by means of which a gas-mask canister, *Zeltbahn* or other item could be carried outside the bag.

19th century, while the World War I Russian rucksack was little more than a canvas bag with a tied top and simple carry slings. A variety of rucksacks were used by German troops in World War I, some of which were adopted because there were insufficient numbers of the standard *Tornister*, while others were used by *Gebirgsjäger*. By 1916 there was a common rucksack with two compartments and a buckled top-closure.

With the first stirrings of a resurrection of German mountain forces, in 1931 a rucksack was adopted specifically for use by *Gebirgsjäger*. Inspired by existing civilian designs and made of olive-green water-repellent canvas, the Rucksack 31 had a double-closure system: a drawstring pulled the bag closed and a flap with three buckles shut over the top. There were three external pockets, one on each side and one to the rear. Five small leather stowage loops were sewn to the top flap, and a further one on each side of the bag. The loops allowed the *Mantel* and *Zeltbahn* to be rolled and wrapped around the top and sides using straps, and provided a space for the *Kochgeschirr* or other items to be secured to the flap. A leather patch with two rings sewn to the bag behind the soldier's back formed a strong locating point for the shoulder straps, functioning in a similar manner to the integral straps of the Tornister 34 by linking to the *Patronentaschen* at the front and passing under the arms to meet with two short straps at the bottom of the bag. It was also possible to attach an additional waist strap, thereby preventing undue swaying of the load when climbing. Up to four smaller linen bags were used with the Rucksack 31 to separate its contents.

During World War II, the advantages of rucksacks were appreciated, being flexible, of greater capacity, simple and often inexpensive to produce. This was particularly significant for Heer branches not issued the *Tornister*, and a quick solution to their needs was found in the *Rucksack für Artillerie*, introduced in early 1940. This was a simply designed oblong canvas bag with a drawstring and small single buckled flap at the top. Its mounting system consisted of a bar of leather across the top edge of the panel behind the soldier's back with two hooks, and a further hook at each corner at the bottom exterior of the bag. The four hooks allowed the little rucksack to be mounted on the support-strap system in the same way as the Tornister 39. Almost identical types are also found with integral straps to be used without the *Koppeltragegestell*. The only real refinement to some *Rucksäcke für Artillerie* are two external buckling straps on the back of the bag. These were used in various ways, but the most obvious was for stowing the gas-mask canister or the *Zeltbahn*, both of which were bulky and could be more conveniently accessed on the outside of the bag.

OPPOSITE Though commonly described as a '1944'-type rucksack, lightly constructed bags with a buckled flap and two exterior pockets had been in use for at least two years by then. The example shown is one of the common varieties.

BELOW Moving station, June 1943. Most of the personal kit has been crammed into rucksacks with gas masks fastened to the outside. Stores are packed into wooden and cardboard boxes. A rifle fitted with a muzzle protector remains close to hand.

From 1940 onward a number of other rucksacks saw use: some were variants of the *Rucksack für Artillerie*, others were inspired by *Gebirgsjäger* rucksacks, or were ad hoc adaptions of civilian types. A *Tropen Rucksack* (tropical rucksack) in tan canvas was used in North Africa and other areas: this was somewhat similar to the Rucksack 31 but had a single buckle to the top flap, and, as originally produced, integral webbing straps in the configuration of the Tornister 34. In another tropical type there were two smaller back pockets. A widespread design, certainly in use by 1942, had a small buckled top-flap closure, again in conjunction with a bag with two back pockets. In yet another model carry straps were fashioned from lengths of the same material used for the internal support straps found in the *Feldbluse*. Some rucksacks had an additional large ring on top for suspension in a vehicle or billet. The morphological stages are unclear, but rucksacks proved more practical than other options, including the *Gefechtsgepäck*, and as a result there was an impetus towards a standard design, increased production and wider issue. Commonly referred to as the '1944' type, the most widely used rucksack at the end of World War II was a bag of relatively thin olive-green material with a drawstring and single-buckle top-flap closure and two back pockets. This was generally used in combination with the separate support straps.

Transshipment in North Africa, c.1942–43: an overloaded war reporter with rucksack and attached bedding roll, belt equipment, rifle, a *Stahlhelm* and a *Tropenhelm* awaits transport. (Bundesarchiv, Bild 101I-419-1900-17A, Foto: Grosse, Helmut)

DIGGING IN AND THE TENT

Next to his rifle the Heer infantryman's best friend was his spade, with effective 'digging in' helping to both conceal and protect the soldier on the battlefield. As the old German military maxim put it, *Schweiß Spart Blut!* ('Sweat Saves Blood!') Throughout the interwar period and much of World War II, the issue digging implement was the *kleines Schanzzeug* (small entrenching tool). This short shovel, mounted on a wooden handle with a rounded finial and a leather carry case with loops to hang from the belt, was first introduced prior to World War I and there were few changes thereafter. The carry case was fitted with a strap which buckled to hold the blade, and was brown leather initially, changing to black later on. Textbook wear was on the left hip, with the bayonet frog attached over the carry

The basic *kleines Schanzzeug* ('small entrenching tool'); this example was made in Berlin in 1941. This short, robust, blunt-ended digging implement was very similar to its World War I predecessor, and is shown here with its belt carry case.

ABOVE The *Klappspaten* (folding spade) had a longer handle and more pointed blade than the *kleines Schanzzeug*, but was rendered just as easy to carry by means of its locking nut and rotating head. The belt carrier has the code 'bdt 40', signifying production by the SALEWA company of Munich (SA: *Sattler* (saddler); LE: *Leder* (leather); WA: *Waren* (wares)) in 1940.

RIGHT Infantry passing through the rubble of Stalingrad, October 1942. Despite the support straps, equipment is carried on the waist belt, where *Kochgeschirr*, *Feldflasche*, *Brotbeutel* and rolled *Zeltbahn* can be seen. (De Agostini/Getty Images)

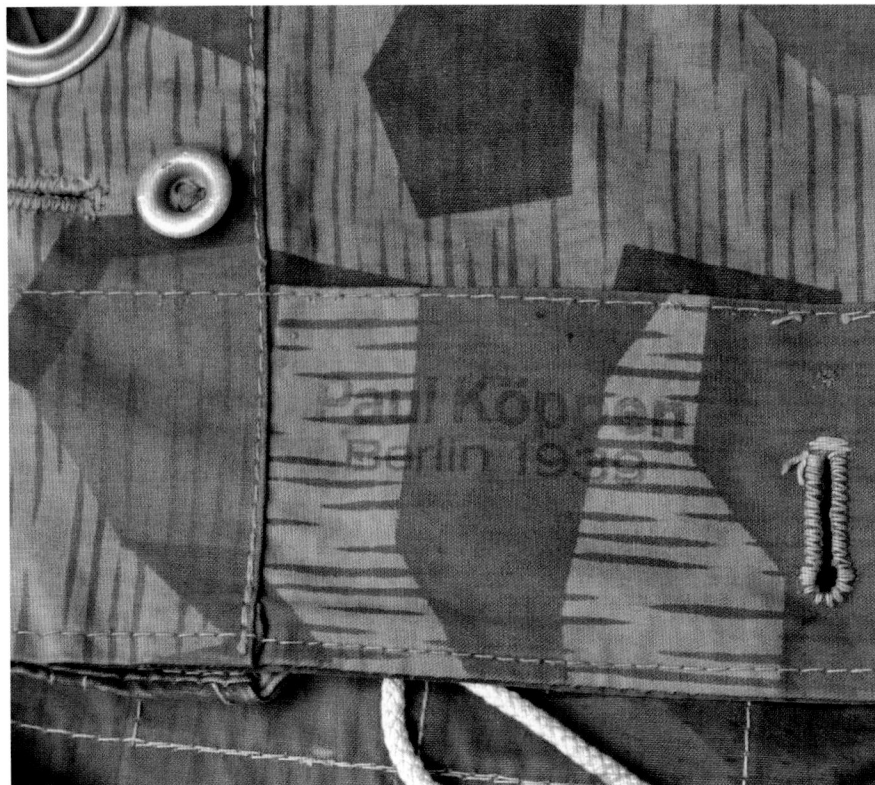

case. Later in the war, the carry case was made from a tough cardboard-like substitute material of cellulose and resin known as *Press Stoff*. The *kleines Schanzzeug* was supplemented by foreign models in German service. These included an Austrian type with a pointed blade, and captures from the enemy.

The most significant innovation was the introduction of a second type of issue digging implement – the *Klappspaten* (folding spade) – in 1938. This digging implement was longer than the *kleines Schanzzeug*, with a pointed blade, but the key difference was a threaded locking nut and pivot which allowed the head to be rotated through 90 degrees to enable the tool to be used as a pick, or through almost 180 degrees so that the head could be folded flat against the handle for carriage. Though the *Klappspaten* functioned in a similar way to the *kleines Schanzzeug*, there was more than one type of carry case for the former, being of leather, *Press Stoff* or canvas, and having different strap arrangements. A loop was usually incorporated to hold the bayonet and *Klappspaten* together on the waist belt. The *Klappspaten* was widely used, but it was relatively expensive to manufacture and so the old *kleines Schanzzeug* continued in production. It is worth noting that other tools were carried by specialist troops, and that engineers and labourers used a range of full-sized spades, picks and saws.

Zeltbahnen buttoned together to create a small field tent. Structures of different shapes and sizes were possible when each man carried a shelter-quarter, with *Zeltpflöcken* (tent poles), *Zeltstöcke* (tent pegs) and *Zeltleinen* (tent ropes) also distributed among the men of the unit.

RIGHT Modern reconstruction (with original items) showing a full load for a rifleman in the field. The *Gefechtsgepäck* is stowed with a *Zeltbahn* and *Kochgeschirr*, the belt with a *Brotbeutel*, *Feldflasche*, *kleines Schanzzeug* and bayonet.

FAR RIGHT The small tent-equipment bag, shown with a slot-together *Zeltpflöcke* (made up of three short sections) and two *Zeltstöcke*.

A German official photograph showing a different combat equipment arrangement for an MG 34 machine-gunner in the field. The *Kochgeschirr* is worn high on the back with a *Zeltbahn* wrapped around it. The belt equipment includes a *Brotbeutel* and *Feldflasche*, and a gas-mask canister is slung to hang near the left hip. (Bundesarchiv, Bild 146-1972-072-25, Foto: o.Ang.)

These drawings from the Reibert manuals show various uses of the *Zeltbahn* as shelter, waterproof cover and poncho, for mounted and dismounted men.

— 268 —

Bild 1.   Bild 2.   Bild 3.

3. Gebirgstruppen, Radfahrer usw.

Die Zeltbahn wird wie für Unberittene geknöpft, die herunterhängenden Zeltbahnecken werden um je ein Bein nach innen herumgeschlagen. Der Knopf auf der schmalen Rechtseite wird in das zweite Knopfloch im doppelten Randstreifen des rechteckigen Unterteils eingeknöpft (Bild 3).

Das Einerzelt. Schon eine Zeltbahn gibt 1 bis 2 Mann notdürftigen Wind- und Wetterschutz (Bild 4).

Das Halbzelt. Aus zwei mit einer Seite zusammengeknöpften Zeltbahnen kann eine Deckung hergerichtet werden, die 2 bis 3 Mann im Rücken und von den Seiten gegen Wind und Wetter schützt (Bild 5).

 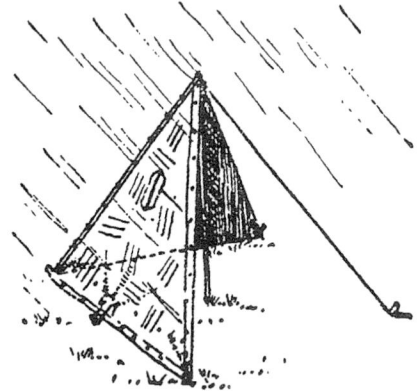

Bild 4.   Bild 5.

Schwimmer aus Zeltbahnen.

Zwei dreieckige Zeltbahnen werden nach Bild 6 zusammengeknöpft und darauf in Richtung des langen Durchmessers (3,43 m) etwa 1½ Bund Langstroh (Schilf, Binsen u. dgl.) gelegt und fest in die Bahnen eingerollt. Dann werden die in der Längsrichtung liegenden Zipfel unter Einschlagen des Stoffes scharf umgeschlagen, straff angezogen und festgeknöpft oder besser noch mit einer durch die beiden großen Knauschen genommenen Leine fest zusammengezogen (Bild 6).

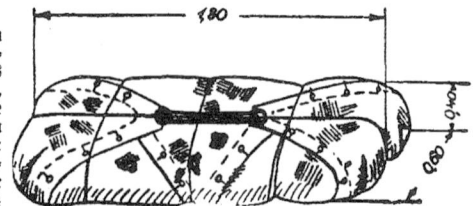

Bild 6.

German soldiers carried tent sections as standard equipment during World War I, but the system underwent various practical changes in the 1930s. As of 1931, a new *Zeltbahn* (shelter-quarter) was introduced. Unlike previous issues this was camouflaged in a pattern of printed irregular angular shapes of grass green and dark brown, on a khaki or light-brownish backing with lines. The new *Zeltbahn* was triangular, 2.5m long on the longest side and 2m on the shorter sides. Four *Zeltbahnen* buttoned together to create a small pyramidal tent known as a *Viererzelt*, but one or two *Zeltbahnen* also made rudimentary shelters. Regulations of 1932 make clear that the *Zeltbahn* was not only part of a shelter, but served as both a form of camouflage and a wet-weather poncho. Manufactured in huge quantities, the *Zeltbahn* was produced in a number of minor variations; the most obvious of these were changes to the colour and detail of camouflage, with, for example, more yellowish tones, or – at the very end of World War II – the inclusion of black overprinting. Buttons and fittings were generally zinc, but other types were also used. Large numbers of Soviet tent sections were also captured from 1941 onwards.

According to the *Taschenkalender* of 1941, the *Zeltausrüstung* (tent equipment) of the individual soldier comprised one Zeltbahn 31, one Zeltleine 1892 (tent rope), one Zeltpflöcke 01(tent pole) piece and two Zeltstöcke 29 (tent pegs). Some earlier 'four-cornered' *Zeltbahnen* still existed and were covered by a separate regulation. Canvas tent-equipment bags with buttoned closures were often used and were manufactured during World War II, though *Soldbuch* records are not usually specific regarding issue, some troops having a *Zeltausrüstung* (tent equipment) entry, others mentioning only the *Zeltbahn*. Larger tents were created by using additional *Zeltbahnen*, and traditional tents of larger sheets were provided separately for staff, horses and other purposes.

ANTI-GAS EQUIPMENT

Prodigious use of poison gas during World War I made gas protection a widespread preoccupation of the interwar period. The Gasmaske 24, introduced in 1924, featured a tube with a flattish filter canister on the end, but this was gradually superseded from 1930 by a new mask, the Gasmaske 30, bearing greater visual similarity to its World War I predecessors of 1915 and 1917. The Gasmaske 30 consisted of a rubberized canvas mask on a leather frame with two eyepieces, onto which was screwed the filter. The mask, which was made in three size fittings, could be slung around the neck ready for use, and a snug fit to the head was achieved by means of a system of elasticated straps. As of 1938 the mask was simplified and updated as the Gasmaske 38, with the face piece now moulded from one piece of synthetic rubber, initially green in colour, later black. The gas-mask canister was also modified, being longer after 1938. According to the 1939 instruction leaflet *Die S-Maske*, the basic-issue mask kit comprised not only the face piece with eyepieces, straps, filter and carry case, but also a pair of *Klarscheiben* (anti-fogging disks) and a *Maskenspanner* (metal former) to keep the face piece in shape when not stowed in the carry case.

The cylindrical sheet-metal gas-mask canister was corrugated lengthwise externally for strength, its lid secured by means of a spring catch and web pull-tab. Under the top of the canister was a small box with hinged lid for the *Klarscheiben*. The gas-mask canister was usually equipped with two web straps, with the longer forming a sling and the shorter ending in a hook. Infantrymen carried the gas-mask canister behind the right hip, with the hook on the rear of the waist belt, but other carrying positions were possible. Issue of a mask was

BELOW Dog-handlers train in gas masks, East Prussia, 1932. The masks of the men are similar to World War I types, those of the dogs more up to date. (Keystone-France/Gamma-Keystone/Getty Images)

BELOW RIGHT *'Meine neueste Aufnahme'* ('My newest snap'): a postcard illustration of a soldier wearing the Gasmaske 30.

Meine neues Aufna

LEFT The Gasmaske 30; the bold number '2' denotes a medium-sized fitting.

BELOW LEFT A Gasmaske 38 canister complete with webbing shoulder sling and belt tab.

BELOW Details of the gas-mask filter, showing the screw-thread fitting and military-acceptance eagle stamping.

TOP Typical anti-gas accessories. Early- and late-war bags for gas capes, and (foreground) the Bakelite container for skin-decontamination tablets (left) and the vibrantly coloured bottle for decontamination ointment (right), this example dated 1944.

BOTTOM Artillerymen demonstrate two different ways to sling the gas-mask canister. The man on the left also wears pre-1939 leather belt support straps without the equipment-attachment rings.

recorded in the *Soldbuch*, with the 'equipment administrator' noting its size, number and date of issue, and signing the entry. A gas mask was a particular encumbrance when worn inside the limited confines of a tank, so extension hose tubes were provided for crewmen so the filter was not permanently in front of the face.

Other anti-gas items on general issue included capes and methods of personal decontamination. The *Gasplane* (gas cape/sheet) was a lightweight sheet of fabric or paper intended to prevent droplets of vesicants, such as mustard gas, settling on skin or uniform. Stowed folded in a flat oblong pouch closed with press buttons until needed, the sheet was pulled over the soldier or equipment on warning of gas. With the progress of the war, *Gasplane* pouches were made more cheaply and simply. Initial orders were that the pouch should be worn on the chest attached to the shoulder sling of the gas-mask canister, but more convenient methods of attaching the *Gasplane* to the canister with rubber bands or straps were widely adopted later. In any event, both *Gasplane* and gas mask were to be kept together.

Losantin skin-decontamination tablets, dissolved in water before application, were supplied in a small rectangular box. The seal of the box showed when the lozenges were manufactured, red signifying production up to 1940, black 1941, light green 1942 and yellow 1943. As can be imagined, mixing tablets in water while suffering the effects of a gas attack would not have been particularly easy, and it was perhaps for this reason that a decontamination ointment was introduced in 1941. Initially issued in a small brown Bakelite bottle, the ointment was later supplied in a bright-orange container. Another decontamination set, distributed in a fibre container and intended for weapons, was marked *Waffenentgiftungsmittel* (weapon detoxification).

Other specialist anti-gas items were not general issue but reserved for troops on particular duties, casualties and the protection of animals such as horses, dogs and messenger pigeons. The Leichte Gasanzug 39 (light protective suit 39), designed shortly before the war and carried in a shoulder bag, consisted of a fibre suit of leggings, trousers with attached apron front, neck protector and gloves. The more durable 'heavy' suit gave better protection and included a jacket with hood, dungaree-style trousers, gloves and boots. Anti-gas protection suits were produced in camouflage finishes towards the end of the war, and were rubberized internally. The *Gazschützehaube* (gas protection hood), enclosing the entire head, was intended for personnel with injuries that precluded the wearing of an ordinary mask. For marking of gas-contaminated areas there was a set of small flags on wire poles and a yellow cloth tape carried in a leather or canvas pouch. The triangular flags were also yellow and bore *Totenkopf* markings in black.

FOOD, DRINK AND THE *BROTBEUTEL*

Ideally, the German soldier was economically fed in barrack canteens using bulk supplies, with officers accommodated in a separate mess. What was provided varied according to both location and increasing shortages, but troops remained better supplied and fed than civilians. As late as 12 February 1945, a weekly *Speizenzettel* ('feeding list') for Grenadier-Ersatz-Bataillon 414, issued at Plauen and preserved by Oberleutnant Kurt Liebeneiner, shows the following. Breakfast consisted of wheat and rye bread and coffee (most likely of a 'substitute' type), with small amounts of honey or jam most mornings, plus 15–20g of either margarine or butter. Very small amounts of beet sugar and 430ml of milk were given daily, and men aged 21 or younger received a 70g piece of sausage on Monday. Lunch was the main meal, and on three days a week the dish was an *Eintopf* (one pot) offering, with 35–50g of pork or veal and either 150g of noodle or 500g of potato plus a little *Suppengrün* (soup greens), gherkin or other vegetable. On two occasions, the youngsters' *Eintopf* included an additional 50g of meat. Other lunchtimes saw 70g of beef or veal prepared with salt or mustard, or as a fricassee, with 500g of potato, and smaller amounts of sauerkraut, red cabbage, gherkin or other vegetable. There was dessert twice a week: semolina on Thursday and a more substantial *Mokkapudding mit Karamel soße* (mocha pudding with caramel sauce) with sugar on Sunday, though this was also

Typical barrack kitchen, *c.*1939. Supervised by an NCO, male and female civilian staff utilize large cauldrons and iron ranges to cook bulk foods.

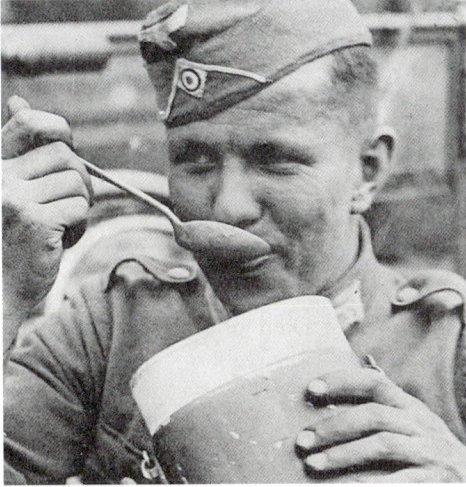

LEFT Metal equipment items could have long periods of use. Here, a large World War I *Kochgeschirr* is still in service, *c.*1940.

BELOW At right, the Kochgeschirr 31. The pot had a 1.7-litre capacity; the lid, doubling as a small pan, had a capacity of 500ml. The 250ml aluminium mug, left, is dated 1940, and also served as a measuring jug. The spoon, with the 'H & KH' maker's mark, was issued in 1941. The sacking 'tablecloth' is in fact a Heer food sack.

NEXT PAGE LEFT The parts of a common type of *Feldflasche*, showing (right) the aluminium inner flask, insulating fibre cover and cap, and (top) the metal *Trinkbecker* (drinking cup) with wire-handle arrangement.

NEXT PAGE RIGHT At left, a *Feldflasche* with a resin-type *Trinkbecker*; at right is the tropical-type *Feldflasche* in which the flask was insulated with a wood-and-resin compound. Its good thermal qualities led to use in various theatres of war.

bolstered with semolina. The weekday evening meal was usually a soup with vegetable or potato and a little sausage or beef, but bread with margarine or lard and coffee were also served. Saturday saw issue of *frische Wurst* (fresh sausage), gherkin, lard and bread. Sunday was again different, with 63g of soft cheese, bread and 30g of butter in the evening.

In occupied Western Europe, Heer food supply was supported by fixed prices and exchange rates, with directions to farmers as to what to produce. France was a prized posting, and until the disaster in the Netherlands of the 'hunger winter' of 1944/45, German forces were adequately fed and outright starvation of local populations was usually avoided. In the Eastern Front war of attrition, however, matters were far less predictable. In the wake of the stalling of Operation *Barbarossa*, Hitler's attack into the

Ukraine was at least in part stimulated by the desire to acquire supplies, but the result was catastrophic. Areas already hard hit by Stalin's brutal collectivization policy were now expected to provide for the Reich, often in conflict with the Nazi political directive to remove local inhabitants to make way for German settlement. Prices were officially pegged, but in the summer of 1942 black-market prices were ten or more times higher. Hordes of starving Soviet prisoners of war for whom no realistic provision was made, the appearance of partisans and the logistical problems associated with ever-stretching lines of supply resulted in deaths on a massive scale, many of them civilians.

Behind the lines, troops were often billeted in households with or without unhappy hosts, and in 1942 OKH provided a set of proven recipes entitled *Östliche Speisen nach Deutscher Art* ('Eastern Dishes in the German Style') using local ingredients. In a version of 'Gulasch', fried diced meat was roasted with onions, tomato and paprika, before being braised in water and flour. Peppers, sauerkraut, pumpkin and other vegetables could be added or substituted according to availability. In a Serbian-inspired dish, rice and meat were mixed in a form of risotto, while meatballs were made with either fresh or canned produce. Mushrooms were of increasing interest, with several civilian guides as to their use published during the war.

When troops were on campaign, but not in direct contact with the enemy, field bakeries and unit field kitchens provided nourishment. Though motorized, train-mounted and even sledge-mounted field kitchens existed, most were horse drawn. The majority were of four models: the Hf 12 and Hf 14 small kitchens and the larger Hf 11 and Hf 13 types; all featured large cauldrons for heating food and drink. Over and above such manuals as the *Feldkochbuch* (1940), field cooks had their own official newsletter *Die Gulaschkanone* ('The Goulash Cannon'), the title being soldier slang for the field kitchen with its cannon-like chimney. A typical issue of the newsletter from 1942 features photos of a train-mounted kitchen along with remarks on tea and substitute coffee, fat, and sunflower oil, and provides statements on the importance of good food in battle against the 'Bolshevik terror'. There is also an article about soya and its calorific content, which was greater than that of steak, eggs, wheat or rye meal. Recipes demonstrate how soya could be incorporated into soups, minced meats and potato dumplings.

That meat was not always available to the field cook is reflected in Richard Schielicke's 1942 volume *Fleischlose und Fleischarme Feldküchengerichte* ('Meatless and Reduced-meat Field-kitchen Dishes') which included such recipes as 'noodles with leek and celery', 'potatoes in herb sauce' and 'Pichelsteiner stew', eking out just 30g of beef with 1,900g of vegetables, salt, pepper and herbs. Accessories accompanying the field kitchen included large drinking-water

flasks; metal containers for condiments and preservatives; utensils and bowls; grinders and food sacks. Collecting rations from the kitchen was often the duty of the deputy squad leader, who carried two or more *Kochgeschirre* to be filled at the kitchen. There were also *Essenbehälter* (metal backpack carriers), enabling details to carry larger quantities of food to front-line positions with hands free.

In combat areas inaccessible to field kitchens, troops were forced to rely on what they carried. According to regulations in the officers' *Taschenkalender*, the soldier's *Brotbeutel* was positioned on the belt or shoulder strap to the right rear side of his body, with the *Feldflasche* secured to it by means of one of its rings. In the *Brotbeutel* were his cutlery, food and *Feldmütze*. This made perfect sense for an inspection with the soldier wearing *Tornister* and *Stahlhelm*, but in the field, with only the tiny bag of the *Gefechtsgepäck* and uniform pockets available to fill, the *Brotbeutel* was apt to become a repository for all manner of things. One of these was a rifle-cleaning kit, and to accommodate this a small pocket was added to the *Brotbeutel* in 1944. The *Kochgeschirr* could also be stowed on the outside of the *Brotbeutel* when neither the *Tornister* nor the *Gefechtsgepäck* was worn.

Also omitted from the original regulation *Brotbeutel* contents was the *Fettbüchse*, a container for butter or spreads formally introduced in 1938 and

Erkennungsmarke of soldier no. 6412, of Sanitäts-Ersatz-Abteilung 12. The *Blutgruppe* (blood group) 'A' is indicated towards the edge of the disc. Infantry- and armoured-unit *Erkennungsmarken* commonly gave the company number ahead of the unit name.

ABOVE Typical pocket items. Top left: German coins and a *Verrechnungsschein* (bill of exchange) note to the value of RM 10 for use by Heer forces in occupied countries, 1944. Top centre: *Urlaubsbescheinigung* (leave-entitlement form) for auxiliaries, Belgium 1940, and whistle. Right: photograph of family and the grave of Gefreiter Wilhelm Mühlenbeck, an anti-aircraft gunner killed at Caen, May 1943. Lower right: cigarette papers and a card commemorating Obergefreiter Johann Wimmer, a *Gebirgsjäger* who fought in Poland, France and Greece before his death in battle at Lake Ladoga in northern Russia in 1942, aged 27. Centre bottom: a *Feldpost* letter and a soldier's German–Russian phrasebook of 1942, including such translations as 'Have the partisans been this way today?' and 'How many chickens do you have?' Bottom left: the *Soldbuch* of Franz Wirtz, promoted *Feldwebel* in December 1943; it is well worn due to spending five years in a *Feldbluse* pocket.

OPPOSITE Military administration. Centre: *Wehrpass* of Georg Esiele, Kraftfahr-Ersatz-Abteilung 12. The *Wehrpass* was the soldier's permanent record, kept at headquarters. Bottom left: *Ausmusterungsschein* (demobilization certificate) of Franz Eichler, certifying the bearer unfit for service, Leipzig, 1941. Left: *Gesundheitsbuch* (medical record) of Gefreiter Jakob Theis, a member of Grenadier-Regiment 9's *Pionier-Zug*, admitted to hospital with shrapnel wounds, November 1943. Upper left: *Entlassungschein* (discharge certificate) of Unteroffizier Edward Schäfer of Kassel on leaving the Heer in September 1940. Top left: *Gestellungsbefehl* (call-up papers) of Rudolph Dickhöfer of Langenfeld, March 1945. Top right: *Sonderausweis* (special pass) allowing Oberleutnant Kurt Liebeneiner, three NCOs and 22 men to retire to Saarbrücken to rejoin their unit, September 1944. Upper centre: official notification to Frau Ida Felske that her husband, missing at Stalingrad more than 18 months earlier, is promoted *Stabsgefreiter*. Right: officer recruitment booklet, *Offizier im Grossdeutschen Heer 1942*. Bottom right: *Wehrpass Notiz* informing Konrad Schäfer of liability to serve, October 1940.

Rapoch

Scheibe: 38

Stegmass: 5840

Wehrmacht-Maskenbrille

Dienst-Brille

Masken-Brille

Name und Dienstgrad:

Truppenteil: Datum:

Maße der Brillenfassung: P. D.:

sphär.	cyl.	Achse, Tabo		sphär.	cyl.	Achse, Tabo	
R			L				

C 1937

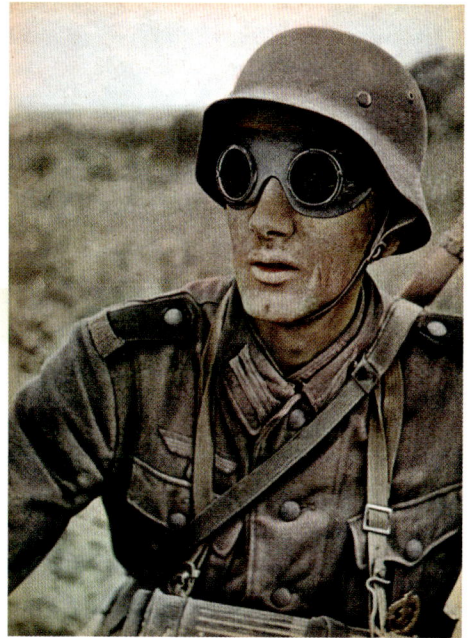

sometimes specified as an issue in the *Soldbuch*. Bread itself was fresh where possible, but a standard ration was the 125g portion of *Knackebrot* (hard tack); sausage and chocolate were popular if available. 'Iron rations' were canned and often of a standard-issue type consisting of concentrated meat, fish or occasionally cheese. The iron ration was regarded as a last resort only to be opened when ordered. Liquids were carried in the *Feldflasche*, but bottled drinks and small vacuum flasks were also sometimes used. (Though the vacuum-flask idea dates to the 19th century, the 'Thermos' name was actually a trademark chosen by a German company in 1904.) Beer was arguably even more popular in the Heer than in other nations' armed services and did feature with rations as well as in home canteens, but rarely reached the front lines.

Matches or lighter and candles could also be found in the *Brotbeutel*. Many soldiers carried an *Esbit Kocher*, a small sheet-metal stand which folded neatly when not in use but opened out to create a platform for solid-fuel tablets. (*Esbit* was an acronym for 'Erich Schumm's Fuel in Tablet Form'. Prolific inventor Erich Schumm (1907–79) of Stuttgart devised this popular system in the mid-1930s and was clearly a complex character, being both a Nazi Party member criticized for his treatment of forced labourers, but apparently also expelled from the Nazi Party for making favourable comments about a Jew.) The tablets were lit and the *Kochgeschirr* or pan was placed on top for heating. Alternatively, small groups of soldiers could work together, when larger cylindrical petrol burners were more convenient than open fires or individual stoves.

OPPOSITE Military eyewear took many forms. Shown here (from top to bottom) are folding tinted dust goggles, standard *Dienstbrille* (service spectacles) in issue metal box with prescription card, and *Maskenbrille*, gas-mask spectacles with elasticated cords rather than rigid side-frames and intended for use in conjunction with the gas mask.

TOP LEFT An NCO wearing the *Maskenbrille* gas-mask spectacles held in place by elasticated cords.

TOP RIGHT A motorcyclist in the Soviet Union wearing tinted goggles, September 1942. His gas-mask canister is worn on his chest in the regulation position for mounted men. (Art Media/ Print Collector/ Getty Images)

PERSONAL AND POCKET ITEMS

A key item carried by all troops was the *Erkennungsmarke* (identification tag). The basic design was a sheet-metal oval with three small holes, two towards the top and one at the bottom. Across the centre horizontally were three slotted perforations, the same information being stamped into both segments. Generally, the soldier's *Stammrollennummer* (personal roll number), unit and *Blutgruppe* (blood group) were recorded, though there were variations. Unlike during World War I, personal names were not included. The *Erkennungsmarke* was suspended around the neck using the two upper holes, commonly with grey-green cord; some soldiers purchased a small leather pouch in which to hold the disc. In the event of a soldier's death, the *Erkennungsmarke* was snapped across the centre and the lower segment returned to company headquarters for casualty recording, while the upper segment remained with the soldier's body. Following incidents in which tank crewmen were incinerated in their vehicles and identification-tag suspension cords were burned, orders were issued in 1942 for armoured-unit personnel to use suspension chains in

LEFT AND BELOW Leather map case, dated 1937, used by Leutnant Willi Karst, together with a large-scale 1941 map of part of the Netherlands, a map of western Russia, a grid square and a marching compass with manufacturer's code 'clk', denoting F.W. Breithaupt & Sohn of Kassel.

ABOVE Leisure items. Top left: smoking materials. Despite the exotic branding, everything depicted here was manufactured in Germany or Austria prior to 1945. Reemtsma Cigarettenfabriken, which was founded in Erfurt in 1910 and later moved to Altona, claimed more than half of the tobacco market under the Nazis. Regie 4 was an Austrian brand, while the Efka company was founded in 1912 in Trossingen. The lightweight chess set was designed for easy postage, and the cards (bottom) are from two different games in which players collected sets depicting weapons and personalities.

RIGHT A selection of popular wartime *Liederbuchen* (songbooks). *Front-Liederbuch*, published in Berlin in 1940, included such classics as '*Die Fahne hoch!*' ('Raise the flag!') by Horst Wessel, '*Ich hatt' einen Kameraden*' ('I had a comrade'), a traditional song of military mourners, the *Funkerlied* ('Signaller's song',) and of course, '*Deutschland über alles*' ('Germany above all').

A soldier wearing the webbing version of the support straps with winter kit in a graphic illustration that confirms webbing items were not used in tropical zones only. Note also the wire-handled mug, grenade, and drum magazine for machine-gun ammunition.

conjunction with the *Erkennungsmarke*. It may be observed that many *Erkennungsmarken* carry the name of an *Ersatz* (replacement) unit. The reason for this is that *Erkennungsmarken* were issued when men joined the Heer, and recruits usually first went into the Ersatzheer. The same *Erkennungsmarke* remained with the individual unless lost, when a replacement might be issued by his current formation.

Another small item carried by all was the *Soldbuch*. The title translates literally as 'pay book', but generally it was not used to record pay, being rather a proof of entitlement to be paid. It was thus, as its subtitle makes clear, a *Personalausweis* (personal identity document). Its pages recorded the name, rank, date of birth, blood type, height, distinguishing features, religion, unit and recruitment details of the holder, as well as the signature of a certifying officer. The *Soldbuch* was numbered to tally either with the individual's *Stammrollennummer* (personnel roster number) in his unit, or with the number on his *Erkennungsmarke*. Additionally, as previously noted, the *Soldbuch* contained pages for recording data including issues of uniform, weapons and equipment. Leave, promotions, inoculations, hospitalization, dental details and pay group were also noted. The cover of the *Soldbuch* was marked with *Hoheitsabzeichen* and made of a tan *Papyrolin*. This material was grained to represent leather, but was actually a composite of paper and fibre.

Curiously, a photograph was not included in the *Soldbuch* until 1944, at which time both a photograph and the signature of the holder were inserted inside the front cover, stamped in such a way as to endorse both image and book. Additional documents were often held inside the rear cover of the *Soldbuch*. Those of Franz Wirtz included official leaflets on dealing with gas, first aid during air raids, typhus, malaria, dysentery and soldierly behaviour. Old habits die hard, as Wirtz was still adding new material as late as 1955, including notes on his escape from Prussia a decade earlier.

Two other identity documents were the *Soldbuch-Ersatz* and the *Truppenausweis*. The *Soldbuch-Ersatz* was a temporary replacement document for a lost *Soldbuch*, as for example when a soldier was injured and taken to hospital. The *Truppenausweis* was a two- or four-page document sometimes used prior to the issue of a *Soldbuch*: it carried basic identification information, usually a photograph, and a note of permission to bear arms. Passes and notifications, travel warrants, military driving licences and tickets were also common.

What else was carried in pockets or tucked among regulation kit varied tremendously – something which interested the US Army during the war. A report of 1944 referred to captured Germans with pockets stuffed with ammunition; wallets; money; food; ointments, foot powders and salves; smoking materials; pocket knives; papers; pencils; string; and condoms. A well-known

The correct way to mark clothing
and equipment. Black oblongs
represent stampings, hatched
oblongs the location of the soldier's
name. From the 1940 edition of
Reibert.

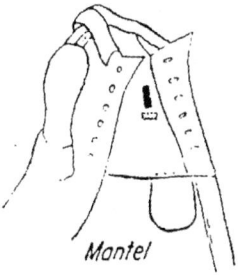

Mantel

Rock

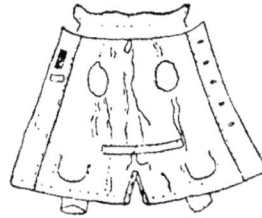

Feldbluse und Drillichrock

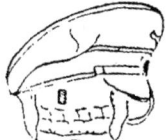

Schirmmütze

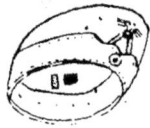

Feldmütze, Bergmütze

Tuchhose, Berghose, Reithose,
Drillich- und Unterhose

Hemd

Badehose

Sporthemd

Sporthose

Kragen-und Halsbinde

Brotbeutel

Feldflasche

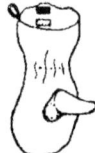

Oberziehhandschuh

Troddel

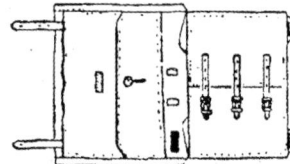

Tornister

Stiefel

Socken

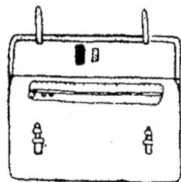

Bekl-Sack und Rucksack

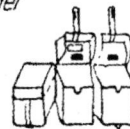

Patronentasche

Meldekartentasche Leibriemen

Sportschuh

Schnürschuh, Bergschuh

Seitengewehr-
tasche

Zeltbahn

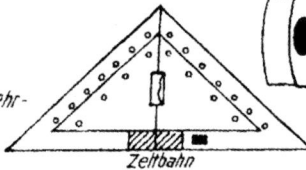

Koppelschloß

Mannschaftsdecke

■ = Stempel

▨ = Namen

photograph of small items gathered from German prisoners of war taken in Normandy shows a bewildering selection including scissors; razor; pills; brushes for shaving, cleaning and polishing; mess and sewing kit; candle; whistle; pocket lamp; compass, and keys. The purpose of a fragment of a female suspender belt was unexplained.

Currency took different forms depending on location, what appeared on pay day and whatever locals gave by way of change. Exchange rates favoured the troops, so a French or Luxembourg franc or a Bohemian and Moravian koruna, for example, were worth just one-tenth of the German Reichsmark. In occupied Jersey in the Channel Islands, many local coins disappeared by 1942, taken away by German soldiers as souvenirs, and were replaced by new notes down to the value of 6d. New money-issuing authorities were set up in places such as Bohemia, Moravia, Poland and Ukraine. Unsurprisingly, barter became normal. There was also occupation currency, issued initially as an emergency measure by the *Reichskreditkasse* following in the wake of armies as national banks collapsed in defeat. From 1942 a new *Wehrmachtbehelfsgeld* (armed forces auxiliary money) was introduced, mainly for use in combat areas, and in 1944 came a new series of *Verrechnungsschein* notes or 'bills of exchange'. Canteen token systems also operated in some places, and in Romania and Bulgaria were operated specifically to avoid undermining the financial systems of Germany's allies.

Reading material for troops was extensive, much of it produced for morale-raising purposes and by way of reinforcing political objectives. The *Tornisterschrift* ('Back-pack Literature') and the *Soldatenblätter für Feier und Freizeit* ('Soldier Pages for Holiday and Leisure') series were both produced by OKH itself. The *Kleine Kriegshefte* ('Little War Volumes'), aimed at civilians and servicemen alike, came from the central office of the Nazi Party, though making use of war reports by the *Propagandakompanien* of the Heer. Versions of popular and classic literature were also reprinted in paperback for sending to the front through the postal system. Songbooks, puzzle books and comic material helped to pass quiet times, though guide and phrase books produced in Germany and locally had more practical aims. *Ein Kleiner Spaziergang durch Saloniki* ('A Little Walk Through Salonika'), commemorating the invasion of Greece in April 1941, for example, was a useful guide and money spinner for a local Italian publisher; but the more substantial *In Bild und Wort durch Bömen und Möhren* ('In Words and Pictures through Bohemia and Moravia'), published in 1940, was aimed directly at the soldier by the armed-forces press in Berlin. Newspapers and magazines enjoyed varying levels of popularity, and publications from occupied countries as well as Germany found their way into baggage. Subject to resources, *Signal*, *Die Wehrmacht* and popular French publications enjoyed significant circulations.

Games and pastimes made their way to war by various routes. Packs of cards for popular games such as *Skat* were easily carried, but could also be found in canteens and the *Soldatenheim* (soldiers' recreation centre). Here, board games and music were played, entertainments enjoyed and newspapers read. Officers had their own equivalent establishments in the *Offizierkasino*. Some board games, such as chess and draughts, were manufactured in compact, lightweight versions for delivery by the field post, and could be carried right up to the front line.

Wenn ich Urlaub hab'!

Worte von Ralph Maria Siegel   Musik von Gerhard Winkler

Heute gehts hinaus, weit fort von dir, für das liebe Vaterland.
Darum reich nochmal zum Abschied mir deinen Mund und deine Hand!
Nun ade, es muß sein, nun ade, bleibe mein
und vergiß nicht, wenn ich draußen bin, präg dir meine Worte ein:

   Wenn ich Urlaub hab', wenn ich Urlaub hab',
   lieber Schatz, dann gehts heim zu dir!
   Wenn ich Urlaub hab', wenn ich Urlaub hab',
   lieber Schatz, dann gehörst du mir!

Halt ich da draußen in der Ferne Wacht, dann gedenk ich immer dein!
Steh ich ganz allein in dunkler Nacht, wird mein Herz stets bei dir sein!
Denn ich weiß, was auch sei, denn ich weiß, du bist mir treu
und ich denk dann nach getaner Pflicht, bin ich ein paar Tage frei:

Wenn aufs neu die Abschiedsstunde schlägt, liebes Mädel, weine nicht!
Ich weiß selber, was dein Herz bewegt, zeig ein lachendes Gesicht!
Sag ade, es muß sein, sag ade, bleibe mein!
Eines Tages kehre ich zurück und ich laß dich nie mehr allein.

Popular song card *Wenn ich Urlaub hab'* ('If I have leave'). The soldier trudges home with a full *Bekleidungssack* in hand and *Gasplane* pouch on his chest.

Photographs, postcards and letters were all highly valued as connections with home, family and comrades. Many soldiers had portraits of themselves taken on enlistment or completion of training for distribution to family and friends, and carried photographs of loved ones with them on campaign. Group photographs were also quite common, and many were printed with lines on the reverse to serve as postcards. Other postcards produced commercially included humour, architecture and landscapes, propaganda, military scenes, art, personalities and erotic subjects. Letters fulfilled both personal and official functions, and, subject to certain limitations, passed between soldier and homeland without need for a stamp.

The *Feldpost* had its own personnel, post offices and transport, and relied on a *Feldpostnummer* system. The soldier used his name, rank and *Feldpostnummer* on correspondence to keep his unit and location secure, and post from home followed his unit by means of the *Feldpostnummer*. A four-digit number was used for Heer manoeuvres in 1937, increased to five or sometimes six digits during the war, with or without letters before or after the number. Mail was marked with both date and location as it left a civilian post office, but field post offices marked letters with only *Feldpost* and date. Censored letters were usually endorsed as having been opened, and scrutiny of letters' content was used as a gauge of morale. The postal system was effective but given troop movements and enemy action, letters were sometimes lost or arrived in the wrong order. For this reason many correspondents numbered their missives consecutively so the recipient would know if something had gone awry.

CHAPTER 4
SMALL ARMS

A member of the *Feldherrnhalle* Division with a Kar 98k bolt-action rifle. The brown *Feldherrnhalle* Division *Ärmelstreifen* on the left sleeve was approved from August 1942, the name commemorating this Heer unit's origins in the *Sturmabteilung* (SA, assault detachment), the paramilitary wing of the Nazi Party. (Roger Viollet/ Getty Images)

RIFLES

In 1939, as the Wehrmacht prepared for war, Heer troops were supposed to be equipped with the latest Mauser-designed 7.92mm bolt-action military rifle. This was the Kar 98k (*Karabiner 98 kurz*, '1898 short carbine'), the designation deriving from the year of introduction of the original Mauser mechanism and the length of the weapon). The Kar 98k was produced from 1935 with the requirements of the fast-expanding Heer in mind. Like its predecessors, it had a five-round integral box magazine and was accurate, more than adequately powerful, well made and robust. It weighed approximately 4kg and was sighted to a maximum of 2,000m.

Though an accomplished rifleman working in perfect conditions might conceivably have hit something, preferably stationary and very large, at such a range, battlefield fire was not usually conducted at more than a few hundred metres. That the Kar 98k was designed with this combat scenario in mind is confirmed by the tangent leaf arrangement of the sights in 100m increments, and a barrel length of only 60cm. The short barrel had the advantages of keeping the rifle's weight manageable and giving it a handy overall length that allowed it to be swiftly aimed and used effectively in confined spaces. It was also determined that the 60cm barrel was not so short a length as to cause unacceptably high muzzle blast and flash, and was thus a good compromise. The Mauser bolt was a tried-and-tested system, being familiar both to old soldiers and increasingly to new recruits because training rifles using the system, some of them in small calibres, were carried by a variety of paramilitary organizations. The new weapon also retained existing types of bayonet fitting and cleaning rod.

A three-man sniper and observation team at work. The observers carry a tubular periscope and binoculars while the sniper uses a Kar 98k fitted with a Zf 41 telescopic sight.

LEFT Detail of a five-round clip of 7.92mm rifle ammunition in the *Patronentasche*. These particular rounds, head-stamped 'emp 44', were made at the Dynamit company's Werk Empelde in Ronnenberg, near Hanover, in 1944.

BELOW A detail view of the Kar 98k showing the loading method. With the bolt fully retracted, a five-round ammunition clip was placed in the guides atop the receiver then depressed firmly with the thumb to charge the integral magazine from the top. Pushing the bolt forward again tensioned the mechanism and fed a cartridge into the chamber. With the safety catch off, the Kar 98k was ready to fire.

The Mauser Gew 98 bolt-action rifle with five-round magazine, as depicted in Hauptmann Friedrich Kühlwein's *Felddienst-ABC für den Schützen* ('Field Service ABC for the Rifleman'), 1934. The pre-World War I Gew 98 survived to serve the Reichsheer. With new barrel bands, sight and side-mounted sling it was rechristened the Kar 98b. Unmodified examples of the Gew 98 were also captured from Polish forces following the invasion of that country in September 1939.

The Kar 98k had many good features and an excellent pedigree, but in retrospect the decision to make such a new weapon a universal arm in the build-up to war is questionable. By contrast, the British had plumped for the .303in Short Magazine Lee Enfield bolt-action rifle, which had an easier action and a ten-round magazine, even before World War I. Of more concern, however, was the fact that while German designers were shortening a weapon whose mechanism dated back to 1898, US specialists were refining a brand-new semi-automatic rifle in the shape of the .30-06 M1 Garand. As if this were not enough, it was soon apparent that there would be insufficient Kar 98k rifles to satisfy demand. Initial production was in the hundreds of thousands per annum, with a figure of 1,351,700 quoted for the year 1940, rising to as many as 2,262,300 in 1944. Total production has been credibly estimated at almost 11.5 million. Perhaps one-third came from the Mauser company's factory at Oberndorf, but other factories including those in Berlin, Erfurt, Steyr (Austria), Brno (Czechoslovakia) and Suhl all produced significant quantities. As in so many other areas, speed and volume of production of the Kar 98k were progressively aided by design simplifications and the substitution of materials. Solid walnut stocks were supplemented first by beech ply and, by the middle of the war, by various sorts of laminate that were heavier than the original walnut stock but strong and significantly reduced wastage. Forged fittings were replaced with stampings, butt plates were simplified, and eventually some examples of the Kar 98k were even made without a bayonet bar or cleaning rod.

The sheer size of the Heer and scale of the war effort meant that though the Kar 98k was the most numerous rifle it was far from the only type in use, particularly in units operating behind the front line. In the case of a single security brigade on the Eastern Front, a return of arms made in 1942 noted that of its 7,694 rifles, only a little over 3,000 were Kar 98k. The remainder were foreign arms drawn from six different countries: Poland, Czechoslovakia, France, the Netherlands, Yugoslavia and the Soviet Union. Captured Soviet rifles alone numbered over 1,000. Czech rifles were of particular significance because their production facilities fell into German hands quite literally lock, stock and barrel with the German occupation of Czechoslovakia in 1939, and no fewer than 11 complete Heer infantry divisions were equipped with the Czech 7.92mm vz. 24 bolt-action rifle, designated the Gewehr 24(t) in Heer

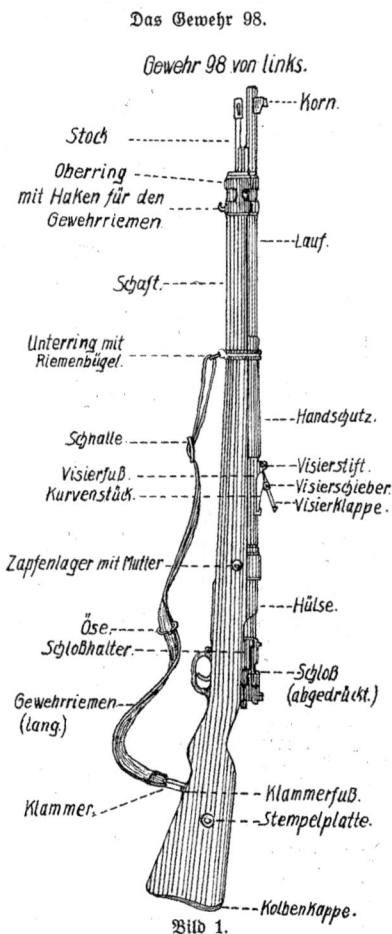

Das Gewehr 98.

Gewehr 98 von links.

Bild 1.

ABOVE LEFT A recruit pictured at Potsdam, *c.*1940, carrying what appears to be a World War I-vintage Gew 98, a noticeably longer weapon than the Kar 98k.

ABOVE Piled Kar 98b bolt-action rifles during an exercise, *c.*1939. Personal kit including *Tornister, Stahlhelme, Kochgeschirre* and gas masks is lined up to the far left and far right of the picture.

LEFT Two different models of obsolescent bolt-action rifle in use with the same unit during the battle for France, summer 1940.

ABOVE Front and rear views of the rifle-ammunition *Patronentaschen* (ammunition pouches). Each of the three small compartments held ten rounds, five each side of a central divider. With 30 rounds in each *Patronentasche*, a Heer soldier carried 60 rounds on his waist belt. Specialists and rear-area troops often carried one *Patronentasche* on the waist belt.

RIGHT Marking detail of the Gustav Schiele Lederwarenfabrik in Loburg on a 1942 *Patronentasche*. Many manufacturers were using code marks by this time.

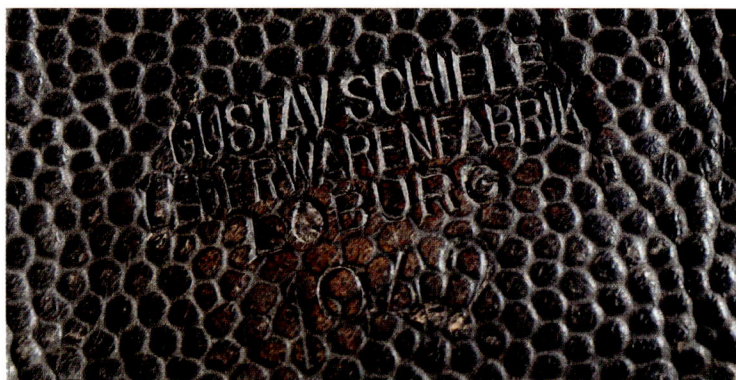

TOP FAR LEFT A well-camouflaged sniper position in the Kuban bridgehead, summer 1943. One man observes while the other aims through, rather than over, the grassy bank.

TOP CENTRE A member of 97. Jäger-Division fires a captured Soviet 7.62mm Mosin-Nagant bolt-action rifle fitted with a telescopic sight. The rifle had a five-round magazine and, when in the hands of a trained marksman and fitted with a telescopic sight, was useful to about 800m.

ABOVE Cleaning the Kar 98k. While the Kar 98k was not a modern design, and a much less significant contributor to the firefight than automatic weapons, it continued to be easily the most numerous firearm in Heer service through to 1945. Well cared for, as a 'soldier's friend' should be, it remained an accurate and deadly weapon.

ABOVE LEFT The Czech-made Gewehr 33/40 bolt-action rifle was one of many foreign-made rifles carried by Heer forces.

LEFT Some typical small-arms accessories. At right, a cardboard box for 15 rounds of *Spitzgeschoss mit Kern* (SmK, steel-cored armour-piercing) ammunition, dated 1943. At left, two muzzle covers; at bottom left, a stripping tool for the P 08 'Luger' pistol.

service. The 7.92mm Gewehr 33/40 bolt-action rifle was also of Czech manufacture. Based on the vz. 33, it had a barrel length of just 49cm and was sighted to only 1,000m maximum; it was used mainly by *Gebirgsjäger* from 1940 onwards. Old German bolt-action rifles also continued to be used. The original 7.92mm Mauser Gewehr 98 (Gew 98) carried in World War I was one such, and was similar to some of the captured Polish rifles, themselves made with German machinery during the interwar period. The 7.92mm Kar 98b was also issued to some personnel, but despite its designation it was the length of the Gew 98, and indeed was only a slightly modified version of the old rifle.

PISTOLS

Pistols were carried by officers, senior NCOs and various officials, as a secondary weapon by machine-gunners and other weapon crews, and for emergency use by specialists. The previous remarks regarding the shortage of rifles and their production applied, if anything, even more to pistols, and the picture was further muddied by private-purchase sidearms. Two pistols, however, both German-made official-issue types, led the field and are most commonly shown in photographs of combat troops.

The 9mm Parabellum P 08 (Pistole 08) semi-automatic pistol, often known as the 'Luger' after its designer Georg Luger, was adopted by the Imperial German Army in 1908. While not at its best in the mud of the trenches it proved practical, easy to point and accurate enough, as well as sufficiently powerful. Key to its success was the 9mm round, eight of which were contained in the P 08's slanting box magazine which slid upwards into the butt of the pistol. The P 08 could be both discharged and reloaded swiftly, particularly in comparison to some of the larger-calibre revolvers then in service. By 1918, production of the Army-model P 08 had reached over 1.5 million. Some continued in private or paramilitary hands thereafter while others were re-marked by the armed forces in 1920, leading to the so-called 'double date' phenomenon when a P 08 carries two dates, one relating to Imperial Germany and the other to '1920'. Though initial P 08 production had been mainly by Deutsche Waffen-und Munitionsfabriken (DWM) in Berlin and the state armoury in Erfurt, it was restarted by Simson & Co of Suhl in 1925. More pistols for commercial sale were also made by Berlin-Karlsruher Industrie-Werke (BKIW), successor to DWM, which kept the old DWM company monogram on the toggle link atop the gun, but it was not until 1934 that large-scale orders were fulfilled by the Mauser company and by Heinrich Krieghoff & Sohn of Suhl. Exactly who was manufacturing what was at least partially concealed by the use of code letters and numbers, but almost 1 million P 08 pistols were made between 1935 and the end of World War II.

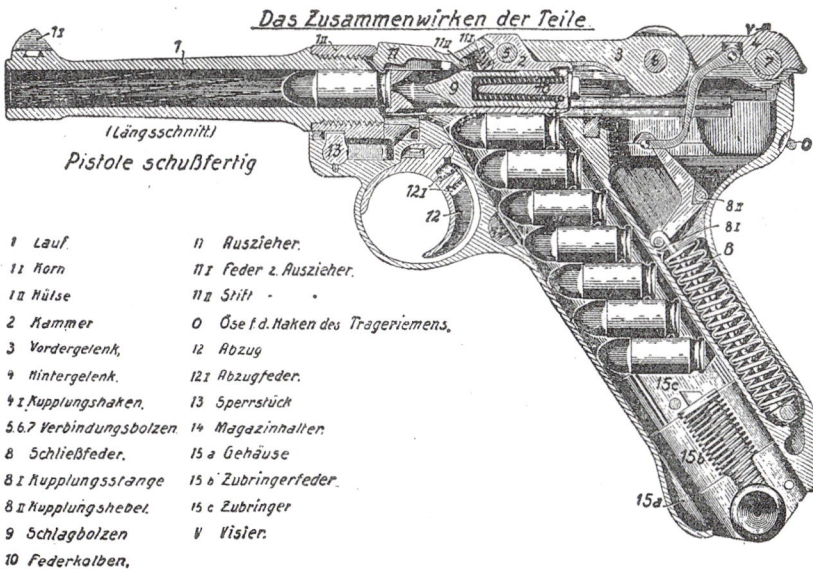

Das Zusammenwirken der Teile

(Längsschnitt)

Pistole schußfertig

1	Lauf.	11	Auszieher.
1 I	Korn	11 I	Feder z. Auszieher.
1 II	Hülse	11 II	Stift
2	Kammer	0	Öse f. d. Haken des Trageriemens.
3	Vordergelenk.	12	Abzug
4	Hintergelenk.	12 I	Abzugfeder.
4 I	Kupplungshaken.	13	Sperrstück
5. 6. 7	Verbindungsbolzen	14	Magazinhalter.
8	Schließfeder.	15 a	Gehäuse
8 I	Kupplungsstange	15 b	Zubringerfeder.
8 II	Kupplunghebel.	15 c	Zubringer
9	Schlagbolzen	V	Visier.
10	Federkolben.		

Bild 57.

Pistole 08 im Längsschnitt.

ABOVE A P 08 semi-automatic pistol, showing how the eight-round magazine was loaded through the butt of the pistol grip. This P 08 is of World War I manufacture, as is the magazine which has the characteristic wooden end detail, later examples being of all-metal construction.

LEFT A sectional manual diagram of the P 08 showing the pistol loaded and ready for use with seven rounds in the magazine and one in the chamber.

Pistol practice with the P 08 for
two NCOs and an officer of
Infanterie-Regiment 24, West
Prussia, *c.*1940. As far as pistols
were concerned, the P 08 was an
accurate weapon with adequate
power for its purpose.
Nevertheless, it was still a last
resort in battle and little damage
was inflicted at much more than
about 30m.

Pistol practice with the P 08 for two NCOs and an officer of Infanterie-Regiment 24, West Prussia, *c.*1940. As far as pistols were concerned, the P 08 was an accurate weapon with adequate power for its purpose. Nevertheless, it was still a last resort in battle and little damage was inflicted at much more than about 30m.

The 9mm Walther P 38 (Pistole 38) semi-automatic pistol came about specifically because the Heereswaffenamt (Army Weapons Office) concluded that the P 08 was too costly and too difficult to manufacture. At the same time, the opportunity was taken to produce a more modern design. Work began in 1935, but an initial suggestion for a pistol without an external hammer was rejected when the Heer made it clear that a weapon was required which could be cocked by means of a hammer and worked single or double action. Though the concept was finalized in 1938, production at Carl Walther Waffenfabrik in Zella-Mehlis did not begin until the following year, with issues from 1940. The P 38 had similar performance to the P 08, and also had an eight-round magazine in the butt, but it was a little cheaper to manufacture and – more importantly – saved machine time. The Mauser company also began to produce the P 38 in 1942 and Metallwarenfabrik Spreewerke of Spandau followed suit in 1943. Between them, they produced more than 1.1 million P 38 pistols during the war.

Production of the P 38 was nowhere near enough to meet demand, and as a result Germany was forced to acquire a mass of other pistols, many of which were produced in occupied nations. According to E.C. Ezell, these pistols comprised 27 different models sourced in Belgium, France, Spain,

ABOVE The P 38 semi-automatic pistol. This example has the code 'AC43', representing Carl Walther Waffenfabrik, 1943. Though the P 38 was intended to be an easier pistol to produce than the P 08, it never succeeded in satisfying demand, with the result that many other pistol types remained in service.

LEFT A 'hard shell' leather holster with flap and push-through tab closure for the P 38.

BELOW Rear detail of the same P 38 holster with Heereswaffenamt (Army Weapons Office) stamp and code 'bdr 42', denoting manufacture by Richard Ehrhardt Lederwarenfabrik of Pößneck, 1942, and Heer acceptance.

RIGHT Manufactured by Fabryka Broni w Radomiu in Radom, Poland, the 9mm pistolet wz. 35 Vis was one of the better foreign pistols in Heer service, and was based on a Browning design. Production continued after the occupation of Poland and the pistol was designated P 35(p): 'Pistol 1935' after its first year of manufacture and 'p' for Polish. This example is shown with its eight-round magazine removed.

OPPOSITE The same pistol in its original leather holster stamped with the German title 'P 35(p)'.

INSET OPPOSITE Detail of a Czech vz. 27 semi-automatic pistol with German manufacturer code 'fnh'. In German service the vz. 27 was designated the P 27(t). During the occupation of Czechoslovakia, the Germans continued to operate the Česká zbrojovka arms factory in Prague as Böhmische Waffenfabrik.

ABOVE Almost 500,000 vz. 27 pistols with eight-round magazines were manufactured during the German occupation of Czechoslovakia.

ABOVE RIGHT The 7.65mm Sauer 38H semi-automatic pistol, manufactured by J.P. Sauer & Sohn of Suhl from 1938; about 200,000 had been made by the end of World War II. The 'H' in its name stands for *Hahn*, a reference to the shrouded or internal hammer mechanism.

RIGHT The 7.65mm Walther semi-automatic pistol, introduced in 1910, was a popular pistol for Heer officers during World War I; some were still in use during World War II.

LEFT The 7.65mm Walther PP semi-automatic pistol was originally intended as a *Polizeipistole (*PP, 'Police Pistol'), but from 1935 it was purchased for use by military, police and political organizations. The PP had an eight-round magazine; the 7.65mm Walther PPK (*Polizeipistole Kriminalmodel*, Police Pistol, Detective Model), which also saw service, was more compact and had only a seven-round capacity. Both pistols were popular and effective weapons, given the limitations of the 7.65mm cartridge.

BELOW LEFT The basic 27mm single-shot signal pistol. This example was manufactured by Erfurter Maschinenfabrik (Erma) of Erfurt in 1939, and is shown in the 'broken open' position for loading.

LEFT A Bakelite container for six star-shells for the signal pistol, manufactured in May 1941. The star on the label indicates the colour of the pyrotechnic.

Czechoslovakia, Norway and Poland as well as Germany and the former Austria. Many were made in the preferred 9mm military calibre, but a good number were 7.65mm: about 2.5 million pistols were gathered by means of these contracts. It is worth noting, however, that this list refers primarily to new weapons from manufacturers, and therefore misses many pistols acquired in other ways – captured Soviet pistols, for example, being a glaring omission. In Italy, Fabbrica d'Armi Pietro Beretta continued to operate under German control, even after Italy capitulated to the Allies in September 1943. Foreign pistols in Heer service received a new designation ending in a lower-case letter in brackets to indicate a pistol's origin. New pistols were marked accordingly, French pistols having 'f', Polish pistols 'p', Czech pistols 't' and Austrian pistols 'ö'. So it was, for example, that the Austrian 9mm Steyr M1912 became the Pistole Modell 12(ö), and the Czech 7.65mm vz. 27 the Pistole Modell 27(t).

SUBMACHINE GUNS

Germany was an early leader in the use of submachine guns, adopting the 9mm Bergmann MP 18/I (Maschinenpistole 18) before the end of World War I. The key features of the MP 18/I were its capacity for automatic fire combined with a pistol-type 9mm round and its compact layout, offering improved firepower and mobility against close-range targets. This made the submachine gun ideal for the conditions for which it was designed: clearing trenches and bunkers, or on the move in close country. Though the Treaty of Versailles hampered development of the German submachine gun it was not entirely curtailed, and an improved weapon in the shape of Heinrich Vollmer's export model, the VMP, appeared in 1928.

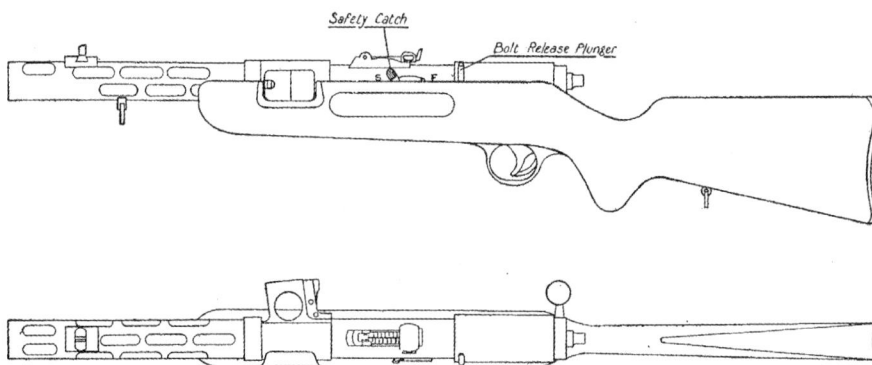

FIG 10—9 mm MACHINE CARBINE MP 34¹ (BERGMANN)

ABOVE The Steyr MP 34(ö) submachine gun in use in Norway. Unusually, it is shown here with the bayonet fixed. (ullstein bild/ Getty Images)

LEFT The Bergmann MP 34 submachine gun. Manufacture of the MP 34, which built on an earlier 1932 model, was contracted out to Carl Walther Waffenfabrik, and the weapon was further improved in 1935.

Two more types of submachine gun appeared in 1934: the Bergmann BMP 34, development of which was assisted by the fabrication of prototypes in Denmark, and the German-designed but Austrian-manufactured Steyr Solothurn S1-100. Both submachine guns saw service with German forces in World War II, and both were 9mm blowback designs with wooden stocks, having the appearance of a short carbine with a projecting box magazine to the side. Beyond this, however, they were very different weapons. The S1-100, referred to as the MP 34(ö) in Heer use, was an exceptionally well-made weapon fitted to take a bayonet, with its bolt handle located forward. Its magazine fed from the left side and could be refilled by means of a charger system. The BMP 34 fed from the right side and had a bolt handle at the breech end of the weapon.

The Spanish Civil War (1936–39) demonstrated the usefulness of the submachine gun, but the conflict also highlighted the lack of an up-to-date, mass-issue weapon in the Heer arsenal as rearmament got into its stride. As a result, Erfurter Maschinenfabrik (Erma) was approached with the requirement for a new submachine gun that took into account the needs of parachute and mechanized forces as well as the role of the submachine gun with the infantry. The result was the then-remarkable 9mm MP 38, designed by Heinrich Vollmer and Berthold Geipel. Obvious new features included a metal 'skeleton' buttstock which folded under the gun for compactness, and the total abandonment of wood, with phenolic resin used for the furniture. Less obvious was the use of Vollmer's telescoping bolt system. Where the old German submachine-gun designs had the appearance of short carbines with side magazines, the MP 38 conveyed modernity with its pistol grip and downward-pointing detachable box magazine. The MP 38 served well in Poland and continued to be used, but early combat experience set in train a number of design improvements and simplifications.

The culmination of these design changes was the 9mm MP 40. Perhaps the biggest savings over the MP 38 were the replacement of the high-grade steel used for the receiver with heavy-gauge sheet steel, and the replacement of the aluminium grip frame with sheet metal. Neither measure detracted from the MP 40's effectiveness, but both saved on materials and manufacturing time. The lack of a safety catch to lock the bolt in the forward position was remedied with a new form of cocking handle

A decorated NCO of the *Großdeutschland* Division alights from his vehicle, MP 38 submachine gun in hand.

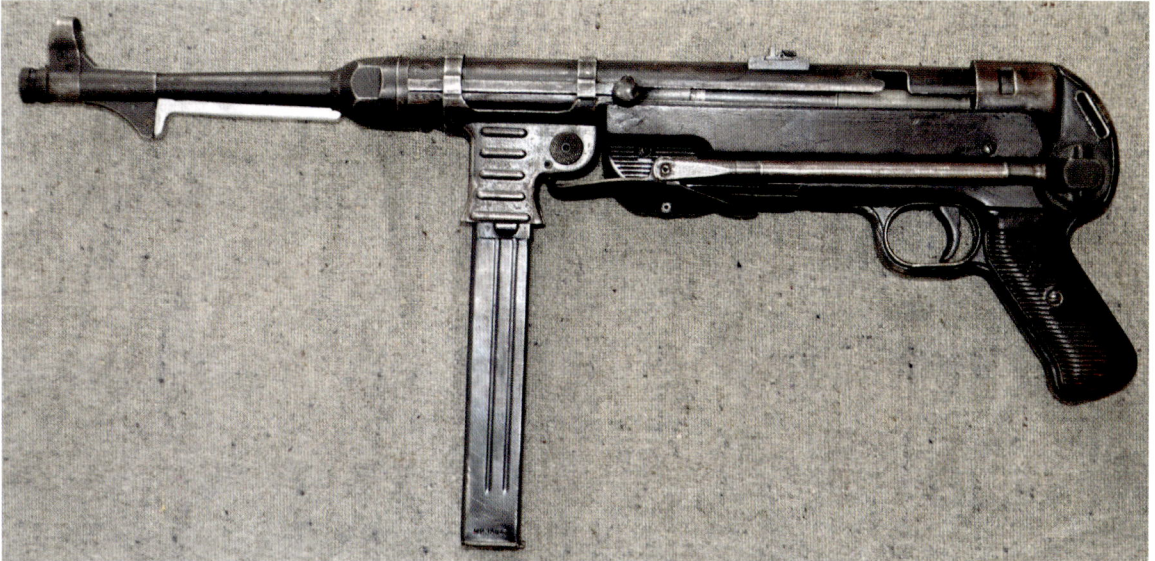

and an internal slot to prevent the bolt moving – something also retrofitted to many existing MP 38s. Both the MP 38 and the MP 40 proved popular and useful weapons, and more than 1 million had been made by the end of the war. These submachine guns had their idiosyncrasies, however, some of which were also common to other weapons. One was that because both designs fired from an open bolt, there was a very short delay as the bolt slammed forward for the first round, and the moving metalwork reduced accuracy. Given short-range use this was probably not too significant, but users also had to be aware that long

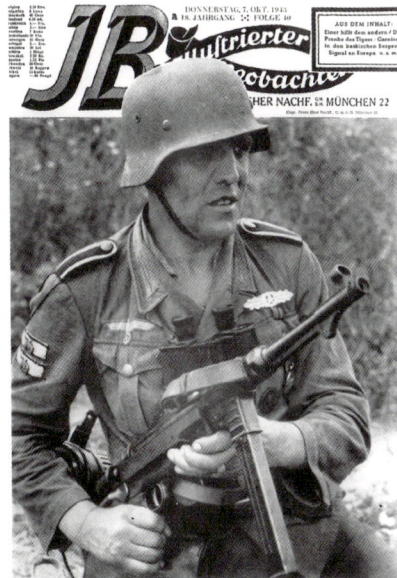

ABOVE Popularly regarded as the iconic front-line infantry squad leader's weapon, the MP 40 submachine gun with its folding stock was a novel weapon at the time of its introduction into Heer service. This example is marked 'bnz', denoting manufacture by Steyr-Daimler-Puch of Steyr, Austria.

LEFT A Munich magazine cover illustration of 1943 showing an *Unteroffizier* armed with the MP 40. His veteran status is underlined by the *Nahkampfspange* over his breast pocket and two *Panzervernichtungsabzeichen* as well as other awards.

bursts of fire tended to cause the muzzle to wander off target and increased the possibility of jamming. Stoppages were not particularly common but could occur, especially if there was any damage to a magazine. The flip-up back-sight arrangement of the MP 40 had two leaves, stamped with '100' and '200' in tiny numerals and thereby giving settings for range in metres. This was realistic because most engagements were likely to be at 100m or less, and because any sort of accuracy was highly unlikely at more than 200m.

Remarkably, one of the most widely used submachine guns in Heer service was not German but Soviet. Approximately 5 million examples of the 7.62mm PPSh-41 were made in the Soviet Union and their aggressive close-range use by Red Army troops caused significant shocks in battle, particularly when Heer troops became aware that whole units within the Red Army were equipped with this weapon, many of them fitted with 71-round drum magazines. Naturally, many captured examples of the PPSh-41 were used just as they were found, but there was also a programme to modify the design to 9mm. The magazine capacity of the PPSh-41 – more than double that of the 32-round MP 40 – was addressed in a short-lived experiment to fit two magazines to what was designated the MP 40/I.

AUTOMATIC AND SEMI-AUTOMATIC RIFLES

German forces made only very limited use of automatic rifles with air units as early as World War I and experiments with auto-loading longarms continued during the interwar period. Most of the weapons examined chambered full-sized rifle cartridges, but from the mid-1930s 'intermediate' rounds were also developed. This ammunition, less powerful than existing rifle cartridges but with a much greater effective range than a pistol bullet, offered the intriguing possibility of new automatic weapons for use on the move by an individual, thus combining the advantages of both rifle and submachine gun. In 1935 the 7.92mm Vollmer M 35 automatic carbine using a reduced-power cartridge was demonstrated to Heereswaffenamt personnel at the Kümmersdorf range, and further trials were held right up until late August 1939.

Nevertheless, no new weapon was adopted at this point, and when the first German semi-automatic rifle of World War II was ordered in 1940 it was the 7.92mm Mauser Gewehr 41 (Gew 41), a weapon that used full-sized cartridges. Both the Mauser Gew 41 and the similar but less complicated 7.92mm Walther Gew 41 semi-automatic rifle, which entered service in 1942, were gas operated and had a ten-round box magazine. Both rifles worked, but at 5kg they were heavy and neither was produced in large numbers. Further redesigns led to the 7.92mm Walther Gewehr 43 (Gew 43) semi-automatic rifle. This was a little lighter, lacked the clumsy muzzle cone of the Gew 41 and incorporated various inspirations from the Soviet 7.62mm Tokarev SVT gas-operated semi-automatic rifle encountered on the Eastern Front. Though about 400,000 Gew 43 rifles were manufactured during the war it was never intended as a general-issue weapon, being regarded as a niche arm for specialists, and indeed many were used as sniping weapons complete with telescopic sight. Useful as they were, none of these rifles ever filled the general role that the .30-06 M1 Garand did with US forces, nor could they be used effectively in the assault role of the submachine gun.

Tunnel Foresight Protector

Release Stud 'Holding Open' Device

Breech Bolt Locking Plunger

Gas Choke

Cocking Cover

Cocking Handle

Safety Catch

Locking Bolt

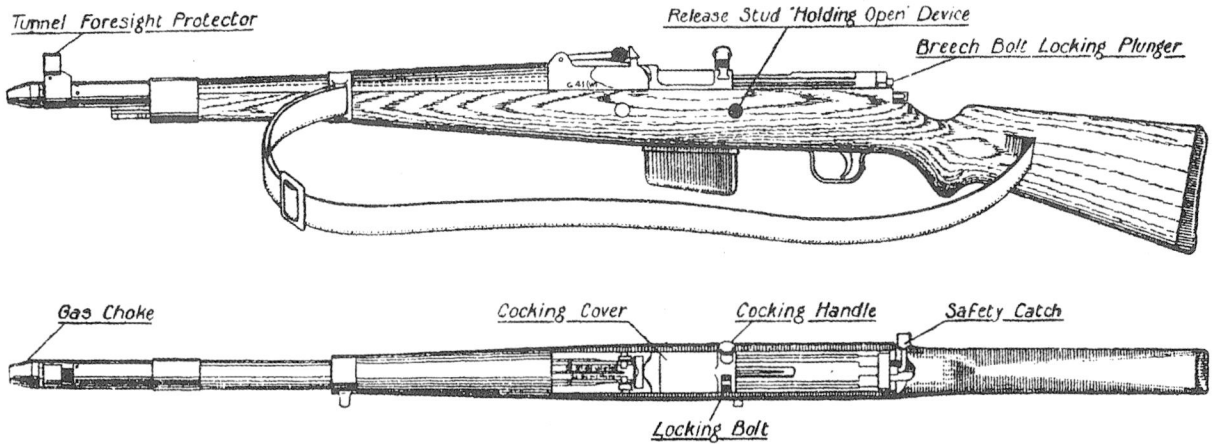

ABOVE The Gew 41 semi-automatic rifle. With a self-loading capability and a ten-round magazine, the Gew 41 had a role in combat, but it was neither well balanced nor particularly popular. Produced only in small numbers, it was gradually superseded by the Gew 43, which had a simpler, piston-type mechanism.

LEFT A squad leader briefing on the Eastern Front. The man in the *Mantel*, foreground left, carries a Soviet Tokarev SVT gas-operated semi-automatic rifle. Though the SVT was not a particularly robust weapon, semi-automatic rifles were at a premium and the Tokarev, like the PPSh-41 submachine gun and the Soviet Maxim machine guns, was very welcome when captured.

Whether the continuation of other experiments with intermediate cartridges and 'machine carbine' weapons is regarded as a duplication of effort or a masterstroke, it was fortunate for Germany that semi-automatic rifles were not the only new development, for given the bolt-action rifle's low rate of fire and the outnumbering of German forces on the Eastern Front, there was now a huge reliance on machine weapons of all types. The appearance of the first intermediate-cartridge 7.92mm Maschinenkarabiner 1942 (MKb 42) was therefore welcome but also controversial. The new weapon was welcomed because it offered an

ABOVE Trial of an MP 43 fitted with a Zielfernrohr 4 optical sight at the *Infanterie-Schule*, October 1943. (Bundesarchiv, Bild 146-1979-118-55, Foto: o.Ang)

ABOVE RIGHT The StG 44 assault rifle in the hands of a well-camouflaged soldier, late 1944. His *Mütze* mounts a face veil of cloth strips and at his side hangs a *Patronentasche*. (Bundesarchiv, Bild 101I-676-7996-13, Foto: Vieth)

RIGHT Detail view of an StG 44 at Wrocław (formerly Breslau) Arsenal, showing the magazine housing, grip and trigger.

increase in firepower and controversial because the manufacture of another type of cartridge and weapon at such a critical juncture might have been considered superfluous, and its tactical niche was as yet poorly defined. At first, Hitler was unconvinced. Test results were also mixed, showing that the MKb 42 could engage at 600m and hit a small target at 400m, but there was criticism of its reliability.

Only very small numbers of the MKb 42 were produced, but 1943 saw the appearance of a refined version now rebranded as a 'machine pistol', namely the MP 43. About 20,000 of these weapons were manufactured during 1943, with extensive combat trials undertaken on the Eastern Front. Not until 1944 was full mass-production achieved, however, with the weapon first redesignated 'MP 44' and then the Sturmgewehr 44 (StG 44). The latter title, meaning 'assault rifle 1944', was significant not only in propaganda terms but in that it signalled the importance of the weapon as a potential replacement for the bolt-action rifle. The StG 44 was, nevertheless, a remarkable departure and after the war many countries adopted 'assault rifles' firing new cartridges. The main features of the StG 44 were a 30-round curved box magazine, an ability to fire either selective single shots or bursts, gas operation and a short (42cm) barrel. The weapon was very simply finished, making extensive use of metal stampings and having a very basic flat wooden buttstock.

Under new plans, Heer infantry platoons were each intended to contain two assault-rifle squads, one machine-gun squad, and a headquarters. Assault rifles would be the main arm, supported by two machine guns and a couple of rifle grenadiers. Though the StG 44 was widely used on the battlefield during the last year of war, fewer than 500,000 were produced and the ambitious plan was never achieved.

GRENADES

The iconic *Stielhandgranate* (stick hand grenade) of World War II was a direct descendant of its World War I predecessor introduced in 1915. The common elements to both were a cylindrical head containing the explosive charge and a wooden handle through which ran a cord linked to the igniter. A pull on the cord activated a friction device – bigger and more robust than a Christmas cracker, but functioning not unlike one – thereby lighting the fuze. After a delay during which the *Stielhandgranate* was thrown, the fuze activated the detonator, exploding the main charge. The key effect was blast, making the *Stielhandgranate*, which could be thrown about 30m, particularly useful for assault situations in which the thrower was not himself under cover, or where the *Stielhandgranate* could be lobbed into trenches or bunkers. During the war, some *Stielhandgranaten* were fitted with a wide metal collar around the cylinder, converting them to heavier and more effective fragmentation bombs. *Stielhandgranaten* were transported unfuzed for safety, being armed behind the front lines, and infantryman Reiner Nieman recorded convalescent troops in the Soviet Union being paid a small bonus for final assembly work.

Various other hand-thrown bombs saw widespread use. Almost identical in design to the basic *Stielhandgranate* was the Nebelhandgranate 39 (smoke grenade 1939). Identified by a white band and the lettering 'Nb. Hgr', this did not burst but emitted clouds of smoke, ideal for screening an attack. Also dating to 1939 was a new form of *Eiergranate* ('egg' grenade), the Eiergranate 39. Made of sheet steel with a fuze activated by means of a turning button attached to a pull cord on top, this was lighter and smaller than the *Stielhandgranate*, making it easy to carry in numbers. In 1943, production was streamlined by the introduction of a hybrid between *Stielhandgranate* and *Eiergranate*. This was a

ABOVE Grenade training at the Infanterie-Schule Berlin, December 1938. These *Stielhandgranaten* are practice types, the holes drilled through the heads showing that they do not contain explosive. (Keystone-France/Gamma-Keystone/Getty Images)

ABOVE RIGHT An officer giving small-arms instruction with a *Stielhandgranate*, and a pistol wrapped in cloth under one arm. The World War II *Stielhandgranate* was simple to use and essentially similar to that used from 1915.

RIGHT A battle position with two *Stielhandgranaten* and an *Eiergranate* as a back-up to the rifle.

small cylinder also with the top-mounted button and cord ignition arrangement, but which could be used with or without a stick. This bomb was made in both explosive and smoke varieties, the latter being identified by the same markings that appeared on the Nebelhandgranate 39. Rather less robust was the glass smoke bomb: this required careful packing and handling, but smashed easily when thrown into buildings or against any hard surface. Some use was made of hand grenades from other countries, notably Czech, Soviet and Dutch types. There were also a couple of unusual emergency *Stielhandgranaten*; in one that apparently first appeared in North Africa the head had a concrete outer casing. In another, produced late in the war, the main material was wood.

Grenade, Egg, Hand, Smoke, 42.

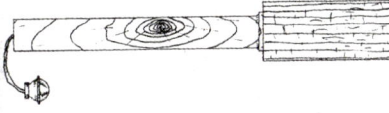

Grenade, Stick, Hand, All Wood.

Grenade, Stick, Concrete, II.

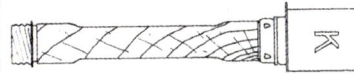

Grenade, Hand, Stick, H.E., Cold-zones.

Grenades projected from firearms had a long history, and Germany remained wedded to the concept during World War II. More than a dozen different models of rifle grenades were projected from a small 3cm-bore discharger cup clamped to the muzzle of the rifle. Many of these were high-explosive bombs intended as a form of light infantry-support weapon, but there were also several models of anti-tank round, a smoke bomb, a parachute illuminating flare and even a grenade to deliver leaflets. The smallest of the anti-tank bombs was

Packkasten für 30 Eihandgranaten 39 mit 30 Brennzündern
für Eihandgranate 39 und 30 Sprengkapseln Nr. 8
geöffnet und mit herausgehobenem Einsatz

Nr. 1 und 4 = Sprengkapseln Nr. 8   Nr. 2 und 3 = B. Z. f. Eihgr.

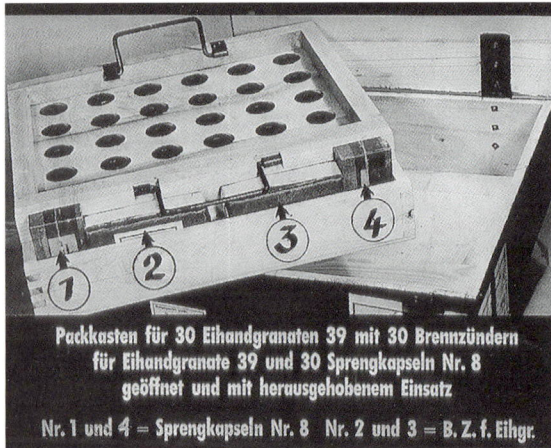

ABOVE A manual illustration of the wooden packing box for the Eiergranate 39, showing holes for bombs and slot for fuzes and detonators.

ABOVE RIGHT A *Panzergrenadier* of the *Großdeutschland* Division firing an anti-tank rifle grenade from a rifle discharger, November 1943. (ullstein bild/Getty Images)

RIGHT The leather carry box and sling for the standard rifle-grenade discharger.

claimed to have an armour penetration of 40mm, but attempts to increase the effectiveness of anti-tank rifle grenades against more heavily armoured vehicles saw the appearance of larger anti-tank rounds with a purported penetration of up to 125mm. Firing such bulbous-headed monsters, which extended well beyond the mouth of the discharger cup, can hardly have been comfortable.

Motive force for firing rifle grenades was provided by special bulletless rounds, and cartridge and grenade were often supplied taped together for convenience. A surprising amount of effort was expended on improving the accuracy of rifle grenades by provision of special sights for firing at up to 250m and by rifling within the discharger cup, or by bands on the grenade. The official instruction pamphlet, *Merkblatt über Handhabung, Mitführung und Verwendung der Gewehrgranaten* ('Leaflet on Handling, Carrying and Using the Rifle Grenade') of October 1942 describes eight different forms of launching cartridge and gives a table by means of which the range of lighter and heavier rifle grenades may be estimated. As well as the discharger, carry case and sights, the pamphlet also mentions a harness for carrying rifle grenades consisting of a pair of oblong bags joined by straps.

Rifle grenades appear to have been limited contributors to the firefight, but they were not the last word in grenade ingenuity, which title may arguably be taken by those projected from pistols. Before the war one of the basic signalling methods of the Heer was the smooth-bored *Leuchtpistole* ('light' or signal pistol) firing coloured flares. Standard equipment to go with the *Leuchtpistole* included a holster, and cartridge pouches holding either 12 or 18 rounds. A more simply manufactured flare gun also entered service in 1942. Made of stamped zinc with Bakelite or wood grips, this was either supplied unpainted or painted black. The adoption of a special tubular 'projector stem' made of plastic or wood allowed issue flare guns to be used as simple grenade throwers. The basic projectile was a small egg-shaped high-explosive grenade, the Würfkorper 361 LP, but there was also a smoke round: the range of both was about 100m. Cartridges were also designed to throw a smaller explosive round further, and for use from armoured vehicles. The *Sprenggranatpatrone LP mit Zeitzünder* round was shot out of a vehicle port and exploded after a short delay, thus discouraging enemy infantry. Allied intelligence described its range as 'a few yards'.

Remarkably, the whole idea was deemed worthy of further development, and so an improved version of the *Leuchtpistole* with rifled barrel was introduced. This *Kampfpistole* (battle pistol) looked much like the ordinary *Leuchtpistole*, but was marked with a 'Z' to denote the rifling and had a special sight. A new selection of at least ten cartridge types, including explosive rounds, smoke, parachute illuminating flares and a 'target indicator' round, were made for this weapon. Dated examples show that the *Kampfpistole* was in existence by 1942. Finally, an improved version of the *Kampfpistole* was developed, referred to in some sources as the *Sturmpistole* (assault pistol). This elaborate piece was rifled and had a folding metal buttstock and a 'bubble' sight not unlike a spirit-level. Perhaps the most extraordinary projectile used with any of the pistols was the Panzerwurfkörper 42 LP, a hollow-charge anti-tank grenade introduced in 1942; this had a range of about 50m.

Another interesting development was *Nipolit*, devised by the Westfälisch-Anhaltische-Sprengstoff AG (WASAG) company of Reinsdorf in mid-1944. *Nipolit* was a plastic explosive, made using fewer resources than conventional munitions, which could be cast and set hard: grenades could thus be made from a solid lump of explosive without the need to make and fill a casing. The main effect of a *Nipolit* bomb was blast, but fragmentation characteristics could be enhanced with a metal sleeve or intrusions of other material cast into the explosive. How many *Nipolit* devices reached the battlefield is unclear, but a *Stielhandgranate* and two different small cylindrical grenades, one having a fragmentation sleeve, appeared in Allied investigations. A flat *Nipolit* disk bomb was also developed, ideal for posting through the vision slits of tanks and bunkers.

EDGED WEAPONS

The Heer used four types of bladed weapon in World War II: *Seitengewehre* (bayonets), *Säbel* (sabres), *Dolche* (officers' daggers) and *Kampfmesser* (fighting knives). Of these, bayonets were easily the most numerous and most frequently carried in action, and naturally there were many different models to match the various rifles in service, foreign as well as German. The commonest bayonet, however, was the basic type for the Kar 98k rifle, the Seitengewehr 84/98 (S 84/98, 'Sidearm 1884/1898'), used by cavalry, field artillery and technical troops as early as 1915. The S 84/98 had a single-edged blade 25cm long, a slot-and-press spring catch for attachment and a steel scabbard. Initially, grips were of plain wood; later, ribbed Bakelite in various shades of brown was used.

During the ramping up of weapons production in the mid-1930s, the identity of *Seitengewehr* manufacturers was concealed by the adoption of the code stamping 'S' followed by a three-digit number; so, for example, a bayonet marked 'S/155' was made by E. & F. Hörster of Solingen in the period 1934–37. After 1937 until approximately 1941, the manufacturer's name appeared in full or in the form of initials on the blade, before the new letter codes as used on the majority of equipment were applied. Many *Seitengewehr* manufacturers were based in Solingen, but there were others, for example, in Chemnitz and Magdeburg. The code 'jwh' denoted *Seitengewehre* made at Châtellerault in occupied France during 1941–44; 'dot' and 'dov' indicated Czech-made vz. 24 *Seitengewehre* modified to fit the Kar 98k at Brno. The S 84/98 was carried in a black leather frog of slightly varying design, reflecting the dozens of manufacturers all over Germany and in Austria, Poland and the Netherlands. A tropical-version bayonet frog was made of webbing.

In addition to issue *Seitengewehre* there was a lively trade in private-purchase bayonets, particularly in the late 1930s and the early part of World War II. These approximated to official patterns but boasted highly polished blades and fittings, plated finishes and decoration. They were not particularly functional, and in some instances not even capable of being attached to a rifle, but were worn to enhance uniform on parade or 'walking out'. Sometimes the blade was etched, and some manufacturers went so far as to offer a range of mottoes and patterns suitable to particular branches of service. The Ernst Pack und Söhne company of Solingen, for example, offered damascened blades with the legend *Zur Erinnerung an meine Dienstzeit* ('In memory of my service time'), accompanied by an image of a tank, infantryman, cavalryman or artillery piece, or a regimental title.

Sabres had been part of the equipment of officers and senior NCOs, as well as all ranks of the cavalry, since well before the unification of Germany in 1871. In the German armed forces of the early 20th century, sabres and sabre knots

TOP The Seitengewehr 84/98 for the Kar 98k rifle with 25cm blade and brown Bakelite grips.

CENTRE Two different types of *Seitengewehr* for the Kar 98k. Above, a pre-war example with wooden grips, held in its leather frog for attachment to the belt; below, a wartime example with Bakelite grips.

BOTTOM Details of the same bayonets showing the manufacturer's marks: Dürkopp, 1938; and '43 fze', for F.W. Höller of Solingen, 1943. Dürkopp Werke of Bielefeld previously produced bicycles, sewing machines and cars; F.W. Höller also made sabres and *Dolche* (daggers).

TOP LEFT A studio portrait of an NCO aspirant with cavalry sabre and decorative knot, c.1936.

TOP CENTRE A *Feldwebel* recipient of the *Eisernes Kreuz* with his sabre and decorative knot. Like officers, certain grades of NCO were entitled to sabres as a distinction of rank.

TOP RIGHT An officer in a *Mantel*, with the suspension strap of his sabre passing through a slit in the coat pocket, so that the hilt may be accessed without fumbling under the coat.

RIGHT A manual drawing depicting the *Troddel, Faustriemen* and *Portepee* decorative knots for bayonets and sabres.

Troddel, Faustriemen und Portepee: wie Bild 7, 8, 9 und 10.

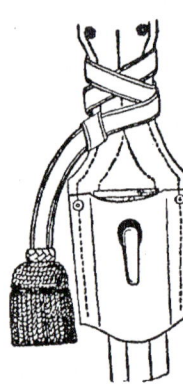
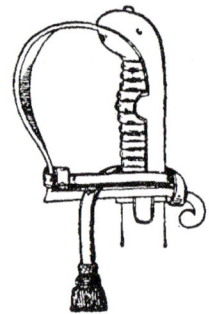

Bild 7.   Bild 8.   Bild 9.   Bild 10.

were so accepted as part of the trappings of rank that grades were defined as with or without 'épee', that is having or not having the right to carry a sword. Orders of 1932 drew a distinction between officers and senior NCOs who carried sabres, and junior officer candidates and junior NCOs who did not, and the 1936 official tables of rank accorded the *Portepee* (decorative sabre knot) to all NCOs down to the level of *Feldwebel*. Sabres themselves were not usually worn except on parade or at specific special occasions.

Though types varied considerably in detail and were both issued and obtainable from manufacturers or private outfitters, Heer sabres were based on the slightly curved light-cavalry pattern with stirrup hilt which appeared in the late 18th century, and which was still worn in battle in the 19th century. Blade width was 20–25mm, but length was graduated according to the height of the

A joint advertisement for military blades by some of the major Solingen cutlers with the marks of the different manufacturers.

OPPOSITE Members of an
infantry squad ride on a tank on
the Don front in the Soviet Union,
July 1942. Some men wear the
camouflaged *Zeltbahn*. (Roger
Viollet/ Getty Images)

wearer. Typical decorative elements included scrolled finials, twisted wire around
the leather grip, lion or panther-head pommels, and occasionally a small
enamelled panel or shield. With the advent of the National Socialist regime,
eagle-and-swastika armed-forces insignia became the norm.

Sabres were manufactured, or finished, in various places but the epicentre of
the trade was Solingen, where blades had been made for centuries and a cluster
of famous firms operated. These included: WKC (Weyersberg, Kirschbaum und
Cie), formed by the amalgamation of the Gebrüder Weyersberg company with
W.R. Kirschbaum & Cie, in 1883; Eickhorn, with its squirrel mark, founded in
1864; E. und F. Hörster; and Ernst Pack und Söhne. The idea of Solingen as a
centre of excellence was fostered both by joint advertising, and by the trade
journal *Die Klinge* ('The Blade'), published from 1933 to 1941. An idea of the
diversity in Heer sabres can be gleaned from WKC's catalogue, which listed 13
different private-purchase officer models, priced from RM 14,65 to 17,50; for a
further RM 0,55, animal-head pommels were enhanced with red eyes. The
same publication offered an NCO sabre in five different grades, priced from
RM 10,50 upwards, having options on bluing, engraving and etching.

Given the general use of sabres and bayonets, the introduction of the Heer
officers' *Dolch* in 1935 appears superfluous, and needs to be understood in the
context of the growing use of dress daggers in other services and political
organizations. The Heer dagger was 40cm in length with eagle-and-swastika
cross guard, and like private-purchase sabres and bayonets could be purchased
at varying prices for different qualities of finish, extra features including etched
decoration or a genuine ivory grip. It was worn with a *Portepee* knot on a double-
strapped braided hanger, below the left hip, on formal occasions. Cessation of
production of both *Dolche* and sabres was ordered in mid-1943, but the wearing
of both continued until September 1944.

German *Nahkampfmesser* (close-combat knives) of World War II owed much
to their predecessors in the trenches of World War I, but in stark contrast to the
new officers' *Dolch* they were strictly practical. Blades were generally short,
single-edged and in the range of 135–175mm in length, though a few larger,
double-edged types have been identified. Short blades made fighting knives
handy compared to a bayonet, and many were worn tucked into the boot top,
or on the waist belt. A few were of a locking design with folding blade. 'Boot
knives' can sometimes be identified by the presence of a spring-tensioned hook
or clip on the scabbard. Grips were often made of wood – plain, or inscribed
with diagonal lines to improve grip – but there were also some all-metal designs.
Metal scabbards and grips were commonly blackened, making the weapon less
prone to corrosion and less reflective or obvious, particularly during night
actions.

CHAPTER 5
SUPPORT AND
SPECIAL WEAPONS

The 5cm leGrW 36 light mortar in use. The prone team wear Tragegestell 39 tubular metal frames for the transport of ammunition boxes as well as their *Kochgeschirre* and *Zeltbahnen*. The man closest to the camera also wears his gas-mask canister attached to the harness.

MACHINE GUNS

As technology advanced and the war progressed, the German soldier was expected to carry an increasing selection of support and special-purpose weaponry. Arguably, none was more important than the machine gun, the ideal weapon to balance numerical odds and defend the vast perimeter of territory conquered in the first two years of war. This was particularly important because bolt-action rifles were not well suited to creating volume fire, so the machine gun also performed a crucial tactical role within the infantry squad.

Easily the most significant German machine gun was the 7.92mm MG 34. Developed in the early 1930s, this weapon was remarkable in that it was intended to be an *Einheitsmaschinengewehr* ('universal' or 'general purpose' machine gun), without the need for water cooling but having a quick-change barrel. Design was by Rheinmetall-Borsig of Sömmerda under chief designer Louis Stange on instructions from the Heereswaffenamt, and the weapon drew on various pre-existing weapons and ideas including the 7.92mm Solothurn MG 30 as well as Mauser and Maxim machine guns. The result was an effective, well-finished and accurate design, but because it had many components it was elaborate in production terms. Tested in the Spanish Civil War, the MG 34 underwent fine-tuning in time for the German invasion of Poland. Key to its flexibility were the bipod and tripod *Lafetten* (mounts) and different methods of feeding ammunition. As a heavy machine gun the mount was the Laffette 34, a tripod with an optical sight and a traverse mechanism, with feed from 250-round ammunition belts. When the MG 34 was employed as a light squad weapon, the integral bipod was lowered and ammunition drums could be used to avoid the inconvenience of trailing belts. The MG 34 was also used as an anti-aircraft and vehicle-mounted machine gun.

Though more than 500,000 MG 34s were eventually produced in several factories, there were never enough to satisfy demand and as a result old weapons continued to be used, particularly by second-line units. Two of these weapons were veterans of the Imperial German Army of World War I: the 7.92mm MG 08 heavy machine gun and MG 08/15 light machine gun. Both were water cooled, belt fed and based on a pre-1914 mechanism designed by Hiram Stevens Maxim. Though many of these weapons were reused unmodified, the MG 08 was revisited in the interwar period with various improvements including a feeder capable of taking both the original fabric ammunition belt and new metal belts, and a squeeze-actuated trigger. New mountings were introduced, including a tall anti-aircraft tripod and a low tripod for the crew to shoot at ground targets while prone, kneeling or seated. Short tubular metal poles were also used in conjunction with the original *Schlitten* (sledge mounts) to allow anti-aircraft fire. The MG 08/15 – essentially a much-slimmed-down version of the original

LEFT The MG 34 in its light-squad role – mounted on the folding light bipod, with gunner and a loader feeding from a 250-round ammunition box to the left of the breech.

BELOW LEFT A *Gebirgsjäger* demonstrates the MG 34 with anti-aircraft tripod, 1939. The gunner's rucksack contains a pair of wooden snowshoes.

BELOW A *Richtschütze* or machine gun 'No. 1' carries an MG 34 during the advance in France, June 1940. On his waist belt are a holstered semi-automatic pistol for close defence and the gunner's belt pouch containing a spare bolt, oil bottle and small tools. An assistant gunner usually carried the spare barrel and an ammunition box in addition to his own personal weapon.

Wiege
Schellenverschluß
Ausgleichsgelenke
Druckplatte
Zapfen für Lafettenaufsatzstück
Lieffermrohrhalter
Winkelhebel
Lagerzapfen
Befestigungsbolzen
Flügelmutter
Kralle
Höhenbegrenzer
Oberpolster
Handrad
Seitenbegrenzer
Gleitbahn
Unterpolster
Riegel
Vorderstütze
Kittelstrebe
Flügelmutter
Hinterstütze
Rasthebel
Trägeriemen
Lafettenaufsatzstück
Spannblech

Bild 5.

Bild a   Bild b

Bild c   Bild e

Bild d

Bild d

Ansicht von unten.   Ansicht von oben

George Petersen

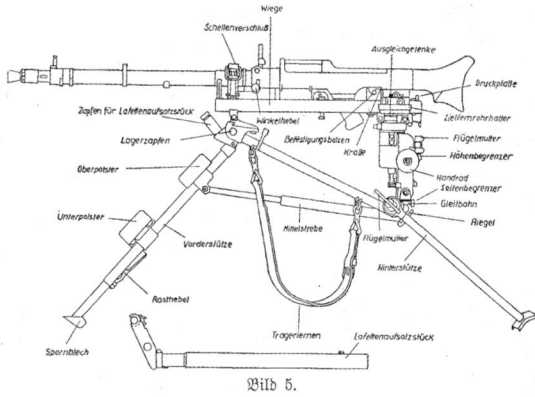

ABOVE This diagram from Hauptmann A. Weber's *Unterrichtsbuch für Soldaten, 1941* ('Instruction Book for Soldiers, 1941'), shows the MG 34 on the tripod *Lafette* mounting for use as a heavy-support weapon complete with traverse and elevating mechanism. The height of the *Lafette* could be adjusted down to match kneeling and prone gunners or left high. The strap and pads were intended to make the awkward load easier to carry.

RIGHT An illustration from a manual showing weight-distributing shoes for use with machine guns and other equipment in snow conditions. Some are oblong boards, while others are circular-frame constructions similar to those worn by troops.

BELOW An MG 34 covering a waterway on the Eastern Front. The weapon has a folded *Lafette*, but is mounted on a board; a common device to spread weight in snow or mud, or to enable several men to carry the equipment stretcherwise.

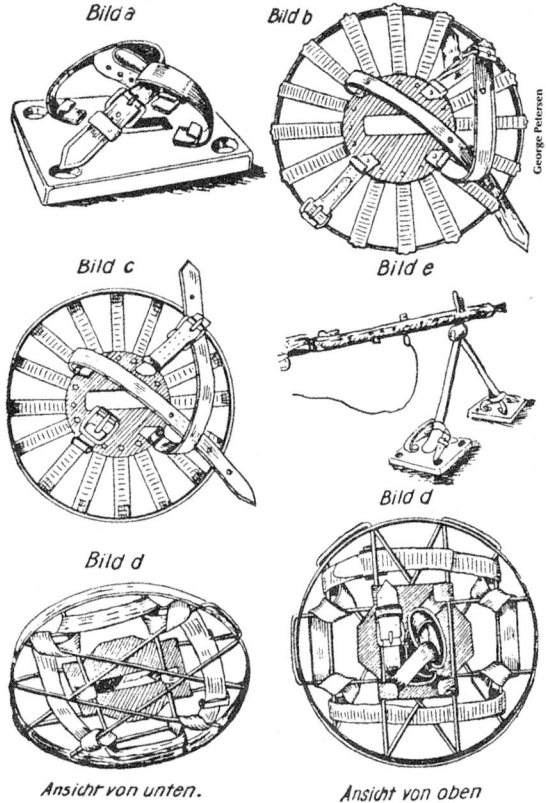

TOP LEFT A squad takes cover during the battle for Stalingrad. The machine-gun team are on the left, while the squad leader carries an MP 40.

ABOVE A squad column advances in loose battlefield formation with, typically, the machine-gun team towards the front.

LEFT A supporting machine-gun team advancing at Stalingrad. The tripod *Lafette* alone weighed about 20kg; the soldier in the foreground carries a *Klappspaten*, with *Kochgeschirr* and *Zeltbahn* on his belt equipment.

MG 08 with the addition of a wooden shoulder stock and a conventional trigger – was the commonest German machine gun of World War I, being designed in 1915 and widely used from 1917 with approximately 130,000 produced, mainly for use with the infantry. A substantial number survived World War I, and this fairly hefty 'light' machine gun was also subject to modifications during the interwar period including the provision of a large ring-shaped sight for anti-aircraft use, and the moving of the bipod from the rear end of the water jacket up to a new bracket near the muzzle where it provided a steadier support for a prone-position machine-gunner.

An MG 34 in its heavy-support role pictured on the Eastern Front in December 1942. Improvised snow camouflage and ammunition boxes are apparent. (Roger Viollet/Getty Images)

An MG 34 in its heavy-support role pictured on the Eastern Front in December 1942. Improvised snow camouflage and ammunition boxes are apparent. (Roger Viollet/Getty Images)

The German World War I Maxim machine guns were later joined by several similar types captured from the enemy, particularly during the 1939–42 period. The most numerically important of these were the Soviet M1905 and M1910 medium machine guns, large numbers of which were taken during the Operation *Barbarossa* campaign on the Eastern Front in 1941. Both of these machine guns, which had a familial resemblance to the MG 08, were often mounted on the distinctive 'Sokolov carriage'. This was a wheeled mount, usually combined with a crew shield, dragged along by the machine-gun team or propped up on legs for use by a seated or kneeling crew. Some Soviet Maxims were even taken complete with multiple anti-aircraft mountings that improved coverage of the sky and saturation of aerial targets by the simple expedient of mounting two or even four Maxims side by side on the same swivel mount.

Though often overlooked, another weapon that supplemented the MG 34 was the MG 13 machine gun. Development of this weapon commenced during World War I and its starting point was as an air-cooled, magazine-fed, lightweight version of a Dreyse design. Work continued in secret after 1918 by Rheinmetall-Borsig, and testing was carried out in the Soviet Union during the late 1920s. The MG 13 entered regular service at the beginning of the 1930s and for a while was the standard-issue German machine gun. Its greatest strength was in many ways also its greatest weakness, for its usual ammunition feed was via 25-round box magazines, inserted on the left side of the mechanism. This was a strength because the MG 13 remained flexible and relatively light on the battlefield, unencumbered by long ammunition belts or large boxes, but it constituted a weakness because 25 rounds was nowhere near enough for sustained fire.

TOP LEFT An old MG 08 heavy machine gun in the hands of a reserve formation almost 40 years after its introduction. The *Schlitten* is of the same design as that taken to war in 1914.

TOP RIGHT Anti-aircraft practice conducted by Infanterie-Regiment 67 at Fort Hahneberg barracks, Berlin, 1937. The machine gun is a Maxim type, modified for use with a drum magazine. (FPG/Hulton Archive/Getty Images)

ABOVE Devised in 1915, the water-cooled, belt-fed MG 08/15 light machine gun continued to see limited use in World War II.

LEFT In this photograph from late 1942, an MG 08/15 on an anti-aircraft tripod has been fitted with the large ring-shaped sight introduced in the interwar period for anti-aircraft use.

ABOVE The distinctive neck-harness magazine carrier for the MG 13. Each ammunition pouch carried four 25-round magazines, two accessible from either end of the canvas container. The magazines shown here are dated 1938.

CENTRE A Heer field postman with an MG 13 machine gun in France, 1940. Developed from Dreyse-type weapons of World War I, the air-cooled MG 13 fired from 25-round box magazines feeding into the left side of the receiver. It had a metal bar the machine-gunner could grip with his left hand. While generally satisfactory, the MG 13 was not suitable for sustained fire. Remarkably, some remained in service throughout World War II, and the bipod and a few other features were retained in the new MG 34.

RIGHT An infantry squad supported by an MG 13, *c.*1937. The machine-gun crew members wear the ammunition-carrying neck harness, the man on the left having two sets, totalling 16 magazines (400 rounds).

Troops in tropical uniform with a Czech ZB vz. 30 light machine gun fitted with anti-aircraft sight. The ZB vz. 26 and ZB vz. 30 were reliable and influential weapons, used in significant numbers by second-line German formations in particular.

With the Czech armaments industry having been taken over before the outbreak of World War II, Czech machine guns also entered service with the Heer. Most of these were manufactured at the Zbrojovka Brno, or Brno armaments factory. Unsurprisingly, given that British designers also built upon Czech models, the 7.92mm ZB vz. 26 (designated the MG 26(t) in German service) and 7.92mm ZB vz. 30 light machine guns show similarities to the .303 Bren gun. All three have top-mounted detachable box magazines, quick-release barrels and cyclic rates of fire of approximately 500 rounds per minute. A heavier Czech weapon, the belt-fed, air-cooled 7.92mm ZB-53 medium machine gun, was also used by German forces, as well as being manufactured under licence in the UK as the Besa. In the Czech and German armies there were three slightly different models of ZB-53, intended for infantry, fortifications and tank use, respectively. Machine guns from a number of other countries were also adopted in varying quantities by the Heer. Notable were large numbers of the French 7.5mm Châtellerault M1931 with its bulky 150-round drum magazine, used mainly in fixed defences; a few 6.5mm Lewis guns, obtained mainly from the Dutch; and the 6.5mm Breda MG 099(i) light machine gun from Italy.

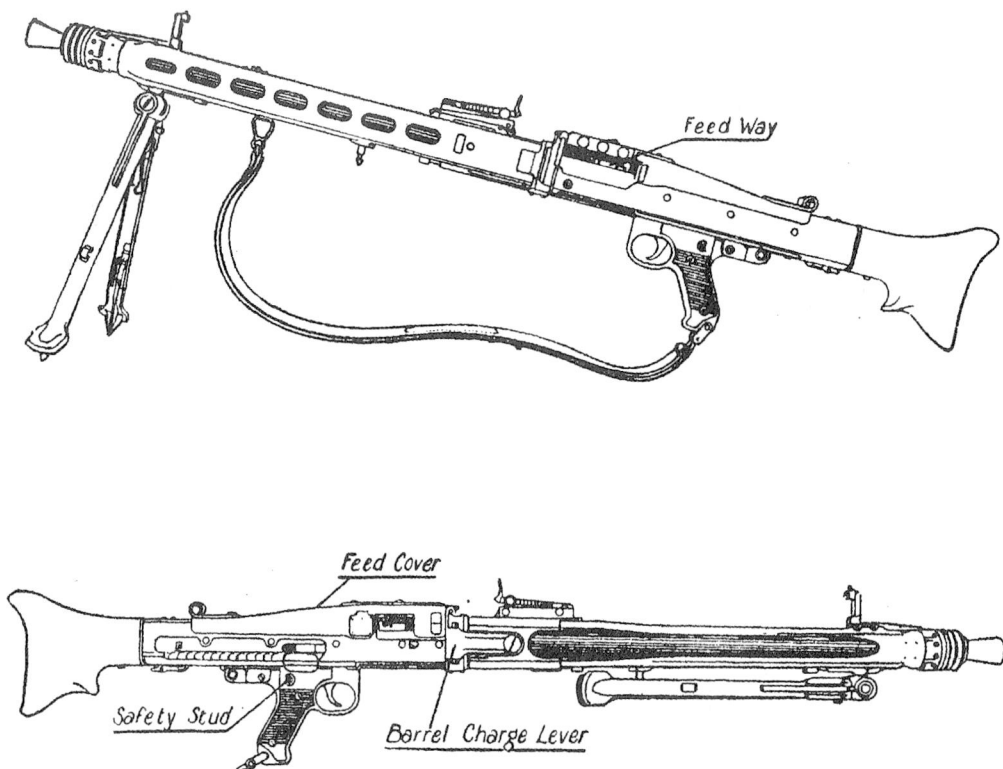

Manual drawings of the highly effective, if ammunition-hungry, MG 42 general-purpose machine gun. It is shown here in its squad configuration with bipod and carry sling attached.

While the MG 34 proved effective and, by the standards of its time, a very good machine gun, the problems of manufacture, material and labour costs, which impacted upon virtually everything supplied to the Heer, were also very much at work here. Criticism of the MG 34 from the production point of view commenced even before the outbreak of World War II and full issue of the weapon, and a parallel study programme addressing the use of pressed parts to substitute for much of the machining and forging ran from 1935 to 1937. While this programme had a limited impact on the MG 34 itself, it paved the way for requests to manufacturers for proposals for an entirely new machine gun, and three experimental models were produced in 1938. That offered by the Grossfuss Metall und Lackierwarenfabrik company of Döbeln, featuring a breech-locking device with rollers, was selected as the most promising of the three experimental models, and it was from here that development of what would later become the 7.92mm MG 42 general-purpose machine gun really commenced. Various experimental pieces were now created, with the new weapon provisionally christened the 'MG 39', but further modifications led to the new machine gun being used in large-scale troop trials in 1941 under the title 'MG 39/41'. Favourable reports swung the decision for formal adoption early in 1942 and accordingly the final designation 'MG 42' was applied.

LEFT Firing the MG 42 in its heavy-support role from a tripod, the ammunition belt blurring as it moves more quickly than the shutter of the camera. The machine-gunner aims through an optical sight and uses a remote trigger on the mounting.

ABOVE A well-known photograph of the MG 42 in use by *Gebirgsjäger*. The machine-gun team wear the *Bergmütze* and the *Windjacke* with the cuffs buttoned against the weather.

LEFT A 1943-manufactured example of the 50-round belt drum used with both the MG 34 and the MG 42. This was handy on the move, but was quickly exhausted and could unbalance the weapon. These ammunition drums were often transported in pairs in a small metal-framed hand carrier.

BELOW The standard 250-round metal-belt ammunition box used with both the MG 34 and the MG 42; the offset handle allowed two to be carried in one hand. The empty 250-round metal belt shown here was manufactured by Schmidt Brothers of Idar-Oberstein.

Descriptions of the MG 42 usually focus on its very high rate of fire, a surprising 20 rounds per second, the reports of which sounded more like a whirring machine or a very loud tearing of fabric than a succession of individual shots. This certainly made the MG 42 more effective in defence or against low-flying aircraft, but there was much more to this very successful weapon. The MG 42 was air cooled and, mounted on a tripod fitted with an optical sight, had a maximum effective range of almost 3,000m. In the squad role on its much handier bipod with basic iron sight, range was reduced to about 800m. The MG 42's roller locking, combined recoil booster and flash-hider, feed action and cold-weather reliability were all noteworthy features. While mountings were not identical, the MG 42 was intended to be compatible with as many accessories from the MG 34 system as possible, and it could use many of the same ammunition belts and drums as previously. Given this all-round usefulness the MG 42 was produced in as a great a volume as possible, with about 400,000 being made before the end of the war by several manufacturers including Mauser, Gustloff and Steyr as well as Grossfuss.

MORTARS

The smaller German mortars were capable of being moved into battle by their teams, and formed part of the standard equipment of the infantry. These were initially inspired by the many different types of *Minenwerfer* (trench mortar) used during World War I. The 5cm leichter Granatwerfer 36 (leGrW 36) mortar

RIGHT A Granatwerfer 36 mortar team in snowy conditions, *c*.1939. The crewman in the foreground has a partially used metal box of 51mm mortar bombs and a short entrenching tool to hand and carries binoculars to observe the fall of shot. The 51mm was a platoon standard until the middle of the war.

OPPOSITE An 81mm mortar team in a well-prepared field position, accessed by a trench to the rear. The 8cm Granatwerfer 34 remained a standard of German forces throughout the war. Packing a much bigger punch than the 51mm platoon mortar it had a good range and rapid rate of fire.

Manual diagram of the
Granatwerfer 34 mortar. This
flexible weapon could shoot a
range of different projectiles
including high explosive, smoke,
and at least two different types of
training round.

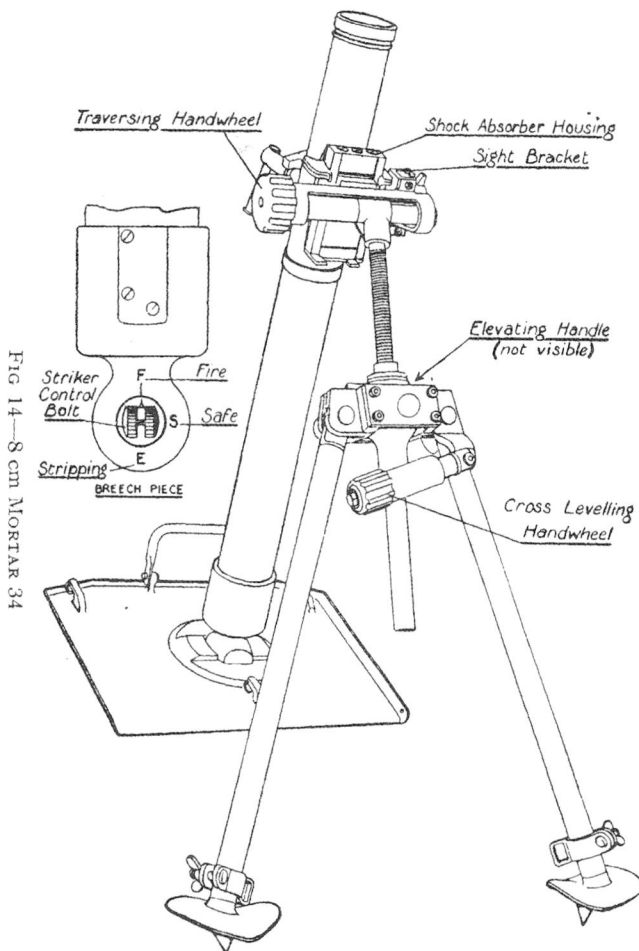

Traversing Handwheel

Shock Absorber Housing

Sight Bracket

*Elevating Handle
(not visible)*

*Striker
Control
Bolt* F Fire

S Safe

E

Stripping

BREECH PIECE

*Cross Levelling
Handwheel*

FIG 14—8 CM MORTAR 34

30

The 8cm GrW 34 mortar, shown
here in action at Smolensk in July
1941, was a much more effective
support weapon than the 5cm
leGrW 36. The team includes an
NCO commander observing with
binoculars, men to aim and fire the
mortar, and enough
supernumeraries to move
equipment and ammunition on the
battlefield. (ullstein bild/Getty
Images)

was standard issue (one per infantry platoon) in 1939 and saw significant use in the French campaign of May–June 1940, though its overall impact must have been limited because by the middle of the war it was being phased out of front-line infantry service. Nevertheless a version of the leGrW 36 was retained for use as a fixed-defence piece, and some use was also made of similar captured French and Soviet types. According to the manual, the leGrW 36 had a three-man team, one of whom carried the weapon while his colleagues had sheet-metal containers of bombs.

Rather more important was the 8cm Granatwerfer 34 (GrW 34), two of which were allotted per rifle company. This mortar broke down into three parts for man portage on the battlefield, each element weighing about 19kg. It was not the weapon itself which was the most limiting factor, however; mortars quickly expended ammunition and even a basic allocation of 21 bombs added more than 73kg to the load. Nevertheless, the GrW 34 was an effective contributor to battle, having a range of more than 2,000m against barely 500m for the leGrW 36, and the larger bomb was much more destructive. Several different sorts of projectile were used, including types which were designed to hit the ground, thereby detonating a small charge which bounced the bomb back into the air before the main charge exploded, thus maximizing the chance of hitting enemy personnel with fragments. As with most mortar and artillery projectiles, this feature was most effective on firm ground.

ANTI-TANK WEAPONS

As of 1939, German handheld anti-tank weapons were of limited capacity, as, to be fair, were the defensive strengths of many tanks of the time. Though there were grenades, engineer charges and mines, the key infantry anti-tank arm was the *Panzerbüchse* (anti-tank rifle). In 1918 Mauser had produced the world's first anti-tank rifle, effectively a giant bolt-action rifle with an equally impressive cartridge, and anti-tank rifles were still the most important portable anti-armour weapon some 20 years later. On the outbreak of World War II the key models were the Panzerbüchse 38 (PzB 38) and Panzerbüchse 39 (PzB 39). The PzB 38 had, for the time, a good performance firing a 7.92mm bullet from a 13mm cartridge and achieving up to 25mm armour penetration at 300m. The vertically sliding breech was operated by means of swinging the pistol grip forward, and some of the massive recoil was absorbed as the barrel moved back within the stock on firing. A simpler weapon more suited to mass production, the PzB 39 entered service before the invasion of France. The absence of a recoiling barrel in this weapon was partially compensated for by the addition of a muzzle brake. The most obviously different feature of the PzB 39 was the addition of two side

panniers, each holding ten rounds of ammunition, with one on either side of the breech. These were not strictly 'magazines' since they did not feed the mechanism directly, but kept ammunition conveniently to hand for the operator.

While progressive improvement of tank armour rendered anti-tank rifles less useful, such weapons continued to be able to engage enemy troops through cover, up to and including brick walls, and to knock out light vehicles. Two additional arms of the general type used during the war were the Panzerbüchse S18-1000 and the Granatbüchse 39 (GrB 39, 'grenade gun 1939). The Panzerbüchse S18-1000 was actually a Swiss design and something of a monster, being semi-automatic, weighing approximately 55kg, and firing a 2cm explosive round. Its 35mm armour penetration was good for this class of weapon and its cumbersomeness was sometimes lessened by the use of a little two-wheeled mount, but the weapon was never used in large numbers. The final German weapon was a sideways acknowledgment that the anti-tank rifle had had its day, for the Granatbüchse 39 (GrB 39) was a conversion of the PzB 39 to discharge grenades. The barrel of this weapon was shortened to 60cm, and fitted with a small discharger cup, but though a range of up to 500m was claimed there were few other advantages over an ordinary rifle fitted with a grenade discharger. In addition to the German and Swiss models, some use was also made of captured anti-tank rifles, notably the Polish 7.9mm Karabin przeciwpancerny wzór 35 (wz. 35), and, from 1941, Soviet types. The wz. 35 was interesting in that it was similar to the original German *T-Gewehr* of 1918, but much lighter, and used the small bullet and large cartridge method to achieve high velocity. Captured Soviet anti-tank rifles included the new 14.5mm PTRD-41: this had a crude tubular appearance, but boasted a recoiling barrel which unlocked the breech as it slid back after firing and ejected the empty cartridge case. The PTRD-41's penetration was about 25mm at 500m.

ABOVE *Panzerfaust* instruction, September 1943. The NCO instructor shows how the sight is raised before use. (Bundesarchiv, Bild 101I-700-0258-21A, Foto: Muck, Richard)

LEFT A well-camouflaged soldier armed with both rifle and *Panzerfaust* practises battlefield concealment, June 1944. (Bundesarchiv, Bild 101I-586-2219-31, Foto: Thönessen (nn))

PANZERFAUST (Klein)-30m

PANZERFAUST -30m

PANZERFAUST -60m

PANZERFAUST -100m

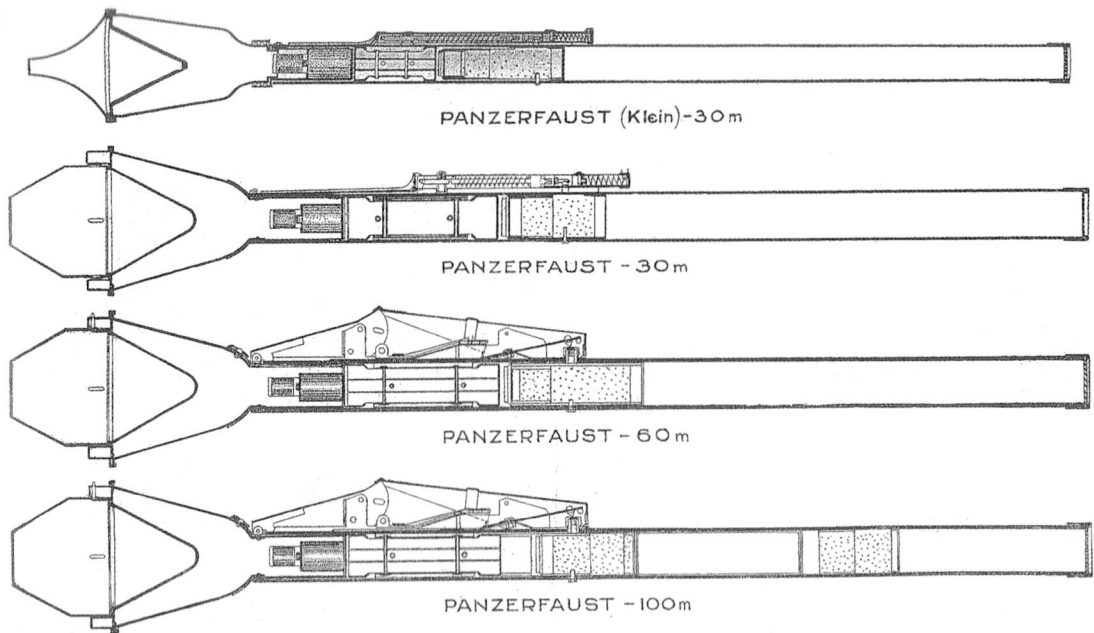

This British Intelligence diagram shows the different *Panzerfaust* models arranged, top to bottom, in order of increasing range and power.

The real step change in portable German anti-tank weapons came in 1942 with the design of an effective hollow-charge, handheld, recoilless, single-shot projector with much better anti-armour capability. The genesis of the *Panzerfaust* (literally translated as 'tank fist') was studied by British Military Intelligence in September 1945, when Major Martin and Captain Hitchins of MI 10 interviewed the inventor, Dr Heinrich Langweiler of HASAG, and others. Martin and Hitchins determined that the new weapon had been produced directly in response to new Soviet tanks, and specifically the T-34 medium tank. The first trial version of what became the *Panzerfaust*, initially known as the *Faustpatrone*, had only a short tube and no sights, but in December 1942 the *Panzerfaust (klein)* was developed. This had a longer tube, sights and a small bulbous projectile 10.5cm in diameter, and was capable of penetrating about 140mm of armour. Key features were: the tube, open at both ends to allow gas to escape and eliminate recoil; a simple trigger mechanism; a black-powder charge to propel the projectile; and, crucially, a bomb with a liner which melted on impact and detonation, producing a jet of molten metal to cut through armour. Hard on the heels of the *Panzerfaust (klein)* followed the Panzerfaust 30 (gross) and Panzerfaust 60, both of which were in service before the end of 1943, with increases in range, velocity and penetration. The Panzerfaust 100 and Panzerfaust 150 would follow before the end of the war and while all the types mentioned above were single-shot and regarded as disposable after discharge, a reloadable Panzerfaust 150 was under development in 1945. This was described as a 'ten-shot' weapon, and a carrier for three or four spare rounds was designed as part of the equipment.

Die *Panzerfaust!*

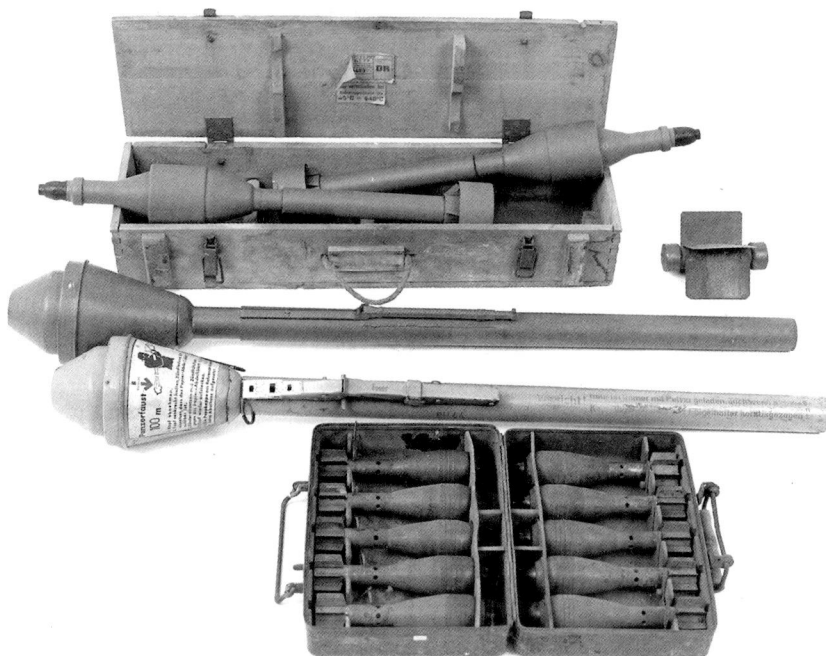

ABOVE LEFT An officer demonstrates the warhead of the *Panzerfaust*. Though wartime production models were single-shot, there were plans to introduce a durable tube for issue with ten separate warheads so the *Panzerfaust* could be reused.

ABOVE *Panzerfaust!* 'The anti-tank gun of the grenadier', a morale-raising cover to the 29 June 1944 edition of the *Berliner Illustrierte Zeitung* (*Berlin Illustrated Times*).

LEFT Typical munitions. Top, two *Panzerschreck* rockets; centre, two *Panzerfäuste*; and bottom, a metal carry case of ten 5cm bombs for the platoon mortar.

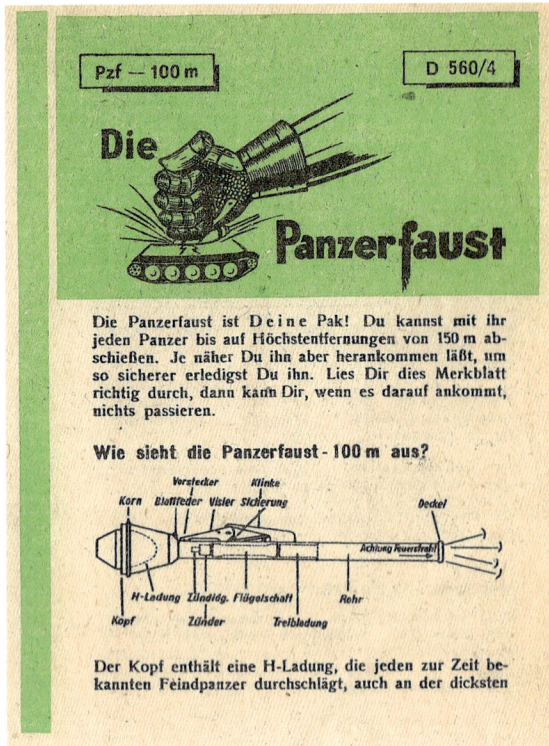

Instruction leaflet for the Panzerfaust 100, with a very literal illustration of the 'tank fist'. While the '100' designation stood for an effective range of 100m, the leaflet suggests that engagement at up to 150m was possible.

In April 1944, a Heer request for a *Panzerfaust* with improved anti-personnel characteristics was put forward, leading to the development of the *Sprengfaust* ('bounding fist'), trialled at Döberitz that June. This unusual weapon married the projector tube of the Panzerfaust 60 with a fragmentation warhead. The new projectile lacked the hollow charge; instead a small charge exploded when the projectile impacted, causing the bomb to bounce, then explode about 1m above the ground. The *Sprengfaust* was declared impractical, however, and instead the Heer demanded a simple fragmentation sleeve to be fitted over the ordinary hollow-charge projectile as required.

Though they differed in detail, firing procedures for the various *Panzerfaust* weapons remained similar. When ready to engage, the soldier removed the safety pin locking the trigger mechanism and raised the sight. He then adopted a firing position with the weapon over or under the shoulder, preferably in cover but definitely with the rear of the tube well clear of obstructions. With aim on target, the trigger was squeezed. The spring-loaded mechanism then snapped down, causing a striker to hit a percussion cap, igniting the projecting charge and throwing the bomb from the tube. The fin-stabilized projectile moved slowly compared to bullets from conventional firearms, but exploded on impact; in so doing its hollow inner shape focused the force on a metal liner, melting it and concentrating the massive power of the weapon on a very small patch of the target. A good strike on armour with any of the later models of *Panzerfaust* was claimed to be able to penetrate 200mm.

German propaganda billed the *Panzerfaust* as the 'anti-tank gun of the grenadier' and in the closing stages of the war, tanks were successfully engaged by raw recruits, men of the Volkssturm and even boys with their *Panzerfäuste* carried into battle on bicycles. Direct close-range hits were dramatic indeed, and frequently resulted in the total destruction of Sherman or T-34 tanks alike, and total production of all *Panzerfaust* models was about 8 million pieces. Compared to other hand-held weapons and grenades the impact of the *Panzerfaust* during battle was huge – even so, it was not the 'wonder weapon' it was sometimes claimed to be. Major disadvantages were its relatively short range and the dangerous back blast, the latter acknowledged to be fatal to anybody standing

LEFT The first version of the *Raketenpanzerbüchse* or *'Panzerschreck'* was a disconcerting anti-tank weapon to fire, the operator being advised to wear a gas-mask face piece to protect against hot particles and smoke from the weapon nicknamed the 'stove pipe'. Here, a soldier in winter dress practises with the weapon in March 1944. (Bundesarchiv, Bild 101I-279-0943-22A, Foto: Bergmann, Johannes)

CENTRE Later *Raketenpanzerbüchsen* were fitted with a shield to protect the two-man team from their own weapon, as is evident in this manual drawing, which also details the sighting arrangements.

BELOW The second version of the *Raketenpanzerbüchse*, showing how the operator aimed through a window in the shield. While the firer hid as much of his body as possible from the enemy, the tube of the *Panzerschreck* had to be kept clear of all obstruction so as to avoid any trapping of the vicious back blast.

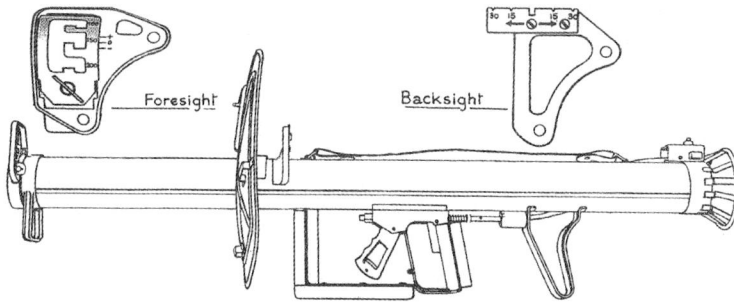

Depicting one of the more desperate methods of tank engagement, this illustration from the 1942 manual *Panzerabwehr aller Waffen* ('Anti-Tank Defence All Arms') shows how a smoke grenade, piece of cord and some wood could be thrown over the barrel of a Soviet tank, temporarily blinding the crew and so allowing other friendly weapons to engage.

Abbildung 2.

Pioniere (combat engineers) needed to carry a range of equipment on the battlefield, including not only weapons and explosives but also other demolition equipment, digging implements and wire cutters. For this reason, a special *Pioniersturmgepäck* (combat engineer assault pack) was designed in 1941. Made of olive-drab canvas, the pack attached to the ordinary support straps and included side pouches as well as a main container for two 3kg explosive charges. The *Pionier* depicted here, in the summer of 1943, shows how grenades could be stowed in the side pouch. (Bundesarchiv, Bild 101I-294-1511-11 and 101I-294-1511-12, Foto: Kurth, Bernhard)

within about 3m of the rear of the tube, and hazardous to about 10m. The *Panzerfaust* could not therefore be used in very confined spaces, or with troops immediately to the rear. Combined with the weapon's limited range, this made the job of the *Panzerfaust* operator very difficult, and requiring of the highest degree of courage. Nor was the *Panzerfaust* the most effective anti-tank weapon on the battlefield: early in 1944, the percentage of enemy tanks knocked out with the *Panzerfaust* was approximately 3 per cent of the total; and more than 2,000 *Panzerfäuste* were issued for each destroyed enemy tank, roughly double the number of anti-tank gun rounds needed to achieve the same result.

TOP The 'J-Feder' time-delay unit allowed *Pioniere* to set up demolitions and booby traps using a clockwork mechanism, activating explosives long after friendly troops had left the scene; a time-lapse of anything up to three weeks was possible.

ABOVE Combat engineers in tropical uniform board a PzKpfw III medium tank in North Africa, 1941. The soldier at top left carries a flamethrower. (ullstein bild/Getty Images)

LEFT A *Pionier* NCO uses a Glühzündapparat 37 exploder to initiate a demolition charge, 1943. The field demolition kit also included a neon test tube, galvanometer, 40 detonators, two spools and four drums of cables, crimpers and other small tools, and insulating tape.

ABOVE A *Propagandakompanie* image of the Flammenwerfer 35 at work. This type had both its fuel and compressed nitrogen in a single tank and weighed 35kg. The Flammenwerfer 41 used two separate tanks, but was slightly lighter. The Flammenwerfer 42 also used two tanks.

RIGHT A manual illustration of a magnetic hollow charge. Made in various sizes, these bombs could be thrown, but were preferably placed on their target, usually an armoured vehicle. The magnets on the base adhered the device firmly to any ferrous metal and the cone-shaped charge focused the force of the explosion onto a small spot for maximum penetration. A delay fuze gave the user time to get clear before the powerful explosion.

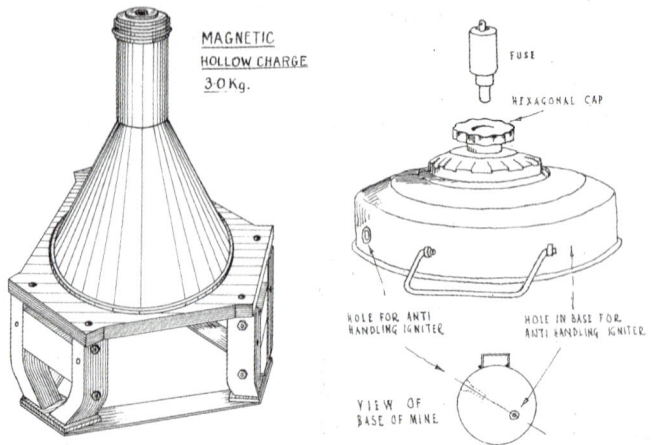

FAR RIGHT The Tellermine 42 had a pressed-steel body with a pressure-plate assembly on top and small ports underneath and on the side for igniters so that the mine would explode either when a heavy weight passed over the top, or when the device was pulled. The payload of this mine was 5.5kg of TNT, when 1kg of this explosive was more than enough to destroy a light vehicle.

BOTTOM A manual diagram of the S-Mine 35. This device consisted of one steel cylinder within another. When the igniter (not shown) was activated by pressure or a pull, a small propellant charge shot the inner container into the air. The main charge exploded when the bomb was 1m or so above the ground, shooting out a shower of steel balls. Not for nothing did American servicemen call this the 'Bouncing Betty'.

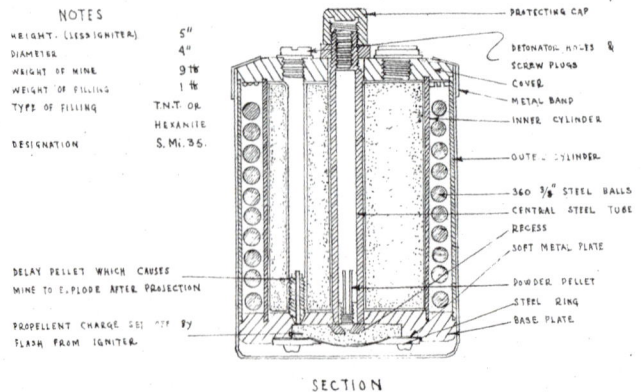

MAGNETIC
HOLLOW CHARGE
3·0 Kg.

FUSE

HEXAGONAL CAP

HOLE FOR ANTI
HANDLING IGNITER

HOLE IN BASE FOR
ANTI HANDLING IGNITER

VIEW OF
BASE OF MINE

NOTES

WEIGHT. (LESS IGNITER)	5"	
DIAMETER	4"	
WEIGHT OF MINE	9 ℔	
WEIGHT OF FILLING	1 ℔	
TYPE OF FILLING	T.N.T. OR HEXANITE	
DESIGNATION	S. Mi. 35.	

PROTECTING CAP

DETONATOR HOLES &
SCREW PLUGS

COVER

METAL BAND

INNER CYLINDER

OUTER CYLINDER

360 ⅜" STEEL BALLS

CENTRAL STEEL TUBE

RECESS

SOFT METAL PLATE

POWDER PELLET

STEEL RING

BASE PLATE

DELAY PELLET WHICH CAUSES
MINE TO EXPLODE AFTER PROJECTION

PROPELLENT CHARGE SET OFF BY
FLASH FROM IGNITER

SECTION

Operating a small rangefinder, *c*.1940. Both stereoscopic- and coincidence-type instruments were used by the Heer, different models forming part of the equipment of machine-gun, mortar and artillery units.

According to Martin and Hitchins, the idea for the *Panzerschreck* (tank terror) anti-tank rocket projector was in place as early as March 1943 when a US bazooka rocket launcher captured in North Africa was returned to Germany, examined and fired. As a result, it was decided to design a similar but larger weapon. The new anti-tank weapon, properly known as the *Raketenpanzerbüchse* (anti-tank rocket weapon), was developed quickly and was in action on the Eastern Front before the end of 1943. The new weapon was nicknamed the *Ofenrohr* (stove pipe) by its users, a tag by no means inappropriate for a large metal tube 163cm long firing a 3.3kg hollow-charge rocket accompanied by a gout of flame and smoke. 'Tank terror' was not inaccurate either, as the *Raketenpanzerbüchse* could penetrate 100mm of armour at 150m – a performance considerably better than that of the bazooka. Like its inspiration, the German rocket launcher boasted electric ignition and was commonly used by a two-man team, with a loader inserting the fin-stabilized rocket from the rear. As with the *Panzerfaust*, there was a vicious back blast, so the loader was well advised to

move smartly to one side having performed his task.

Perhaps because of its rapid introduction, the first version of the *Panzerschreck* was less than perfect. The commonest complaint was that with the rocket motor still burning as it left the tube, hot particles were apt to shower the operator. As an improvised solution, gas masks, gloves and *Zeltbahnen* were worn as personal protection, but with the development of a second version a shield was added to the tube to protect the face of the firer. This increased the weight of the unloaded weapon to 11kg, and did not actually reduce the issue of the smoke and flame which also betrayed the position of the *Panzerschreck* team, who were trained to change position frequently. Finally, a smaller version of the rocket launcher was developed with a shorter barrel, an improved rocket and an effective range of about 180m. While the *Panzerfaust* was essentially a weapon of the individual infantryman, the *Panzerschreck* was regarded as a substitute for small *Panzerabwehrkanonen* (PaK, anti-tank guns) and accordingly issued to anti-tank units, usually complete with a small cart or limber on which six weapons and 30 rounds were carried into action, pulled by either a horse or the *Panzerschreck* crew.

ABOVE A soldier moves to lay *Tellerminen*, Soviet Union, summer 1941. Intended mainly to destroy tanks and vehicles, the *Tellermine* was so-called because of its plate-like shape. It entered service in 1929, with new models being introduced in 1935, 1942 and 1943. (Arthur Grimm/ullstein bild via Getty Images)

OPPOSITE The Schützenmine 42 was an anti-personnel device with a spring-loaded igniter. The wooden box with hinged lid was simple to produce in large numbers, and the payload was just 200g. The mine activated when the hinged lid was depressed, releasing the spring in the igniter. The Allied term 'Shoe mine' was, however, a complete misnomer since this was a misreading of the German abbreviation *Schü*, which actually means 'defensive'.

CHAPTER 6
SPECIAL CLOTHING AND EQUIPMENT

The issue lightweight *Drilljacke* in green was frequently used as summer combat uniform. This example has infantry other ranks' *Schulterklappen* and is worn with a belt with a subdued finish applied to the buckle, and a short leather loop and ring for attachment of equipment.

Sonderbekleidung (special clothing) was a recognized term in the Heer during World War II and generally taken to mean garments used in addition to basic uniform. Sometimes such items were a unit or temporary issue, and in most instances not recorded in the individual *Soldbuch*. What was 'special' changed over time, however: and so it was, for example, that the black Panzer uniform, initially used only for duty in tanks, was later used generally by armoured formations. *Sonderbekleidung* existed principally for two reasons: either because it was required for a particular duty, or to meet conditions of climate and terrain. For convenience we also include here a selection of the many pieces of portable equipment used by specialists.

TANK AND MOTORIZED UNIFORMS

Early in the 20th century, black tank clothing was adopted by several nations for the same practical reason: vehicles were oily and dirty, and black was least likely to show stains. The German version introduced in 1934 was not initially referred to as 'armoured' uniform because until repudiation of the Treaty of Versailles there were, officially at least, no tanks. The *Panzerjacke* was unusual in that it was double-breasted, and though it could be closed up to the neck was commonly worn open at the top with a grey shirt and black tie or a sweater underneath on active service in cold weather. The *Panzerjacke* was lined in grey, most wartime linings being of artificial silk, and there were two interior breast pockets. Reasonably close fitting and without exterior pockets or buckles, it was designed not to catch on the many obstructions to be found inside a tank. The *Hoheitsabzeichen* worn on the right breast was backed in black.

The distinctive collar badges of the *Panzerjacke* were black rhomboid-shaped patches with a stamped metal *Totenkopf* in the centre, mounted to appear upright with the collar open. The patches were piped in the *Waffenfarbe* as was the collar itself, at least until 1942 when collar piping was deleted. For tank crews and heavy anti-tank units the *Waffenfarbe* was pink; armoured signals units wore lemon yellow; armoured reconnaissance units pink or golden yellow depending on their origin, and Panzer-Regiment 24 golden yellow in honour of its descent from Kavallerie-Regiment 1. Logically, armoured engineers should have worn black *Waffenfarbe*, but because this did not show up on a black uniform it was changed to black interwoven with white. As of 1942 the armoured engineers' *Waffenfarbe* was again black when worn on field-grey uniform. *Dienstgradabzeichen* appeared on *Schulterklappen* and on the left sleeve of the tank uniform, but NCO braid was not applied to collars. The combination of *Totenkopf* insignia and distinctive black uniform was doubtless regarded as smart but perhaps more importantly was redolent of historic Brunswick and Prussian hussar uniforms.

TOP LEFT This NCO veteran of the Eastern Front campaign wears the black Panzer uniform, complete with dark-grey shirt and black tie and the usual Heer leather waist belt, c.1943. Black was adopted by the tank corps of several armies for practical reasons.

TOP NCOs of Panzer-Regiment 3 pictured in their 'bandit's lair' at the Grafenwöhr training area in northern Bavaria, summer 1937. Most possible uniforms are depicted, including the old field-grey *Dienstrock*, the new *Feldbluse* and the black Panzer uniform. At far left is the *Sportanzug* (sports training suit) with its zippered jacket; one man even wears a light-coloured and probably civilian sweater. The regiment was part of 2. Panzer-Division and fought in Poland, France, Greece and before Moscow and at Kursk, seeing action in Normandy and being almost completely destroyed at Falaise. Even so the division was rebuilt and also campaigned in the Ardennes and finally on the Rhine.

ABOVE LEFT Although the popular image was pristine black Panzer uniforms, a more accurate portrayal is provided by this photograph of a PzKpfw III crew taken near Erfurt. The dirt and mixture of costume are obvious.

LEFT An armoured soldier in black working *Drillichanzug* paints the *Balkenkreuz* on the turret of a captured French Char B1 tank, June 1940. (ullstein bild/Getty Images)

The crew of a Tiger I heavy tank sort their kit during maintenance on the Eastern Front, September 1943. Rucksacks, blankets, bread and jerrycans are just a few of the items visible. (ullstein bild/Getty Images)

The black trousers to match the *Panzerjacke* had a waistband, slash side pockets and tapered legs at the bottom tied with tapes. Boots of various types were worn by tank crews, but hobnailed soles were forbidden as being slippery on metal surfaces. Individually tailored tank uniforms were also made, particularly for officers and many NCOs, and, as with field grey, the tank uniform underwent changes to the quality of materials and details of manufacture as the war progressed. Jacket collars, which had tended to increase in size before 1939, were made smaller and with more rounded points in the latter part of the war. Provision to support belt hooks was also omitted. Until 1940 tank crews were issued with both the black and an ordinary field grey uniform, but thereafter received only the black. As a result the black uniform was now used for 'walking out' and other orders of dress.

Armoured troops wore a number of other garments in addition to the black *Feldanzug*. One was a lightweight work suit in black drill material. From 1941 this was widely supplemented or substituted with a suit of reed green of similar cut to the black *Feldanzug*, but usually with an exterior breast pocket to the jacket and patch pockets on the trousers. The reed-green outfit was versatile enough to be used with a shirt as summer dress, or over other clothing as a less conspicuous combat option. Some crewmen also adopted unofficial garments made from a variety of fabrics including Italian camouflage material, groundsheets or *Zeltbahn* canvas. A one-piece protective suit of grey-brown twill was worn as an overall, particularly in cool weather. This offered plenty of stowage, having breast, side and seat pockets, and was worn with *Schulterklappen*, rank insignia and breast eagle.

As many assault and self-propelled guns and tank destroyers were open on top it was apparent that black uniform was conspicuous if worn by the crews. Accordingly, a field-grey cloth version of the *Panzerjacke* with matching trousers was approved in 1940 for motorized gun crews of the artillery, and this was progressively extended to all crews of similar vehicles. When first trialled, the jacket had a bluish-green collar, but this was quickly deleted. Piping was never worn on the collar edges, but it did appear around the collar patches. Collar badges varied with *Litzen* for artillery units, though *Totenköpfe* were worn by anti-tank and many assault-gun crews. Regulations of 1941 make it clear that the assault-gun ensemble was to be worn with ankle boots and gaiters.

Motorcyclists were entitled to special clothing which consisted of a coat; long woollen leggings or 'over stockings'; a pullover and waterproof gauntlets.

BELOW LEFT An NCO of an assault-gun unit wears the 'wrap over'-style field-grey jacket of his arm of service. His decorations include the ribbon of the *Eisernes Kreuz 2. Klasse* and the *Infanterie-Sturmabzeichen*.

BELOW Scouts clad in camouflage smocks report to an officer of an assault-gun unit in Normandy, July 1944. (Roger Viollet/Getty Images)

ABOVE Members of a motorcycle team early in the war, most of whom are wearing the *Kradmantel* and gauntlets.

RIGHT Deutsches Afrikakorps motorcycle combinations on the way to the front in North Africa, March 1941. They wear the new tropical uniform with *Tropenhelm*. Baggage stowed on the backs of the sidecars is covered in camouflaged *Zeltbahnen*. (ullstein bild/ Getty Images)

The *Kradmantel* (motorcyclist's coat) was long and double-breasted with an external half-belt and cape top. For maximum weather protection the skirts of the *Kradmantel* could be buttoned around the rider's legs, and cuffs closed tight with buttoned tabs. The coat was of rubberized fabric but the collar changed in approximately the same sequence as that of the *Feldbluse*, being field-grey cloth initially, then bluish-green, and finally field grey again from 1940 onward. In a

Packtasche 34

rechte - Reitergepäck -

linke - Pferdegepäck -

(dreiteilig)

überwurf

Fleischkonserve
Putzbürste

Laufschuh
Hemd u. Strümpfe in Badehose ein-gerollt
Zwiebackbeutel
Nähzeug
Putzzeug } *dahinter Gewehrreini-gungsgerät*
Wasch-und Rasierzeug
Zeltleine

In der Hufeisentasche:
Anbindering
16 Nägel
Stollenschlüss
8 Stollen
2 Hufeisen

Kardätsche
Kochgeschirr 31

Striegel
Deckengurt

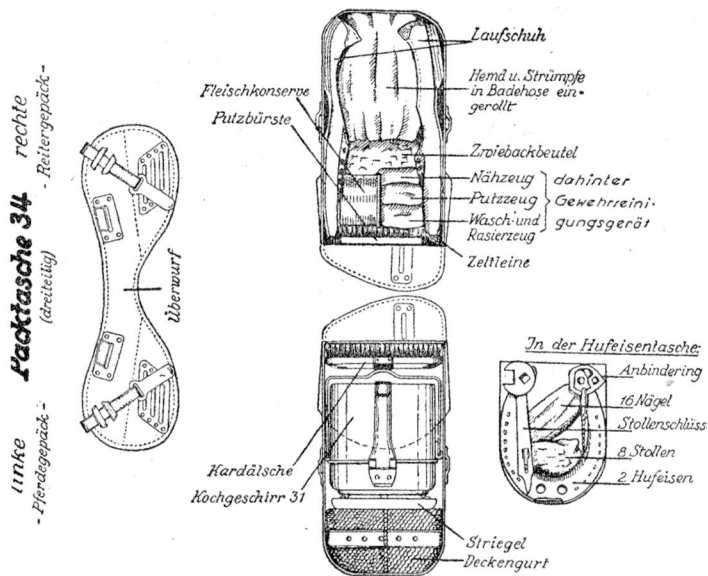

tropical version of the *Kradmantel* worn in Africa, southern Europe and southern Russia, the coat was of olive-green canvas. Drivers and co-drivers of open-cabbed vehicles were generally permitted *Mäntel*, woollen leggings and gauntlets, those in closed-cab vehicles foregoing the leggings.

TROPICAL UNIFORM

With the projected deployment of Heer assets to North Africa, the need for a cooler uniform more suited to the camouflage requirements of the terrain became pressing. As a result, tropical uniform was hastily designed in late 1940 with the assistance of the Hamburg *Tropeninstitut* (Tropical Institute), drawing inspiration from colonial experience and the cut of field-grey clothing. With new campaigns opening in the Balkans, Greece and southern Soviet Union in 1941, tropical uniform would be widely used, and sometimes influenced developments in other theatres. The wear of tropical uniform was even permitted in Germany in summer when a soldier was on leave or specific detached duties. Though the tropical kit was conceived as stand alone, it was habitually worn together with the field-grey *Mantel* and ordinary boots in the Mediterranean, the Balkans and the Soviet Union, and even in North Africa some temperate headgear and garments were worn. Officers and officials were initially permitted to claim the expense for a tailor-made tropical uniform for North Africa consisting of a jacket, one pair each of trousers and breeches, and a *Tropen Feldmütze* and *Mantel*, but the wearing of issue clothing by officers in theatre was commonplace.

ABOVE LEFT The Packtasche 34 saddle bags for mounted troops. The small container held a horseshoe and related items, the two larger bags a *Kochgeschirr*, rope, iron rations, spare shoes for the soldier, brushes and other small objects. The kit for the man was on the right-hand side, that for the horse on the left.

ABOVE An equine gas mask in use early in the war. There were several models, the 1938 type being a bag-like device, later examples having different arrangements of cones and filters. In the 1941 model, two cones were inserted into the nostrils of the animal.

The *Tropen Feldbluse* was of similar design to the field-grey equivalent with four large patch pockets, but was made from unlined olive cotton twill and its sand-brown-painted buttons were secured with rings, rather than sewn in place, to allow for washing. *Tropen Feldbluse* pockets were originally pleated, a feature later deleted. There was also an inside field-dressing pocket and provision for belt hooks, but there were only two, one positioned on each hip. The collar of the *Tropen Feldbluse* was designed to be worn open, with a shirt and tie for any formal occasion. Neck cloths, scarves and shirts were all worn on service and photographs even show some personnel, particularly artillerymen, in action bare-chested despite the risk of sunburn.

Tropical insignia were again similar to those worn with temperate uniform, but backed with sand- or mustard-coloured fabric, and braid for rank insignia was worked in copper-brown: *Litzen* were generally of bluish-grey thread. Standard embellishments were sometimes used, however, and even on an issue other-ranks' *Tropen Feldbluse*, officers frequently wore temperate-type officer distinctions. Curiously, breast eagles on tropical uniforms usually slightly overlap the right breast pocket of the jacket, as if the designer of the uniform had not taken into account the possibility of the open neck obscuring the insignia. From mid-1941, members of the Deutsches Afrikakorps became entitled to a *Ärmelstreifen* with AFRIKAKORPS presented in silver capital letters on a dark-green backing, after serving two months in theatre. The cuff-titles *AFRIKA* and *KRETA* were campaign awards.

Stiefelhose (breeches), *Hose* and *Kurze Hose* (shorts) were all worn with the *Tropen Feldbluse*. The commonest legwear appears to have been long trousers in the same material as the *Tropen Feldbluse*, with integral fabric belt and sometimes tied at the ankles, worn with gaiters and laced brown ankle boots. Shorts were of similar design but terminated above the knee: ribbed twill shorts were also worn. Long socks and ankle boots were usually worn with shorts. The standard *Stiefelhose*, technically 'boot trousers for dismounted personnel' with a tight buttoned lower leg, were initially intended for wear with braces but an integral belt was soon included. Tropical *Reithose* for mounted personnel with a reinforced seat were also produced, seeing particular use in Italy. Worn mainly in North Africa, the knee-high tropical boots with green canvas legs were particularly distinctive and these were often worn with breeches. Given supply issues in North Africa, use of captured equipment and food was commonplace. Shorts, boots and goggles were particularly useful as demand for them was high, and wearing them was not likely to lead to being confused with the enemy.

BELOW LEFT A tropical uniform shirt used as outerwear with the *Hoheitsabzeichen* over the right breast pocket. (© IWM UNI 12883)

BELOW The distinctive tall laced canvas-and-leather tropical boots worn by many of the Deutsches Afrikakorps. (© IWM UNI 12886)

German troops advancing during the Tunisian campaign of 1942–43. Some, including the machine-gunner in the foreground, wear the tall tropical boots. (Roger Viollet/Getty Images)

With nights sometimes cold, even in desert areas, the *Tropen Mantel* was very necessary, and the issue type was similar to the temperate version save that it was in olive brown and had tropical insignia. Given that leather was prone to drying out in very hot weather, and to rot in damp conditions, equipment straps for tropical use were made of webbing. Nevertheless, black leather straps were still used with tropical kit, particularly on the European mainland, and the advantages of webbing were soon apparent, leading to its more general adoption. Later in the war in particular, web support straps and other items could be seen even in cold areas. Equipment items such as gas-mask canisters and helmets were often painted sand colour.

GEBIRGSJÄGER UNIFORM

Mountain warfare was not new and Germany deployed *Gebirgsjäger* during World War I. German alpine expertise, already focused on Bavaria, was considerably enhanced after the Anschluss when whole divisions of Austrian mountain troops were integrated into the Heer. After the war spread to cold climates and mountains, some of the lessons learned by the *Gebirgsjäger* were adopted by the Heer as a whole.

As of 1939 the basic field-grey uniform of *Gebirgsjäger* appeared to be little different to that of the rest of the Heer, save for the *Bergmütze* and the Edelweiss badge worn on the right upper arm. The *Gebirgsjäger* was also issued with *Berghose* (mountain trousers), however, initially made of stone-grey and later field-grey wool. These were high waisted with wide-cut legs to allow freedom of movement in climbing, reinforced at the seat, and with buttoned flapped pockets. Cloth stirrups under the foot held the trousers firmly in place. The *Berghose* tapered at the ankle for wear with gaiters, thick socks or *Wickelgemaschen* (a form of puttee of elasticated woollen cloth) and laced boots. As of 1943 new trousers, the *Rundbundhose*, were introduced for all troops, including *Gebirgsjäger*; these integrated many of the useful features from the *Berghose*.

Another specialized garment was the *Windjacke*, literally 'wind jacket' but better translated as windcheater, or windbreaker. This was the latest in a line of mountain coats dating back to before World War I and was lightweight, double-breasted, short and made of waterproofed cotton fabric. Though items could be worn over the *Windjacke*, it was cut generously enough to fit over the belt equipment. A fabric half-belt at the back of the *Windjacke* allowed its girth to be expanded or reduced, and tabs under the large falling collar and at the cuffs were fastened for improved weather protection. There were side pockets in the lower skirts with additional slanted pockets above. Shoulder rank insignia were often worn. Issue *Windjacken* were marked internally in a similar fashion to the *Feldbluse* with maker's details, size, clothing-depot letter and date.

BELOW LEFT *Gebirgsjäger* on a high peak in the Caucasus, October 1942. The *Windjacke* is worn and rope, rucksacks and googles are all in evidence. (De Agostini/ Getty Images)

BELOW A *Gebirgsjäger* NCO with ice axe, climbing rope, gloves and binoculars. His decorations include the ribbon of the *Eisernes Kreuz 2. Klasse* and a marksman's lanyard.

An MG 34 deployed at high altitude, with the machine-gunner in camouflage suit and snow goggles.

Good footwear was crucial and *Gebirgsjäger* were issued with two main types. The *Bergschuh* was a general-purpose laced boot with steel cleats and studs, good for rugged terrain but also capable of being worn with ski bindings. For serious climbing, the *Kletterschuh* was worn. This was a flexible, flat-soled, low-laced boot of grey canvas and brown leather. Later versions made entirely of suede can also be encountered. With the *Kletterschuh* good grip and balance could be achieved on rock faces. Interestingly, the *Kletterschuh* and similar 'hut boots' were also used as a form of general-purpose slipper, reducing wear and tear indoors or on transports.

Because *Gebirgsjäger* frequently operated above the snow line, white camouflage clothing existed for their use even before the outbreak of war. The basic garment was a *Windbluse*, a lightweight hooded oversmock with three pockets across the chest. Laces around the waist and hood, and at the throat were tightened for a good fit after the *Windbluse* was pulled on over the head. Tapes and buckles closed the wrist openings. The original *Windbluse* was single sided, but as of 1942 a reversible version was introduced allowing a grey-brown side to be shown making the item useful all year round. Both versions of the *Windbluse* were worn with loose white trousers, later types also being reversible. Given its usefulness and versatility, the *Windbluse* was extended to arms other than the *Gebirgsjäger* during the war. Other snow-camouflage items used by the *Gebirgsjäger* included long, front-buttoning, hooded smocks, and cap and rucksack covers. The use of white smocks was quickly extended to other troops,

and substitutes made from white cloth or bed sheets were also widely worn.

Gebirgsjäger also had many tools of their trade. The ice axe was used during both climbing and walking, creating holds or as a brake on slopes. Snowshoes saw widespread use and were of several different models, generally constructed from rope on a wooden frame with canvas straps to retain the boot. Issue skis were painted white with a green stripe down the front part, and were provided by various manufacturers, which helps to account for the variation in bindings used. However, there was usually a metal base for the boot with adjustable metal cheeks to the sides; the rear of the foot was held by a metal

ABOVE The medic's belt-pouch *Verbandtasche* (first-aid kit). Produced in either black or brown leather, these boxes were worn on the belt in place of one or both *Patronentaschen*. A paper label under the lid gave the regulation contents. Here we see a selection of field dressings in different-coloured fabric packets dating from 1940 to 1945.

LEFT The oversized *Feldflasche* (field flask) with insulating fabric cover and suspension strap was issued to medical personnel and *Gebirgsjäger*.

ABOVE A selection of the many armbands used by specific personnel. The red Geneva cross (centre) was for medics and stretcher-bearers, and was often endorsed with a unit stamp. The *Deutsche Wehrmacht* bands (top and bottom) denoted those 'in the service of the German armed forces' and were often given to persons in supporting roles who did not wear uniform.

ABOVE RIGHT *Gebirgsjäger* transfer baggage to mule transport for work in rough terrain. The boxes of the medical team can be seen at centre left.

RIGHT *Gebirgsjäger* NCOs aboard ship en route to Norway, 1940. Soft climbing shoes are being worn as deck shoes and several different types of life vest are in evidence. This photograph is from the album of Ludwig Pöltl of Graz, a driver with Gebirgs-Pionier-Bataillon 83 who fought at Narvik.

spring and the toe by a strap. Ski poles were of wood or bamboo with a leather grip and wrist strap, and were fitted with a metal ferrule and an open wooden ring at the tip. The ring could rest evenly on the surface of the snow even when the pole was at an angle. Crampons were useful for moving over snow and ice during climbing and there were types which covered the entire foot for high-mountain work as well as smaller four spike models. Even so, full climbing kit was not carried as often as might be expected, but when required was often issued on the basis of one set between two men: one rope; one piton hammer; three pitons for vertical cracks and one for horizontal; one ring and one wafer piton; four karabiners; two pairs of climbing shoes; three cord slings; two small first aid kits; rucksack; compass; torch and altimeter.

WINTER CLOTHING

As of 1939 there was little specialist clothing for cold weather outside the *Gebirgsjäger* formations. Exceptions were *Wachtmäntel* (watch coats) and *Ubermäntel* (overcoats) worn by sentries and drivers whose tasks necessarily exposed them to the elements for long periods. The sentry's *Wachtmantel* had a long history, having existed in various forms in different armies for a couple of centuries by the outbreak of World War II. The German version of the 1930s was essentially an oversized double-breasted *Mantel*, which could in fact be worn over the standard-issue *Mantel* and belt equipment. It was blanket-lined with large flapped hip pockets and vertical hand-warmer or 'muff' pockets higher up. A leather yoke panel reinforced the shoulders. In a *Pelzmantel* (fur coat) variation, a similar garment was lined in black sheepskin which showed clearly around the collar, particularly if left open. Theoretically, both these coats were superseded by a general-purpose *Übermantel*, without leather shoulder reinforcement or sheepskin and with a fabric hood concealed in the collar during the late 1930s. The demand occasioned by expansion of the forces and the durability of heavy-duty coats not in constant wear meant all three continued in use, however, as did the *Mantel*. Variant *Pelzmäntel* were also produced with other colours of sheepskin lining. While all these garments were useful, they shared the significant drawbacks of weight, unsuitability for strenuous movement and high visibility against snowy terrain. The *Mantel* in particular was of only modest thermal efficiency. Cumbrous sentry boots with wooden soles, worn over ordinary footwear and also very similar to those used in World War I, compounded difficulties of movement.

BELOW LEFT Clad in *Pelzmantel* and felt sentry boots, a rifleman guards a bridge in winter.

BELOW General der Artillerie Walther von Brauchitsch (1881–1948), wearing the officers' optional leather coat, studies maps at his command post. Commissioned into the Imperial German Army as early as 1900, Brauchitsch fought throughout World War I. A *Major* by 1918, he was chief-of-staff to a division by 1927, becoming chief-of-staff of I. Armeekorps in 1935. Ultimately commander-in-chief of the Heer, he was promoted *Generalfeldmarschall* in 1940, but was dismissed from command at the end of 1941 as the Axis invasion of the Soviet Union stalled before Moscow. (Bettmann/ Getty Images)

TOP RIGHT Combat in snow camouflage; identification bands are worn on the upper arms, with uniform details being obscured by the suits and hoods.

BELOW LEFT A modern reconstruction using original uniform and issue snow camouflage coat. The coat is hooded and voluminous, reaching almost to the ankle, but being thin the fabric has almost no thermal quality. The detailing is similar to that found on uniforms, the buttons pebbled but painted white.

BELOW RIGHT *Wacht im Osten* ('Watch in the East'), 1943, a painting by Emil Dielmann (1897–1954), once in the Haus der Deutschen Kunst, Munich. The artist captures the details not only of snow camouflage worn over *Mäntel* but also weapons, and even a helmet interior.

The impact of the Russian winter on the clothing and appearance of the German soldier at the end of 1941 is difficult to exaggerate. Not only were the troops dressed for a far less severe climate, but an optimistic assumption had been made that fighting would be over by late autumn. As it was the temperature dropped to -20°C by early December with the Heer just short of Moscow. Generaloberst Franz Halder, chief-of-staff of the OKH, claimed that the OKH had given some thought to the possibility of winter fighting during the late

ABOVE Marching with skis during training. While *Gebirgsjäger* undertook ski training as a matter of course, the huge demand for skiers on the Eastern Front led to the training of many additional ski companies to act as scouts and skirmishers for other units.

LEFT Felt and wood sentry boots made by the Herman Müller company, 1942.

summer, and some skis were requisitioned in the autumn. Yet there was much else to consider, and it would doubtless have appeared defeatist to make elaborate preparations for an eventuality the *Führer* had already ruled out.

As cold and frostbite ravaged the Heer, a call went out to the home front through the *Winterhilfswerk* (winter relief organization) for emergency donations of clothing. Sweaters, coats, blankets, mittens and all manner of apparel poured in, but as much of it did not arrive at the front until well into the New Year the misery continued, and many troops had to rely on their own resources. Clothing was purchased or looted from Soviet civilians, and enemy dead were stripped of boots, coats, shirts and hats. German supply dumps close to the front disgorged everything they had and soldiers donned it all at once, often wearing multiple sets of underwear, while outsized *Mäntel* were valued as something to put on top of an entire wardrobe. Cloth ties or string were used to bind skirts of *Mäntel* to legs trapping a little extra heat, but footwear was arguably the most pressing concern, and felt boots particularly prized. Failing this, overshoes of plaited straw or boots wrapped in cloth were worn against extreme cold. Soviet propaganda was not slow to find opportunity, inventing a character called 'Winter Fritz', a grim figure of fun whose uniform was padded with newspaper and who wore stolen mittens and ladies' drawers.

Not until 1942 were significant improvements in winter clothing achieved, and even then results were patchy given the scale of the task. Some of the motley stockpile of material previously gathered was disinfected, cleaned and repaired against the next winter, and various literature prepared, including the important manual *Taschenbuch Für Den Winterkrieg* (Pocket Book for Winter Warfare). According to the *Taschenbuch*, troops were to avoid tight footwear and clothing, use layers to create insulation, make inner soles of cloth, paper or straw to prevent frostbite of the feet, and collect garments abandoned by the wounded. Where two pairs of socks were worn, one set was rolled down like ski socks. Footwear was to be kept clean and dried slowly if wet to avoid cracking. Motorcyclists were instructed to wear a second sweater and put layers of newspaper over the shirt. A Soviet suit of quilted jacket and trousers was captured in some quantities and widely used, often under other clothing. Mittens with leather reinforcement, a separate trigger finger and wool lining, first introduced in November 1941, were distributed. Photographs and surviving artefacts demonstrate that locally made sheepskin coats and short rabbit skin jackets, worn as liners under issue coats, were also used.

At the same time a more effective permanent solution to cold was worked out with the Joseph Neckermann company, now commissioned to devise better winter uniform and to act as an interface with textile manufacturers. Following work in cold chambers and durability tests in Finland, a prototype kit was exhibited to Hitler for approval in April 1942. Inspired by *Gebirgsjäger* and civilian clothing worn in arctic regions, the new *Winteranzug* (winter suit) was of revolutionary appearance. It consisted of a jacket with large hood, trousers

LEFT The new padded *Winteranzug* photographed at Saarbrücken, December 1942. This is the initial-issue winter suit in grey.

BELOW LEFT One of the several patterns of felt winter boots with leather foot sections and detailing. Unlike ungainly sentry boots with wooden soles, these were practical for marching and fighting.

BELOW A fitting for a privately purchased sheepskin coat on the Eastern Front.

OPPOSITE Jacket from the camouflaged version of the winter uniform, dated 1944.

LEFT The same jacket shown open revealing the white side, the uniform worn underneath, and the fastening of the interior fabric belt, which also contributed to creating a pocket of warm air around the chest.

ABOVE *Propagandakompanie* photograph of the work of the field postman in winter, *c.*1943. Both the postman and the addressee wear winter uniform over field grey.

LEFT A view of the gauntlets for the grey version of the winter uniform, showing inner and outer fabrics.

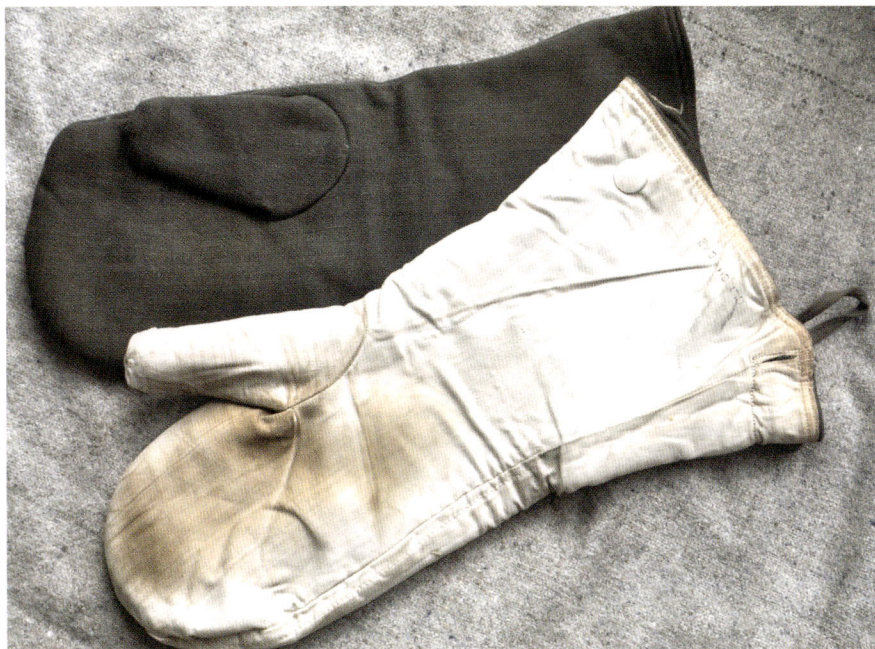

ABOVE A detail of the camouflaged trousers from the winter camouflage suit, 1944. Toggles and large buttons make for greater practicality with cold hands. Note that the braces used here predate the trousers, being of the first-pattern camouflage, which is the same as that used on the *Zeltbahn*.

RIGHT The officers' optional cold-weather *Mantel* with fur collar, here worn by a *Hauptmann* of the artillery during the winter of 1939/40.

OPPOSITE Table of rank insignia, woven in black, white, green and yellow thread introduced in the latter part of the war, mainly for use with camouflage garments. Though quite widely used, this system was never universal.

supported by braces, mittens, leg warmers and snow boots, plus a separate and more closely fitting hood. The outer fabric of the suit was water- and wind-resistant and warmth was assured by one or more layers of padding within: the main materials were rayon, synthetic wools and recycled cloth.

As it was produced later in 1942 the *Winteranzug* was fully reversible to white for snow camouflage, with a plain-grey exterior. Nevertheless, photographs show variations as well as hooded jackets with quilted exterior, and initially at least the *Winteranzug* may have been made in more than one weight to suit different conditions. It also appears that the jacket and trousers were sometimes

Unteroffizier

Leutnant

Generalmajor

Unterfeldwebel

Oberleutnant

Generalleutnant

Feldwebel

Hauptmann

General d.Inf. ect.

Oberfeldwebel

Major

Generaloberst

Stabsfeldwebel

Oberstleutnant

*General-
feldmarschall*

schwarz weiß grün gelb

Oberst

worn over both basic uniform and a quilted under-suit in the most extreme conditions. An illustration in the US Army's TM-E 30-451 *Handbook on German Military Forces* (1945), shows such a padded, quilted under-suit consisting of jacket and trousers. The under-jacket has a snug wrap-over front fastened with two tapes, a short upper tape, and a much longer one running externally around the waist. The trousers terminate just above the ankle to accommodate boots and socks or foot wraps.

What is certain is that nowhere near enough sets of winter uniform were distributed by the onset of cold weather at the end of 1942, as is attested by images of the Stalingrad campaign, during which many troops appeared in *Mäntel*. Heer sources also make it clear that there was still significant reliance on fur coats, overshoes, woollen blankets and foot wraps. *Deutsche Uniformen-Zeitschrift* explains that as a result of shortage of materials it was 'real combat troops' who received the new winter outfit, others making do with traditional garb plus 'paper garments' and straw overboots for 'unexpected' demands.

The year 1943 saw changes and improvements to the *Winteranzug*, the most obvious of which was replacement of the grey exterior fabric with a printed camouflage material of similar design to the 'splinter' pattern found on the *Zeltbahn*. Usually this reversed to white: there were variations, however, including non-reversible camouflaged winter jackets and trousers lined in grey or blue-grey, and camouflage material where the pattern lacked the previously sharply defined edges or had colours reversed. Another camouflage material, apparently introduced in 1943 and extensively used in production in 1944, in at least two slightly different forms, was described as *Sumpfmuster* or 'marsh' pattern.

There were also different sorts of fastenings to suits but large buttons, usually of resin, and small wooden toggles for braces were preferred on the grounds that these were easier for a soldier whose hands were numb with cold or encased in

A *Panzerfaust* operator in camouflaged winter padded uniform, winter 1944. (Bundesarchiv, Bild 101I-709-0337A-10A, Foto: Gronefeld, Gerhard)

gloves. Suits were manufactured in batches in different sizes, but not to the multitude of different measurements applied to the field-grey uniform. On issue, complete suits of the same pattern were distributed to each man and often an entire unit received matching outfits. Nevertheless, uniformity gradually broke down, not only because subsequent issues were of differing types but because the *Winteranzug* was not necessarily regarded as a permanent issue to an individual, and could be handed in again, and perhaps repaired, during warmer seasons. Strict uniformity was not in any event most conducive to effective concealment, nor was it likely that the matching of camouflage patterns was viewed as more important than availability of warm clothing. The *Winteranzug* was a huge improvement, but it was not perfect, being surprisingly heavy and not easy to clean, and if completely saturated taking a long time to dry.

OTHER CAMOUFLAGE CLOTHING

For the Heer, the starting point for much of the camouflage clothing developed during the war was the pattern first employed on the *Zeltbahn* in 1931, and used on a suit consisting of baggy smock and trousers in 1942. This suit was widely used, becoming more common over time, but far from a universal issue even to the infantry, and in practice the smock appears to have been much more common than the trousers. As the *Handbook on German Military Forces* explained in 1945, camouflage clothing was usually 'organizational', being issued to snipers, personnel of outposts and similar troops. As in the case of winter uniforms, updated and variant-pattern cloths were added to the repertoire

RIGHT In this photograph, marked '1942', the soldier in the centre wears a pair of trousers cut from camouflage material and featuring large buttoned front thigh pockets.

FAR RIGHT Made of Zeltbahn 31 cloth, this infantry single-breasted jacket has stand-and-fall collar, concealed buttons to the front fly and one lower button exposed at the waist. There is a single slanted pocket to the left chest, secured by an exposed button with a flap. On the shoulders are *Oberfeldwebel* insignia with subdued grey cloth NCO lacing to the edges. (© IWM UNI 3535)

as they appeared, and different patterns of material continued to be used in parallel. The basic smock to the issue camouflage suit was simple, made of printed drill material, pulled on over the head, and lacked external pockets or collar. Buttoned tabs closed the cuffs, there was a drawstring at the waist, and a laced vertical slit from the neck to mid-chest. Smaller slits either side allowed access to pockets of garments worn underneath. The trousers featured a pronged strap serving as belt, and side pockets. The very shapelessness of the outfit and its lack of detail or badges were distinct advantages, not only in that the suit was more difficult to see, but also in that it was simple to produce.

In addition to the basic form there were a number of variations to the smock, both official and unofficial, and examples are found that were not factory produced but run up by unit or local tailors. The most obviously different type features a hood and occasionally an integral face veil, allowing the wearer to see while obscuring the obvious tone and features of his face. Most smocks were designed to be worn single sided only, even though the reverse of the cloth was usually an unprinted white, but in another variation some were constructed fully reversible for snow camouflage. Interestingly, there are also instances of mismatches of material, where, for example, a smock is lighter or darker than usual, or even has a part of a different-pattern fabric. Where these are original features it is unlikely they are deliberate, being the result of fading, which is obvious in some photographs, repairs, or an 'economical' use of materials.

A selection of camouflage gear worn by officers and men of the *Großdeutschland* Division. The officer, centre, has a camouflage smock, while others wear winter uniform or the *Zeltbahn* poncho.

Camouflaged winter uniforms and a selection of headgear worn on the Eastern Front, 1944. (Roger Viollet/Getty Images)

An unusual camouflage garment of a distinctly ad hoc appearance was the body apron. This consisted of a simple oblong of printed camouflage fabric somewhat over 2m in length with a hole near the middle. The wearer's head went through the hole, and tapes fastened the side openings. The camouflaged apron is generally described as a sniper accessory: another was the body net. While manufacture and distribution are unclear, photographs from France in 1944 show German infantry using netting, again donned over the head through a hole. Natural camouflage materials garnish the net, which is held in place around the body by the leather waist belt. The result was quite effective as the form of the soldier was effectively broken up and the foliage matched the local environment. The idea was ingenious though not completely new, and would later become a starting point for many different types of sniper suit.

Remarkably, camouflage material, both German and Italian issue, was also put to a wide variety of uses in more or less unofficial bespoke garments. Jackets were usually cut to approximate to the various patterns of *Feldbluse*, but there were also trousers, shirts and – occasionally – field caps. In rare instances, zip fasteners were even incorporated in camouflage garments, the first 'slide closure' having been invented in the United States in the 19th century, and a patent registered in 1909 in Germany, where production on a significant scale was under way by the interwar period.

WOMEN'S UNIFORMS

The role of women in the Third Reich was viewed as traditional, perhaps best summed up by *Kinder, Küche, Kirche* – 'Children, Kitchen, Church' – a form of words current before the end of the 19th century. Though the Heer employed women in various civilian capacities they did not fight in World War I, nor was it expected they would do so in 1939. Only after the opening campaigns in World War II did the need for more active engagement of German women becoming pressing. The Nachrichtenhelferinnen des Heeres (Female Signals Auxiliaries of the Army) was founded in October 1940, Betreuungshelferinnen (Female Welfare Auxiliaries) following in 1941, Stabshelferinnen (Female Staff Auxiliaries) in 1942 and a female remount corps for horse training, the Bereiterinnen, in 1943. All were intended to release men for front-line service. Uniforms were not necessarily worn initially, but deployment of women to occupied countries made distinctive clothing and communal living under military conditions more and more commonplace. Participation, initially voluntary, became subject to compunction in December 1941.

Females were not combatants, but as in Britain women with anti-aircraft units, the manpower crisis, and the willingness of some to take more active roles blurred official boundaries later in the war. Women's costume closely reflected the nature of their roles, with work smocks worn for practical tasks and smart uniform, approximating to a business suit, for 'walking out' and formal occasions. The full outfit of the signals auxiliary in the middle period of the war consisted of cap; greatcoat; rain cape; suit with one jacket and two skirts in stone grey; four blouses (one white and three 'service'); two woollen vests; three pairs of stockings; two black ties; rubber overboots; two work smocks with three collars; handbag; and brooch with distinctive *Blitz* symbol to be worn on the tie. For winter this was supplemented by a cap with ear protection; two pairs of woollen stockings; scarf; two chemises; two pairs of woollen underwear and gloves. In extreme cold climates, fur vest, ski trousers and mittens might be included. In warm weather a summer dress was worn. Make-up and jewellery were not entirely banned, but had to be discreet.

Female Heer auxiliaries dressed for 'walking out' in their smart grey suits with field cap and regulation handbags, *c.*1942.

Photographs show that the Heer eagle emblem was usually, but not always, worn over the right breast. The signals auxiliary and the staff auxiliary had different cuff-titles, though not always worn. New regulations for rank insignia were introduced in March 1941, and were expanded to ten different grades a year later. These ranks approximated to the male equivalents, from *Schütze* to *Oberstleutnant*. The lowest-grade *Nachrichtenhelferin* had no rank badge, and the next grade up, the *Vorhelferin*, a pip on the left upper sleeve below the *Blitz* insignia. More senior ranks bore a system of chevrons in aluminium, silver or gold on the left arm, and braid embellishments on the collar as female uniform jackets lacked *Schulterklappen*.

Much of the work undertaken by welfare auxiliaries after October 1941 had previously been undertaken by the Red Cross, but the foundation of the new corps brought these tasks under Heer jurisdiction. Many staff auxiliaries were also employed prior to the foundation of their corps in 1942, some being civilians, others already part of the signals auxiliaries. The immediate result was a somewhat confused situation, with some already having a uniform and others only civilian dress. This was partly remedied by the use of armbands and badges and the *Stabshelferin des Heeres* cuff-title. New uniform for staff auxiliaries was formally introduced in 1943, being essentially the same as that worn by the signals auxiliaries with appropriate badges. The female auxiliary remount corps worked mainly in equestrian schools, and photographs show them in single-

ABOVE A Heer field radio station, *c.*1937. Communications equipment remained heavy and delicate, even in 1945, though more compact radios were progressively introduced, particularly for battlefield units.

ABOVE RIGHT Artillery signallers on the Eastern Front operating a backpack radio, *c.*1942. Larger radio sets were mounted in tanks and radio vans, another version forming pack equipment for a horse. (Trautvetter/PhotoQuest/Getty Images)

RIGHT General der Panzertruppe Heinz Guderian (1888–1954) in his command vehicle with 19. Panzer-Division. His signallers operate various equipment including a coding machine, foreground left. (Roger Viollet/Getty Images)

BELOW Signalling the old-fashioned way, *c.*1939. A soldier attaches small pigeon baskets to the harness of a dog, for the birds to be released from the front line with messages.

The distinctive signallers' backpack was issued to signals teams in three slightly different versions numbered 1, 2 and 3, as is evident here. Each type carried a different load, teams needing objects such as cable reels, ground-marking panels, small tools and poles for holding wires. Hooked pole-climbers were worn on the feet for adjusting wire in trees and on telegraph poles.

Signallers on the Eastern Front lay out wire from a backpack reel, field telephones with cables being particularly useful for communicating over shorter ranges from static positions. The downsides were that cables were difficult to retrieve quickly and apt to be severed by bombardments.

Pioniere (assault engineers) use an inflatable boat during the crossing of the River Meuse, 1940.

Pioniere (assault engineers) use an inflatable boat during the crossing of the River Meuse, 1940.

breasted jacket with eagle insignia, shirt and tie or sweater, breeches and riding boots. Side caps were later supplemented by a soft peaked cap resembling the *Einheitsfeldmütze*.

Because women had no place on the battlefield and clothing supply was increasingly limited, re-equipping female auxiliaries was low priority. There was, however, a belated attempt to regularize the position. The various women's auxiliary services of the Heer, Kriegsmarine and Luftwaffe were combined at the end of 1944, and at some point female kitchen staff and other support staff were also recognized as auxiliaries, even though not uniformed. For those in uniform, new rank insignia consisting of bands of braid around the lower left sleeve were introduced in early 1945. There were also intended to be cuff-titles with the wording *Wehrmachthelferin-Heer* for Heer auxiliaries.

Interestingly, a female version of the final men's *Feldbluse*, the Helferinnen-Tuchbluse 44, was described in the January 1945 edition of *Deutsche Uniformen-Zeitschrift*. Similar in general outline to the male *Feldbluse*, and also of the new universal cloth, it differed most obviously in that it closed right over left and the waistband was narrower, having only one of its six front buttons on the band. There were no *Schulterklappen*, but the *Hoheitsabzeichen* was worn over the right breast, or on the left arm. The *Bluse* was to be worn with a skirt, the Helferinnen-Rock 44, and an overcoat. The outfit was intended for all uniformed females attached to all branches of the Wehrmacht, as well as the labour service and Red Cross. It is unlikely that many of these uniforms were made.

ABOVE LEFT Regulation Heer sports kit, consisting of a singlet with eagle insignia and dark shorts, is worn during a competition at Hanover, 1939.

ABOVE There was even a regulation pattern of Heer swimming trunks, worn here, incongruously, with *Feldmütze* or steel helmet.

LEFT An observer using stereoscopic binoculars from a plank-lined field position.

CHAPTER 7

HEER MEDALS AND AWARDS

A well-made though unmarked *Infanterie-Sturmabzeichen* on the left breast pocket of a *Feldbluse*.

It is often said that the proliferation of medals, badges and other awards under the Third Reich was a morale-boosting exercise, as indeed it is for many nations at times of crisis. Yet it was also the case that the longer the war went on, and the more varied its combat theatres, the greater was the demand to mark important events and deeds: and like coins, medallic art carried messages.

As of 1933, Germany had a rich heritage upon which to draw. The states subsumed into the German Empire in 1871 already had orders and medals, the *Eisernes Kreuz* (Iron Cross) and the *Pour le Mérite* (Blue Max) of Prussia being particularly significant; but with a small Reichsheer, little to celebrate and award of the *Eisernes Kreuz* suspended after World War I, innovation in awards and commemorative regalia was left largely to associations and political bodies, not least the Nazi Party. An important exception to this was the *Ehrenkreuz des Weltkriegs 1914/1918* (Honour Cross of the World War 1914/1918) introduced under the auspices of Reich President Hindenburg on 13 July 1934. This acknowledgement of the sacrifices made in World War I was produced in different versions granted to combatants, non-combatants and war widows. There were many different manufacturers, and the *Ehrenkreuz* was produced in both bronze and oxidized finishes. More than 4 million *Ehrenkreuze* were awarded in the first year with a final total of more than 8 million, distribution continuing until as late as 1944. Hitler also authorized a medal in 1934, the *Medaille zur Erinnerung an den 9. November 1923* (Medal to Commemorate 9 November 1923), also known as the *Blutorden* ('Blood Order'), commemorating the failed Beer Hall *Putsch* of November 1923; this was later recognized for wear on military uniform.

The rapid expansion of the Heer in the mid-1930s and the shift of responsibility for orders and decorations to the *Führer* by means of a 'design ordinance' in 1935, and a statute of July 1937 giving Hitler sole right to bestow awards, marked important changes. From this point on there was scope for the politicization of official awards, retrospective authorization of selected pre-existing unofficial badges and awards, and inclusion of overtly National Socialist iconography in new designs. Many orders, medals and badges were abolished, including regimental commemorative crosses, the Bavarian *Kriegserinnerungskreuz* (War Commemorative Cross), the *Langemarck-Kreuz* (commemorating the battle for Landemarck, a village in Flanders, on 21 October 1914 and mythologized by the Nazis as the 'sacrifice of German youth') and various Freikorps pieces, all of which were no longer to be worn. Dr Heinrich Doehle, a Chancellery official and *SS-Oberführer* (colonel), later characterized this Nazi monopolization as a means of correcting the medallic confusion created by 22 state jurisdictions; but it was also a sign of the crumbling of local autonomy.

TOP FAR LEFT The *Ehrenkreuz des Weltkriegs 1914/1918, mit Schwertern*, for a combatant of World War I. This medal could be purchased from a catalogue for as little as RM 1,00, with miniature versions at RM 0,22. Nevertheless, its official status meant that it could be worn with Heer uniform.

TOP CENTRE The Anschluss medal, awarded for participation in the annexation of Austria in March 1938, in its issue box. By the time awarding of this medal ceased at the end of 1940, 318,689 had been issued. The reverse bears the text *EIN VOLK, EIN REICH, EIN FÜHRER* ('One People, One Empire, One Leader').

TOP RIGHT The design for the three 'Flower Wars' medals was shared with the theme of the September 1938 Party Rally in Nuremberg, dubbed the *Reichsparteitag Großdeutschland* ('Rally of Greater Germany'), which promoted the idea of liberating ethnic Germans from other nations.

LEFT An *Oberfeldwebel* with his new wife, *c.*1940. He wears an Anschluss medal (right) and a long-service medal (left).

Medal winners were helped to see the correctness of the latest provisions by official approval of many earlier awards and the reintroduction of the monetary stipends to recipients abolished in the 1920s. Among others, the Prussian *Pour le Mérite* and *Eisernes Kreuz*, the Austrian *Militär-Maria-Theresien-Orden* (Military Order of Maria Theresa), the Württemberger *Militärverdienstorden* (Military Merit Order) and the Bavarian *Militär-Max-Joseph-Orden* (Military Order of Max Joseph) were formally recognized by the Nazi regime, the highest orders and medals for bravery and merit now attracting a monthly payment from the state of RM 20–25. Foreign orders and medals could also be accepted by individuals, but only with permission. A later stipulation was that holders of certain high awards were entitled to be recognized by sentries presenting arms.

RIGHT The reverse of the Sudetenland medal, 1938, with the text *EIN VOLK, EIN REICH, EIN FÜHRER*. There were two issues of the medal: one relating to the occupation of the Sudetenland, the second when German forces occupied the remainder of the Czech lands, thereby creating the Protectorate of Bohemia and Moravia. Altogether, more than 1 million Sudetenland medals were awarded.

FAR RIGHT An ordnance officer wearing the old-style *Dienstrock* complete with aiguillette and *große Ordenschnalle* (large medal bar) for a formal occasion in Breslau, July 1936. Next to the 1914 *Eisernes Kreuz 2. Klasse*, with black-and-white ribbon, is a Saxon *Friedrich-August-Medaille*.

As of 1936, conscription was reintroduced and with it came a new set of *Wehrmacht-Dienstauszeichnung* (Armed Forces Long Service Award) medals on blue ribbons, those for the Heer and Kriegsmarine having a small 'armed services' eagle on the medal ribbon, the Luftwaffe having a flying eagle. The four- and 12-year medals were discs, those for 18 and 25 years, crosses. The lower awards could be authorized at unit level. Anybody who reached 40 years of satisfactory service became entitled to a wreath of oak leaves to be added to the medal ribbon below the eagle.

A signal example of the 'Nazification' of medals was the harvest of awards for the so-called *Blumenkriege* ('Flower Wars') of 1938–39, a series of territorial annexations designed to reintegrate German minorities living inside the boundaries of other states within the Reich. The annexations were also intended to right some of the perceived wrongs of the Treaty of Versailles which had lopped off 13 per cent of Germany's territory, and about 10 per cent of its population. These territorial gains of the late 1930s were at the expense of Austria, which was itself swallowed whole in the Anschluss of March 1938; the Czechoslovak state, which lost its northern, western and southern areas (known to the Germans as the Sudetenland) in October 1938 and was subsequently expunged as a whole in March 1939; and the recently independent Lithuania, which lost Memel in March 1939. While all this entailed political bullying, opportunism, intimidation and some violence, the territorial gains were achieved without triggering a major war. German newsreels showed previously 'enslaved' populations greeting their 'liberators' with bouquets, and there is little doubt these actions were genuinely popular with a significant proportion of the German population. The medals for these events, for both military and civilian participants, rammed home a message of unalloyed triumph.

The awards for meritorious service in the Anschluss of Austria, the seizure of the Sudetenland and the return of Memel were designed by Professor Richard Klein (1890–1967), Director of the Munich School of Applied Arts, also a painter and designer of postage stamps, who had already produced other medals including the long-service medal. All three of the 'Flower Wars' medals shared a common theme and an obverse design of two figures, one with a Nazi banner who is helping the other leap up and shed his chains. The sledgehammer message was difficult to avoid, particularly as the 1938 Party Rally in Nuremberg was dubbed the *Reichsparteitag Großdeutschland* ('Rally of Greater Germany') and the artwork of the two figures featured on the rally's commemorative plaque. Both the Anschluss medal (*Die Medaille zur Erinnerung an den 13. März 1938*) and the Sudetenland medal (*Die Medaille zur Erinnerung an den 1. Oktober 1938*) had the slogan *EIN VOLK, EIN REICH, EIN FÜHRER* ('One People, One Empire, One Leader') on the reverse and the respective date, but the Memel medal's reverse included the inscription *Zur Erinnerung an die Heimkehr des Memellandes, 22. März 1939* ('To Commemorate the Return of the Memel Area, 22 March 1939'). As the Czech lands were denuded first by the Sudetenland debacle, then by complete occupation and conversion to a German 'protectorate', a fresh issue of the Sudetenland medal was made. Where a recipient already had a Sudetenland medal from the first issue, he was awarded a *Spange* (bar) instead. The *Prag Spange*, showing Prague Castle, was worn on both the ribbon of the medal itself and a ribbon bar when the medal was not present.

AWARDS SANCTIONED IN 1939

In hindsight, 1939 was a pivotal year in the history of Heer awards. In January the *SA-Sportabzeichen* (SA Sport Badge) was formally elevated to the status of *SA-Wehrabzeichen* (SA Defence Badge), in three grades. In March came the Memel medal. In April, the *Spanien-Kreuz* (Spanish Cross) was approved for Germans who had served in the Spanish Civil War; also introduced was the *Ehrenkreuz für Hinterbliebene deutscher Spanienkämpfer* ('Cross of Honour for the German combatant survivors of Spain'). The much more widely distributed *Deutsches Schutzwall-Ehrenzeichen* could literally be translated as the 'German defensive wall decoration', but is usually described in English as the 'West Wall Medal'.

ABOVE A new recipient of the 1939 *Eisernes Kreuz 2. Klasse*. This *Unteroffizier* wears the medal from the second buttonhole of his *Waffenrock* where it was often suspended during, or immediately after, the award ceremony. Subsequently, the actual medal was only worn on a ribbon bar on parades, though a ribbon was worn through the buttonhole on uniform, or represented by a shorter piece of ribbon on a small ribbon bar.

RIGHT The *Eisernes Kreuz 2. Klasse* of soldier Ernst Gelhard. The good condition of the medal is attributable to the fact that Gelhard was killed in 1942 and had no opportunity to wear the piece, which was then preserved by his family.

Authorized in August 1939, it was awarded in gratitude to those who gave 'meritorious service' in the design and construction of Germany's western defences. Curiously, holders of the Memel medal were not allowed to have the *Deutsches Schutzwall-Ehrenzeichen*. These awards were merely the curtain-raiser, however, for on 1 September Germany invaded Poland, and with the outbreak of war came rapid developments.

Of central importance was the reactivation of the *Eisernes Kreuz*, an act that was necessary, as Hitler disingenuously explained, due to 'threatening attacks' on Germany. The basic cross was very similar to that of 1914, with an iron centre and a silver frame, in first and second classes. While the 1914 cross was a Prussian award, with its ribbon in the black and white of Prussia, the 1939 cross was national, with a red, white and black ribbon, and the medal itself was adorned with a swastika and awarded 'in the name of the *Führer*'. All World

War II examples of the *Eisernes Kreuz* carry the date '1939', the year of reintroduction of the award, irrespective of when a particular medal was actually made or awarded. There was no 'home front' version of the *Eisernes Kreuz* in World War II as there had been in World War I, but a silver *Spange* (clasp) with an eagle and swastika in an oak-leaf wreath and inscribed '1939' was granted to those who already held the 1914 *Eisernes Kreuz*. The *Spange* for the *Eisernes Kreuz 2. Klasse* was mounted on ribbon; the *Eisernes Kreuz 1. Klasse* was attached directly to the left breast of the uniform.

The same ordinance announcing the reappearance of the *Eisernes Kreuz*, approved on 1 September 1939 and distributed the next day, also introduced a very significant departure in the form of the *Ritterkreuz des Eisernen Kreuzes* (Knight's Cross of the Iron Cross), a grade of award higher than the *Eisernes Kreuz 1. Klasse*. The *Ritterkreuz* looked like an *Eisernes Kreuz*, but was larger and worn around the neck on a red, white and black ribbon. Where uniform made this difficult, recipients were given special permission to leave the top of the *Feldbluse* unfastened. With the *Ritterkreuz* being perceived as an important award from the start, but one which the wearer was expected to display, even in battle, many recipients obtained copies and wore these on active service. Some even mounted an *Eisernes Kreuz 2. Klasse* at the throat and risked losing this rather than their *Ritterkreuz*. From 1939 to 1942 the *Ritterkreuz* was accompanied

FAR LEFT Generaloberst Eduard Dietl (1890–1944), first recipient of *Eichenlaub* (Oak Leaves) to the *Ritterkreuz. Schwerter* (Swords) were added to his cross only after his death on 23 June 1944 in an air crash, and thus never worn. Dietl served in the Königlich Bayerisches Armee (Royal Bavarian Army) during World War I, and was a member of the Freikorps afterwards. He helped organize the 1936 Winter Olympics held in Garmisch-Partenkirchen, Bavaria, and went on to command 3. Gebirgs-Division during the invasion of Norway in June 1940. Subsequently he led an entire *Gebirgsarmee* (mountain army) on the northern sector of the Eastern Front.

LEFT Robert Eichert (1914–44) took part in both the invasion of Poland in September 1939 and the May–June 1940 campaign in the West. After seeing combat in Yugoslavia he participated in the invasion of the Soviet Union in June 1941, subsequently being involved in many major actions, including the battle of Stalingrad (August 1942–February 1943). Already highly decorated, he won the *Ritterkreuz* in April 1943 while serving as an *Oberfeldwebel* platoon commander with 4./ PzRgt 36. Promoted *Leutnant*, he was killed in the Soviet Union on 23 September 1944, aged 30.

ABOVE Erwin Rommel (1891–1944) holding his new velvet-covered *Generalfeldmarschall*'s baton. A favourite of Hitler until his implication in the 20 July 1944 assassination plot, Rommel was one of the best-known and most highly decorated generals in Nazi Germany. His *Pour le Mérite* and both classes of the *Eisernes Kreuz* were won in World War I. His *Ritterkreuz* was awarded for his role as commander of 7. Panzer-Division during the campaign in France in May–June 1940, with *Eichenlaub* being added in 1941, *Schwerter* in 1942 and *Brillanten* in 1943. He also held long-service medals for 25 years' service, a Sudetenland medal with *Prag Spange*, a Memel medal, a *Verwundetenabzeichen* in gold and a clutch of Austrian, Bavarian, Württemberger and Italian medals, as well as the *Panzerkampfabzeichen* in silver.

ABOVE Generalleutnant Fritz Bayerlein (1899–1970) is perhaps best remembered for his service as chief-of-staff to the Deutsches Afrikakorps, but he had a long and eventful military career commencing as a teenager on the Western Front in World War I. He also served in the invasions of Poland and France, and on the Eastern Front commanded 3. Panzer-Division and then the Panzer-Lehr-Division, and was one of the most successful leaders in the Ardennes in 1944–45. His *Ritterkreuz* – just one of his many awards, both German and Italian – was awarded on 26 December 1941, with *Eichenlaub* added on 6 July 1943 and *Schwerter* on 20 July 1944. (ullstein bild / Getty Images)

ABOVE Adolf Vogt (1915–92) joined the machine-gun company of Infanterie-Regiment 15 in 1934. He took part in the German reoccupation of the Rhineland two years later, as well as the 1940 campaign in the West. By 1941 he was an NCO with both classes of the *Eisernes Kreuz* and the *Infanterie-Sturmabzeichen*, fighting in Greece. Badly wounded on the Eastern Front, he was awarded the *Deutsches Kreuz in Gold* on 5 May 1942, and subsequently attended the Kriegsakademie (War Academy) and was promoted *Oberleutnant*. Now a company commander with 12./GR 1085, he fought in the West in 1944, and was awarded the *Ritterkreuz* on 16 October for a successful defensive engagement in France.

by a red-leather binder designed by the architect and interior designer/decorator Gerdy Troost (1904–2003), in which was held the award document bearing the signature of the *Führer*, genuine or facsimile. Hitler also made many presentations personally. The criteria for award of the *Ritterkreuz* varied: with the Kriegsmarine and Luftwaffe, there were tonnages sunk or points systems to consider, but for the Heer – which received the bulk of the crosses – it came down to more brutal

ABOVE Stabsfeldwebel (Staff Sergeant) Ewald Mrousek (1911–81) in tropical uniform after receiving the *Ritterkreuz* in Tunisia, 19 January 1943. The *Ritterkreuz* was usually placed around the neck on a long piece of ribbon during an award ceremony, subsequently being worn at the throat with a shorter length. Mrousek also held the *Infanterie-Sturmabzeichen*, both classes of the *Eisernes Kreuz* and a *Dienstauszeichnung der Wehrmacht*. (Keystone-France/Gamma-Keystone/Getty Images)

ABOVE The *Eisernes Kreuz* family of awards, pictured in *Signal* magazine. Top: the *Großkreuz des Eisernen Kreuzes* (Grand Cross of the Iron Cross), awarded only once in World War II, to Reichsmarschall des Großdeutschen Reiches Hermann Göring. Middle row: *Ritterkreuz mit Eichenlaub*; *1939 Spange* to the *Eisernes Kreuz 1. Klasse*; and the *Ritterkreuz*. Bottom row: *1939 Spange* to the *Eisernes Kreuz 2. Klasse*; *Eisernes Kreuz 1. Klasse*; and the *Eisernes Kreuz 2. Klasse*. The *1939 Spange* was awarded in instances when the recipient had already won one or both classes of the *Eisernes Kreuz* in World War I, and was then awarded a 1939 *Eisernes Kreuz*.

factors: a soldier was expected to show continuous and exceptional bravery; a senior commander to win battles.

If the *Ritterkreuz* was quickly accepted as a prestigious award, the *Kriegsverdienstkreuz* (War Merit Cross), introduced on 18 October 1939 (the 126th anniversary of the battle of Leipzig), made a useful, if less well regarded, acknowledgement of levels of achievement below, or not covered by the *Eisernes Kreuz*. Sometimes derided as 'Iron Cross training', the new medal drew inspiration from both the *Ritterkreuz* and the *Eisernes Kreuz*, being in two main classes, and having a black, white and red ribbon. In this instance, however, the prominent broad central stripe of the ribbon was black, rather than red. As with the

The *Kriegsverdienstkreuz 1. Klasse mit Schwertern*, worn by an NCO in a family portrait. As with the *Eisernes Kreuz*, the *Kriegsverdienstkreuz 1. Klasse* was worn on the breast.

Eisernes Kreuz the *Kriegsverdienstkreuz 1. Klasse* was worn on the left breast without a ribbon, while the *Kriegsverdienstkreuz 2. Klasse* was suspended on a ribbon as part of a group, or represented by a ribbon through the buttonhole on the combat uniform. The medal had crossed swords in the design when given as a combat award, being otherwise without embellishment. The combat version took precedence, so if a soldier won both he wore only the *mit Schwertern* (with Swords) version: civilians were eligible for the *ohne Schwertern* (without Swords) medal. Again, it was given without reference to rank.

Also included in the *Kriegsverdienstkreuz* series were two further awards, coming as something of an afterthought in August 1940. One was extremely exclusive; the other was conferred very widely. The *Ritterkreuz des Kriegsverdienstkreuzes* (Knight's Cross of the War Merit Cross) was awarded with and without Swords; only about 250 were awarded in total, including fewer than 50 to Heer personnel. It ranked below the *Ritterkreuz des Eisernen Kreuzes*, but was much rarer. The other addition was the *Kriegsverdienstmedaille* (War Merit Medal), made in the millions and distributed mainly to munition workers, anti-aircraft auxiliaries and similar personnel, foreigners as well as both sexes being eligible. Soldiers who won this award in civilian life could continue to wear the ribbon on their uniform.

Another relatively humble award, reintroduced in 1939, was a new version of the *Verwundetenabzeichen* (Wound Badge) which existed in World War I, and had also been awarded in small numbers for service in the Spanish Civil War. As approved in September 1939 the *Verwundetenabzeichen* was black for one or two wounds, silver for three or four, and gold for five or more. Wounds received in World War I for which a badge had been awarded counted towards higher grades of award in World War II. Regulations also took into account the severity of wounds, so a soldier might jump straight to the silver award if he had been brain-damaged, facially disfigured, or had lost an eye, hand or foot. The gold badge might likewise be given immediately in the event of complete blindness or very severe brain-damage, or a man might step up from an existing black badge to the gold badge having received serious wounds. An extremely rare variation was the *Verwundetenabzeichen 20. Juli 1944*, awarded only to those injured in the failed attempt to assassinate Hitler in his headquarters at Rastenburg in East Prussia.

FAR LEFT The 1939 *Eisernes Kreuz 1. Klasse*, shown in the approved position on the left breast pocket of the field uniform. The pin of this example is stamped with a tiny 'L/58' indicating Dresdner Medaillenmünze Glaser & Sohn GmbH, but is otherwise devoid of markings.

LEFT Given the vast number of battle wounds suffered by German soldiers in World War II, the 1939 *Verwundetenabzeichen* (Wound Badge) in black was one of the commonest awards. Apart from the swastika, the design was very similar to the *Verwundetenabzeichen* awarded in 1918.

BELOW LEFT 'Greater Germany's War Medals': an illustration from *Signal* magazine. Top row, left to right: *Deutsches Kreuz in Silber*; *Ritterkreuz mit Eichenlaub, Schwertern und Brillanten*; and *Deutsches Kreuz in Gold*. Centre: *Kriegsverdienstkreuz mit Schwertern in Silber*. Bottom row: *Kriegsverdienstmedaille*; *Ritterkreuz des Kriegsverdienstkreuz*; and *Kriegsverdienstkreuz in Bronze*.

BELOW An impressive medal array worn by a veteran Austrian NCO, *c*.1940. The pieces on the bar include Austro-Hungarian medals for 1914–18, the *Ehrenzeichen fur Verdienste um das Rote Kreuz* (Decoration for Services to the Red Cross) and the *Ehrenkreuz des Weltkriegs 1914/1918*. On the pocket of the *Feldbluse* are a World War I *Verwundetenabzeichen* and the *SA-Wehrabzeichen* (originally billed as a sports award).

RIGHT General Wilhelm Keitel (1882–1946) replete with awards before the outbreak of World War II. These include both grades of the *Eisernes Kreuz;* Austrian and various state medals from Oldenburg, Hamburg, Bremen and Brunswick; all three 'Flower Wars' medals and a *Prag Spange;* a long-service medal; and a World War I *Verwundetenabzeichen.* According to Keitel himself, his gold NSDAP badge was personally granted by Hitler in April 1939. Ultimately a *Generalfeldmarschall* and Chef des Oberkommandos der Wehrmacht, Keitel was a Hitler loyalist. He was tried and found guilty by the International Military Tribunal at Nuremberg, before being executed on 16 October 1946. (Hugo Jaeger/Timepix/The LIFE Picture Collection via Getty Images)

FAR RIGHT The *Kriegsverdienstkreuz mit Schwertern, 2. Klasse,* with issue packet and ribbon. Introduced on 18 October 1939, the 126th anniversary of the battle of Leipzig, the *Kriegsverdienstkreuz* consisted of three classes: a *Ritterkreuz des Kriegsverdienstkreuz,* the *Kriegsverdienstkreuz 1. Klasse* and the *Kriegsverdienstkreuz 2. Klasse.* Awards with Swords were for combat; without Swords, non-combat.

RIGHT The reverse of the Austro-Hungarian *Kriegserinnerungsmedaille* (War Commemorative Medal) for service in World War I showing a *Stahlhelm* and the motto PRO DEO ET PATRIA ('For God and Country'). As with the *Ehrenkreuz des Weltkriegs 1914/1918,* many older soldiers in the Heer of 1939 were entitled to this award.

CAMPAIGN AWARDS

A very odd omission from the medals and badges approved in 1939 was anything approximating to a campaign medal. Instead, some specific battles were marked by awards, but in curiously piecemeal fashion. So it was that Narvik, a small but significant engagement in April–June 1940 during the campaign in Norway, was the first battle to be commemorated with an *Ärmelschild* (arm shield) – the *Narvikschild* – but no *Ärmelschilde* were awarded for any battles during the conquests of Poland, France and the Low Countries, nor for battles in North Africa and the Balkans. Similar *Ärmelschilde* were awarded for the defence of Kholm (the *Cholmschild*) and the campaign in Crimea (the *Krimschild*) in 1942, the defence of Demyansk (the *Ärmelschild Demjansk*) and the fighting in the Kuban bridgehead in 1943 (the *Ärmelschild Kuban*). A *Lapplandschild* was authorized, ,made and distributed locally on the orders of General der Gebirgstruppe Franz Böhme at the conclusion of hostilities in Norway in 1945. The *Lapplandschild* shows a map of Lapland, but does not bear a swastika.

Other *Ärmelschilde* were proposed but never worn and only four – the *Cholmschild*, the *Krimschild*, the *Ärmelschild Demjansk* and the *Ärmelschild Kuban* – appear in the price list given in the November 1944 edition of *Deutsche Uniformen-Zeitschrift*. Issue of the *Narvikschild* was officially completed in mid-1943, by which time fewer than 9,000 awards were confirmed, about 10 per cent of them posthumous. This stood in stark contrast to the 250,000 troops eligible for the *Krimschild*. Although awards of *Ärmelschilde* were limited, the actual number manufactured was significantly higher because *Ärmelschilde* could be purchased commercially and an individual might possess several.

BELOW LEFT This pre-stamped commemorative card, which also depicts the *Narvikschild*, was cancelled in Hanover on 12 January 1941 (German 'stamp day').

BELOW The *Narvikschild* was the first, and the second rarest, of the *Ärmelschilde*. Fought during April–June 1940, the battle for Narvik was a series of engagements conducted by air, sea and land which contributed significantly to the fall of Norway.

TOP RIGHT The *Cholmschild* commemorated the defence of Kholm, when a garrison led by Generalleutnant Theodor Scherer held out for three months until relieved on 5 May 1942. Only 5,500 men of the garrison received the *Cholmschild,* many of whom died in subsequent actions, and the last of the *Ärmelschild* awards was made in 1943. The stamped-metal silvered shield was designed by Polizei-Rottwachtmeister Schlimmer, one of the Kholm garrison, and Professor Richard Klein.

TOP FAR RIGHT Generalfeldmarschall Erich von Manstein, who commanded German forces at Sevastopol and the battle of the Kerch Peninsula (December 1941–May 1942), wearing the *Krimschild* in gold: just two gold examples were awarded, the other going to Ion Antonescu, military dictator of Romania (September 1940–August 1944). (ullstein bild/Getty Images)

CENTRE RIGHT The *Krimschild*, seen here on field grey backing, bore a map of the Crimea and the dates 1941–1942.

CENTRE FAR RIGHT The Demjansk shield was not authorised until April 1943, but marked the efforts of the 96,000 troops who broke out of encirclement at Demjansk a year earlier. It appears in both a silvered and a dull finish for wear on combat uniform.

BOTTOM RIGHT An officer of a *Panzerjäger* unit after surrendering to Canadian troops in the Netherlands, April 1945. His awards include the *Sturmabzeichen,* both classes of the *Eisernes Kreuz* and a *Verwundetenabzeichen* in addition to the *Ärmelschild Kuban.* (Keystone-France/Gamma-Rapho/Getty Images)

BOTTOM FAR RIGHT Generalfeldmarschall Ernst Busch (1885–1945) pictured in 1944 with *Ritterkreuz* and *Pour le Mérite* as well as clasp indicating award of the *Eisernes Kreuz* in both world wars, the *Eisernes Kreuz 1. Klasse* and the *Ärmelschild Demjansk.* Busch led armies in Poland and France as well as during the invasion of the Soviet Union, but was relieved of command on 28 June 1944 after the success of the Soviet summer offensive, Operation *Bagration.* Recalled to lead Heeresgruppe Nordwest, Busch surrendered on 4 May 1945.(Bundesarchiv, Bild 101I-088-3724-15, Foto: Thiemann)

FAR LEFT This Panzer unit commander with throat microphone and *Fernglas* wears the *Krimschild*, both classes of the *Eisernes Kreuz* and the *Panzerkampfabzeichen*.

LEFT Joseph Rettemeir (1914–97) won the *Ritterkreuz* as a *Hauptmann* in Panzer-Abteilung 5 in 1943, with Oak Leaves added in March 1944. Here he appears in Panzer uniform adorned with the *AFRIKA* cuff-title.

There would never be any general award for the war in the Soviet Union, though this might have been rectified in the event of a German victory: but there was a significant medal for the winter campaign of 1941/42, a disaster that was arguably an early step towards Germany's eventual defeat. The *Winterschlacht im Osten 1941/42* (Winter Battle in the East 1941/42) medal, conceived by graphic designer and SS-Unterscharführer Ernst Krause, depicts an eagle and swastika on a disk, surmounted by a *Stahlhelm* and grenade. The reverse shows the title of the medal, which was cheaply manufactured in zinc or non-ferrous alloy, in huge numbers and by many companies, with an estimated total number of awards of about 3 million.

It has been claimed that the ordinance instituting the *Winterschlacht im Osten 1941/42* medal specified that the red, white and black colours of the ribbon were intended to represent blood, snow and death. This is not only completely untrue but, on reflection, an extremely unlikely and demoralizing statement for any regime to have made to its own troops. What the document signed by Hitler in May 1942 actually said was that the award was in recognition of the struggle against Bolshevism and the Russian winter, within the period from 15 November 1941 to 15 April 1942. The ribbon colours were mentioned but nothing was said about what they symbolized, any elaboration being superfluous since the German national colours had previously been used on

Awarded in huge numbers, the *Winterschlacht im Osten 1941/42* medal was a symbol of endurance in the face of natural forces as well as the enemy.

other awards. Outlandish ideas regarding the ribbon colours' symbolism may have been inadvertently stoked by Joachim Preß, a journalist writing in September 1942, whose florid and possibly unwise narrative was repeated in the pages of *Deutsche Uniformen-Zeitschrift* on 15 October 1942. Preß was more nuanced than myth suggests, writing that the 'blood red ground' of the ribbon stood for brave lives moving 'inexorably to the east', the white for winter, and the black for 'remembrance and mourning' for fallen comrades. 'Blood, snow and death' is just one of several examples of the black humour which also describe the medal as the 'Frozen Meat Medal' and the *Gefrierfleischorden* ('Order of the Frozen Flesh'), or the ribbon as signifying snow and night – with the Red Army all around.

As if to underline the inconsistency of campaign awards, there were a few which were neither medals nor *Ärmelschilde*. The red *1936 Spanien 1939 Ärmelstreifen* was not an award for an individual but granted as a unit battle honour to I. Abteilung, Panzer-Lehr-Regiment and a couple of other units. The *KRETA* (Crete) title was awarded in 1942 to those who took part in the invasion of the Greek island in May–June 1941. *AFRIKA* was awarded in 1943 to those who served in North Africa for six months or more, or qualified due to illness or wounding there. *KURLAND* was approved for members of Army Group Courland surrounded by Red Army forces on the Courland Peninsula in Latvia during January–May 1945, and saw very limited use. Other *Ärmelstreifen* were proposed but never worn.

COMBAT BADGES

Combat badges were neither bravery nor campaign awards, and despite their physical similarity to the parachutists' badges for the Luftwaffe and Heer authorized in 1937, were not for proficiency either. Instead, combat badges recorded in tangible form a number of actions in which the recipient had participated, or, in certain instances, a number of enemy, or enemy machines, put out of action. The *Infanterie-Sturmabzeichen* (Infantry Assault Badge) was sanctioned by Generaloberst Walther von Brauchitsch, Oberbefehlshaber des Heeres (Commander-in-chief of the Army), on 20 December 1939, but qualification for the new award did not start until the New Year, 1940. As with subsequent Heer combat badges, it was open to officers and men alike. Qualification required participation in three combats on different days, armed

FAR LEFT The *Deutsches Schutzwall-Ehrenzeichen*, with ribbon and packet of issue. Designed by Professor Richard Klein, Director of the Munich School of Applied Arts, this medal (usually known in English as the 'West Wall Medal') was awarded to those who worked on the construction of the western fortifications 'for the protection of Germany'. Initial distribution was in 1939–41, with further production in 1944.

LEFT Obergefreiter Rudi Stelmasik fought on the Eastern Front from 1941 and in the Ardennes in 1944. His awards are the *Panzerkampfabzeichen* for 25 days of action, the *Verwundetenabzeichen* and the ribbon to the *Winterschlacht im Osten 1941/42* medal.

BELOW LEFT Observers in an Eastern Front bridgehead, 1943. Both men wear the *Infanterie-Sturmabzeichen*, and the *Unteroffizier* (left), with rudimentary mud camouflage on his *Stahlhelm*, also has a *Verwundetenabzeichen* and the *Goldenes Parteiabzeichen* (Golden Party Badge). This last was awarded to those of the first 100,000 of the NSDAP Party who boasted unbroken membership, and was formally sanctioned for wear on uniform.

BELOW A postcard sent in 1943 celebrating the *Infanterie-Sturmabzeichen* and repeating Hitler's claim that the German infantry stood above all others in performance.

with hand-held weapons; patrol actions, hand-to-hand combat and counter-attacks all counted. Award was made on recommendation of the company commander authorized by the regimental commander. Also introduced on the same day was the *Panzerkampfabzeichen* (Tank Combat Badge), designed by Wilhelm Ernst Peekhaus of Berlin. The *Panzerkampfabzeichen* was available to tank crew only and depicted a tank as its central motif, but the general criteria were similar, with the tanker having to have participated in three armoured actions to qualify.

RIGHT This veteran *Oberfeldwebel* artificer wears an old-type *Dienstrock* with marksman's lanyard, the *Eisernes Kreuz* ribbon, the *Infanterie-Sturmabzeichen*, the long-service medal and the *Deutsches Sportabzeichen* (German Sports Badge).

FAR RIGHT A young soldier wearing the *Sturmabzeichen* and black *Verwundetenabzeichen*, c.1942.

BELOW A highly decorated *Oberfeldwebel*, ranking as *Der Spiess* (a senior NCO with record-keeping responsibilities for his unit), writing a report, 1944. In addition to several medal ribbons and a *Nahkampfspange* worn over his left breast pocket, he also wears three badges for the single-handed destruction of tanks. (ullstein bild/ Getty Images)

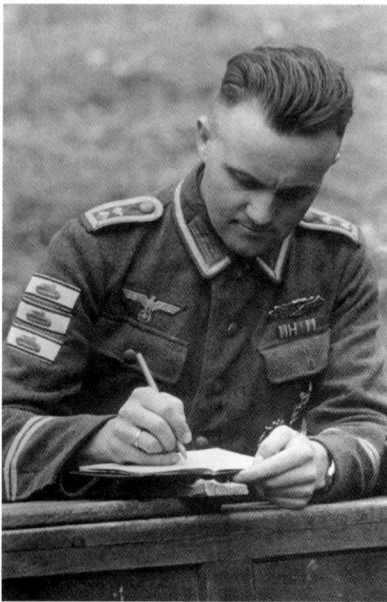

Both infantry and tank awards were tidied up by a directive of 1 June 1940 in which bronze-coloured versions were introduced. The bronze *Infanterie-Sturmabzeichen* was for motorized infantry, the bronze *Panzerkampfabzeichen* for rifle and reconnaissance units of Panzer divisions. Tank signals units could win the original silver-coloured badge. As of 1943, higher *Panzerkampfabzeichen* awards for 25, 50, 75 and 100 days in action were introduced, with these numbers shown on the lower part of the badge. Also introduced on 1 June 1940 was the *Sturmabzeichen*, usually described as the 'general assault badge' because it was available to all other troops taking part in assaults not covered by the tank or infantry badges, for example assault-artillery units. Also designed by Wilhelm Ernst Peekhaus, its motif was a crossed grenade and bayonet. In July 1941 came the *Heeres-Flakabzeichen* (Army Anti-Aircraft Badge), depicting an anti-aircraft gun. This was not easy to win as anti-aircraft gun crews and their commanders needed to bring down five enemy aircraft, higher commanders gaining the *Flakabzeichen* when half of the anti-aircraft gunners under their command became eligible.

An anti-tank award intended to mark individual valour was given the cumbersome title *Sonderabzeichen für das Niederkämpfen von Panzerkampfwagen durch Einzelkämpfer* ('Special Badge for the Single-Handed Destruction of a Tank'), but the award was often referred to as the *Panzervernichtungsabzeichen* (Tank Destruction Badge). The award was sanctioned by Hitler in March 1942, but could be given for achievements from 22 June 1941 onwards. Unlike previous badges it was a ribbon of spun aluminium, on which was mounted the black-metal tank silhouette, worn on the right upper arm. Moreover, another badge was awarded for each enemy tank destroyed, so several could be worn at the same time.

Also distinctly different from the breast badges was the *Nahkampfspange* (close-combat clasp) introduced at the end of November 1942. Taking the form of a decorative horizontal bar with eagle, swastika and crossed bayonet and stick grenade, this was to be worn 1cm above the ribbon bar. It came in three grades – bronze, silver and gold – for 15, 30 or 50 days in close combat. Those wounded required only ten, 20 or 40 days in close combat. The definition of a close-combat day included all instances in which troops were close enough to use close-combat weapons, with participation in major attacks, acting as a runner or defending an artillery fire-position all being likely examples. Troops were supposed to note such days in their *Soldbuch*, then have them authorized by a higher authority. Interestingly, award documents use the word 'brave' and Hitler presented some of the very limited number of gold *Nahkampfspangen* personally, making the award a significant decoration in its own right.

Three further combat badges from the last 18 months of the war require mention, though one was probably never worn, and the others but rarely. The first of these was the *Ballonbeobachterabzeichen* (Balloon Observers Badge), planned in 1944 but not distributed. Heer personnel were eligible for the *Bandenkampfabzeichen* (Anti-Partisan War Badge) publicized in the pages of the March 1944 edition of *Deutsche Uniformen-Zeitschrift*, though this was not primarily a Heer award. It was in three grades, representing 20, 50 and 100 days of combat. In September 1944 the new *Scharfschützenabzeichen* ('Sharpshooter' or Sniper Badge) was also shown, though an illustration of the final form was not released until October. Worn on the right forearm, this cloth badge appeared in three grades for 20, 40 or 60 kills – plain, and with silver and gold cord surround respectively. Given the brutal treatment sometimes meted out to snipers by the enemy, it is readily apparent why this badge was not worn on combat uniforms.

The *Scharfschützenabzeichen* as originally announced in the uniform press in September 1944. In the event the final version differed in detail, and was rarely if ever worn on combat uniform.

SENIOR GRADES OF THE *RITTERKREUZ* AND THE *DEUTSCHES KREUZ*

That the *Ritterkreuz* succeeded in its objectives of marking exceptional courage and providing examples for emulation is obvious. During the war, *Ritterkreuz* recipients were lauded in the German press and postcards celebrated their awards. Even into the 21st century, some surviving recipients circulated signed photographs, and most were little tainted by the acknowledged excesses of the Nazi regime which honoured them. What had not been appreciated in 1939 was that the war would go on so long, or that so many men would perform deeds deemed worthy of the *Ritterkreuz*. As the number of recipients ticked upwards and they performed new deeds, fresh ways were required to celebrate success.

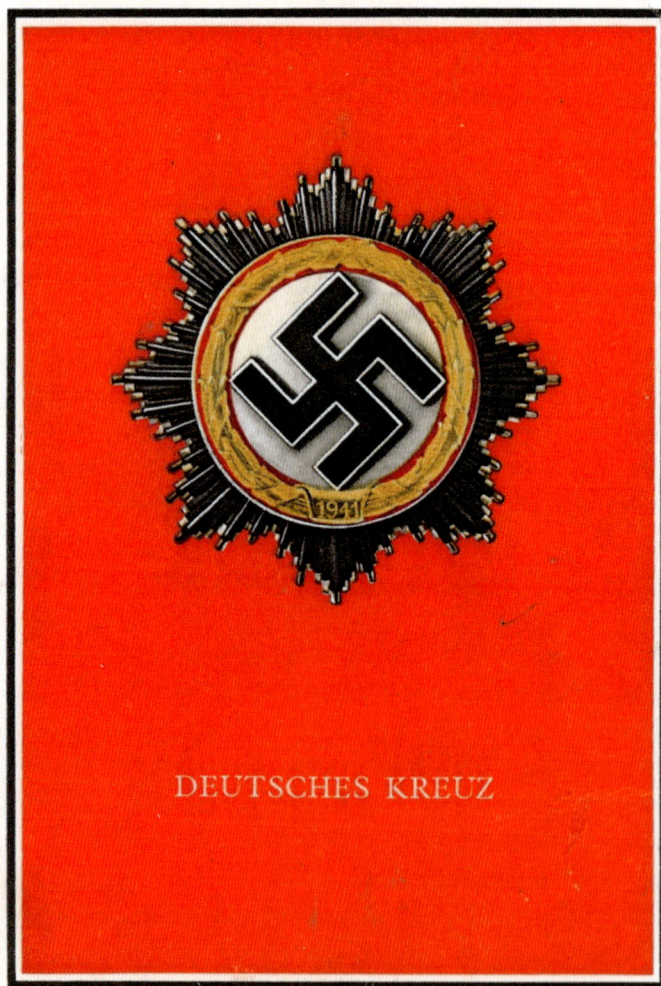

DEUTSCHES KREUZ

The *Deutsches Kreuz in Gold*. Introduced in 1941 and worn on the right breast pocket of the jacket, this decoration ranked above the *Eisernes Kreuz* but below the *Ritterkreuz*, being awarded for multiple acts of outstanding bravery or distinguished leadership. The *Deutsches Kreuz in Silber* was for outstanding non-combat achievements.

The first step came in July 1940, when Oak Leaves were added to the *Ritterkreuz* as a mark of particular distinction. First to receive them was Generalleutnant Eduard Dietl in acknowledgement of his success at Narvik. A year later, another embellishment was accorded when Swords were introduced for those whose achievements were deemed to have outstripped or repeated previous exploits. The first 159 Swords were presented by Hitler personally. A month later came Diamonds. Just 27 men would win the prize of *Eichenlaub mit Schwertern und Brillanten zum Ritterkreuz des Eisernen Kreuzes* (Knight's Cross with Oak Leaves, Swords and Diamonds), with nearly three carats of real stones added to their medal. Only one man would take this further: in a final flourish, in January 1945 Luftwaffe pilot Hans-Ulrich Rudel (1916–82) was awarded golden Oak Leaves (*Goldenes Eichenlaub mit Schwertern und Brillanten zum Ritterkreuz des Eisernen Kreuzes*). Against this singular event more than 7,000 won the *Ritterkreuz* altogether, the precise number being unclear because when the war in Europe ended on 8 May 1945, some medals were yet to be awarded and others not approved.

A further award, introduced in September 1941, was the *Deutsches Kreuz* (German Cross). This was not strictly a 'medal' as the award consisted of a breast badge shaped like an eight-pointed star and resembled the 'orders' of old, but the niche for the *Deutsches Kreuz in Gold* fell between the *Eisernes Kreuz 1. Klasse* and the *Ritterkreuz*, being intended for multiple acts of bravery or achievement in battle. The *Deutsches Kreuz in Silber* bridged a similar gap in the War Merit series, being situated between the *Kriegsverdienstkreuz 1. Klasse mit Schwerter*, and the *Ritterkreuz des Kriegsverdienstkreuzes mit Schwerter*. In the event, many more awards of the *Deutsches Kreuz in Gold* were made than of the *Deutsches Kreuz in Silber*, and the *Deutsches Kreuz in Gold* was also available in cloth for sewing to the combat uniform.

MANUFACTURE, CERTIFICATION AND PRICING

Some of the apparent mystery surrounding awards can be dispelled by an understanding of the mechanisms involved in their manufacture, presentation and wear. Unlike some nations, Germany had no overarching official mint manufacturing its many awards. Medals and badges were made by, and sourced from, private concerns, some of whom contracted with the state; but there was limited control, and awards were ordered privately by individuals from outfitters as well as being officially presented. The natural result was variations.

The Reichskanzlei (Reichs Chancellery) was aware of the problem and in 1940 issued an instruction that only licensed firms should supply. At the same time the *Leistungsgemeinschaft deutscher Ordenshersteller* (LDO, Guild of

German Orders Manufacturers), a self-regulating body, was formed. It was not until early 1941, however, that all the necessary regulations were in place and members of the LDO were given identifying numbers, effectively forcing award-holders to source additional examples from authorized companies producing to more stringent guidelines. Commercial direct sale of the *Ritterkreuz* was forbidden and it now had to be obtained only through official channels. Regulation also extended to the packaging of awards in boxes and packets. The 140 or so concerns which made up the LDO were spread about the Reich, and there were concentrations in Berlin, Munich, Dresden and Vienna. Perhaps less obvious were groups of companies in the towns of Pforzheim in Baden and Lüdenscheid in Westphalia, both of which had metalworking and jewellery traditions. Any firms committing particularly egregious breaches of regulation could have their licences withdrawn. Nevertheless, marking – particularly of cheaper pieces – does not seem to have been rigidly enforced; moreover, the authority of the LDO covered only commercial supply, not state or Heer contracts for the 'original' pieces presented.

Awards were verified by paperwork including *Soldbuch* entries, letters and medical records, but the key document was a *Besitzzeugnis* (entitlement certificate) presented to the award recipient. This is especially significant because almost all World War II German medals and awards were unnamed, and more than one example might be held by an individual. Certificates accompanying the highest awards were elaborate, and a few at least were actually signed by Hitler; many more carried his signature in facsimile. The vast majority of certificates were simple, however, and could be endorsed by relatively junior officers and officials even if they carried the legend *In Namen des Führers* ('In the name of the *Führer*'). *Verwundetenabzeichen* certificates were usually signed off by senior Heer doctors. The common form of the more basic *Besitzzeugnis* was a single sheet of heavy cream-coloured paper, essentially a pro forma with standard wording and the name of the award pre-printed. Spaces allowed for the insertion of the recipient's name and unit and the date of the award, either typed or handwritten, and the endorser's signature. Most certificates were authenticated with a small circular unit or office stamp towards the bottom left-hand corner.

The wearing of awards was subject to detailed regulations even if photographs and surviving ribbon bars show variations or mistakes. According to the rules of 1943, the Bavarian folded medal ribbon and the Austrian tri-folded ribbon were no longer allowed. In service only six classes of decoration were to be worn: permitted German decorations; war decorations of Germany's allies; NSDAP 'Honour Awards'; SA defence badges; authorized *Sportabzeichen* (sport badges); and permitted foreign orders. Other authorized awards could be worn only when the holder was not deemed to be on service.

OPPOSITE TOP Typical ribbon bars. Top left: *Eisernes Kreuz, Winterschlacht im Osten 1941/42* and Sudetenland medal with *Prag Spange*. Top right: *Kriegsverdienstkreuz 2. Klasse mit Schwertern* and long-service medal. Bottom, left to right: *Deutsches Schutzwall-Ehrenzeichen, Ehrenkreuz des Weltkriegs 1914/1918* and Sudetenland medal (first issue).

OPPOSITE BOTTOM The *Deutsches Sportabzeichen in Bronze*. The example on the left is an early issue; on the right is the later type with swastika. Both are by the same manufacturer, Wernstein of Jena: the *Deutsches Sportabzeichen* also existed in silver and gold grades with a special version for disabled competitors.

RIBBONS FOR VALOR AND SERVICE — *These ribbons are a selection of those which may be worn above the left breast pocket by German military personnel.*

1   2   3   4   5   6   7   8   9   10   11   12

1. IRON CROSS, 1914
2. IRON CROSS, 1939
3. WAR SERVICE CROSS
4. WAR SERVICE MEDAL

5. EASTERN WINTER CAMPAIGN, 1941-42
6. WAR CROSS OF HONOR (Front Line Fighter)
7. PARTY SERVICE BADGE (24 Years)
8. PARTY SERVICE BADGE (15 Years)

9. PARTY SERVICE BADGE (10 Years)
10. GERMAN SOCIAL SERVICE
11. MEDAL FOR LENGTH OF MILITARY SERVICE
12. ENTRY INTO AUSTRIA

13   14   15   16   17   18   19   20   21   22   23   24

13. ENTRY INTO SUDETENLAND
14. WESTWALL SERVICE, 1939-40
15. MEMEL RIBBON
16. OLYMPIC GAMES MEDAL

17. GERMAN MOTHER'S CROSS
18. FIREMAN'S RIBBON
19. BALTIC CROSS (1919-20 Freikorps Service)
20. A.R.P. MEDAL

21. PRUSSIAN WAR EFFORT CROSS
22. PRUSSIAN LIFE-SAVING MEDAL
23. SILESIAN EAGLE (1919-20 Fighting vs. Poland)
24. BADEN MILITARY SERVICE CROSS

25   26   27   28   29   30   31   32   33   34   35   36

25. BAVARIAN MILITARY SERVICE CROSS
26. KING LUDWIG CROSS
27. PRINCE REGENT LUITPOLD MEDAL
28. BAVARIAN MILITARY SERVICE BADGE

29. BAVARIAN MEDAL OF VALOR
30. WURTTEMBERG MILITARY SERVICE CROSS
31. AUSTRIAN MEDAL OF VALOR
32. KARL TROOP CROSS

33. AUSTRIAN WAR SERVICE MEDAL
34. TIROL SERVICE MEDAL
35. HAMBURG HANSA WAR CROSS
36. BREMEN HANSA WAR CROSS

37   38   39   40   41   42   43   44   45   46   47   48

37. LUBECK HANSA WAR CROSS
38. BULGARIAN MEDAL OF VALOR
39. BULGARIAN WAR SERVICE MEDAL
40. HUNGARIAN WAR SERVICE (Horthy)

41. CROATIAN MEDAL OF VALOR
42. SLOVAKIAN MEDAL OF VALOR
43. AFRICA RIBBON
44. ITALIAN MEDAL OF VALOR

45. ITALIAN SERVICE MEDAL
46. FINNISH SERVICE MEDAL
47. FINNISH LIBERATION CROSS I CLASS
48. FINNISH LIBERATION CROSS II CLASS

49   50   51   52   53   54   55   56   57   58   59   60

49. FINNISH LIBERATION CROSS III CLASS
50. SPANISH MILITARY MEDAL OF VALOR
51. SPANISH RED MILITARY SERVICE CROSS
52. SPANISH WHITE MILITARY SERVICE CROSS

53. SPANISH CAMPAIGN MEDAL
54. SPANISH WOUND MEDAL
55. SPANISH SURVIVORS RIBBON
56. SPANISH COMMUNIST RIBBON

57. RUMANIAN MEDAL OF VALOR AND LOYALTY
58. RUMANIAN FAITHFUL SERVICE CROSS (Peace)
59. RUMANIAN MEDAL OF VALOR
60. RUMANIAN ORDER OF THE CROWN (Post 1932)

61   62   63   64   65   66   67   68   69   70   71   72

61. RUMANIAN ORDER OF THE CROWN (Pre-1932)
62. RUMANIAN FAITHFUL SERVICE CROSS (War)
63. RUMANIAN MEDICAL SERVICE CROSS
64. RUMANIAN FAITHFUL SERVICE MEDAL (War)
65. RUMANIAN ANTI-COMMUNIST SERVICE

66. CROSS OF QUEEN MARIE OF RUMANIA
67. RUMANIAN FLIERS' MEDAL OF VALOR
68. RUMANIAN FLIERS' ORDER OF VALOR
69. STAR OF RUMANIA

70. BRONZE CROSS OF VALOR AND SERVICE
    (For Eastern Volunteers)
71. SILVER CROSS OF VALOR AND SERVICE
    (For Eastern Volunteers)
72. GOLD CROSS OF VALOR AND SERVICE
    (For Eastern Volunteers)

For the neck, the highest war orders took precedence, being worn above peace orders. Decorations without ribbons, such as the *Eisernes Kreuz 1. Klasse*, were arranged on the breast so that war decorations were above wound badges, with other awards and NSDAP Party decorations below and *Sportabzeichen* at the lowest point. For medals worn on ribbons, or represented by ribbons on a bar above the left breast, the order of seniority was military decorations first and closest to the centre of the chest. These were followed by orders, the old state awards, and next the commemorative awards of World War I. These last were the *Ehrenkreuz des Weltkriegs 1914/1918*, the Austrian *Kriegserinnerungsmedaille* and then – for the extremely elderly – any commemoratives for Otto von Bismarck's 19th-century campaigns. Colonial, life-saving and long-service medals were then followed by other state and NSDAP decorations, the 'Flower Wars' medals, the *Deutsches Schutzwall-Ehrenzeichen*, Olympic and Red Cross awards. Last were foreign orders and decorations, arranged in the chronological order they were received.

A few decorations were represented by a longer piece of ribbon when the actual medals were not worn. These included the *Blutorden*, the *Eisernes Kreuz*, the *Kriegsverdienstkreuz* and the *Winterschlacht im Osten 1941/42* medal, all of

OPPOSITE A very large number of medals were worn by German soldiers. The US Army's TM-E 30-451 *Handbook on German Military Forces*, shows the ribbons of 72 of them, awarded not only by Germany and the old German states, but by nations as diverse as Finland, Bulgaria, Italy, Romania, Spain and Croatia.

BELOW LEFT A typical *Winterschlacht im Osten 1941/42* medal citation, here to Oberfeldwebel Willi Raabe.

BELOW *Verwundetenabzeichen* citation of Gefreiter Markus Passegger, II. Bataillon, Infanterie-Regiment 468, January 1942, endorsed by his doctor at Michelstadt military hospital.

IM NAMEN DES FÜHRERS
UND
OBERSTEN BEFEHLSHABERS
DER WEHRMACHT

IST DEM

Oberfeldwebel

Willi R a a b e

AM 18. August 1942

DIE MEDAILLE
WINTERSCHLACHT IM OSTEN
1941/42
(OSTMEDAILLE)
VERLIEHEN WORDEN.

FÜR DIE RICHTIGKEIT:

Metz, den 15. Juli 1943   Major u. Inspektion-Chef

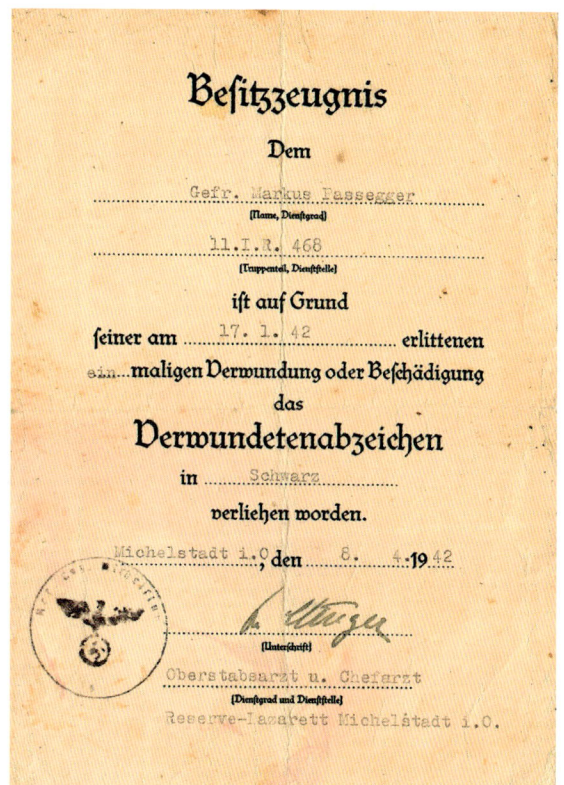

Besitzzeugnis

Dem

Gefr. Markus Passegger
[Name, Dienstgrad]

11.I.R. 468
[Truppenteil, Dienststelle]

ist auf Grund

seiner am 17. 1. 42 erlittenen

ein...maligen Verwundung oder Beschädigung

das

Verwundetenabzeichen

in Schwarz

verliehen worden.

Michelstadt i.O., den 8. 4. 19 42

[Unterschrift]

Oberstabsarzt u. Chefarzt
[Dienstgrad und Dienststelle]

Reserve-Lazarett Michelstadt i.O.

which could be attached to the second buttonhole of a uniform jacket. The regulation order of wear made the *Ritterkreuz* and *Eisernes Kreuz* family of decorations particularly apparent, while the large swastika badge of the *Deutsches Kreuz* stood out bold and solitary on the right breast pocket.

Orders and medals purchased commercially were not expensive. According to the November 1944 edition of *Deutsche Uniformen-Zeitschrift*, the official price of the 1939 *Eisernes Kreuz 1. Klasse*, boxed with a pin back, was just RM 3,64 wholesale, with RM 1,61 added for the retail customer. A black *Verwundetenabzeichen* in a packet was RM 0,45 wholesale, with a mark-up of a further RM 0,25 for retail, the combined cost being similar to the official price of a loaf of bread or an hour's pay for a factory worker. Combat badges varied in price according to whether they were silvered and polished, zinc finished or 'bronze coloured': so it was that the *Infanterie-Sturmabzeichen*, tank and *Sturmabzeichen*, silvered and in packets, each cost RM 1,85 retail. The *Infanterie-Sturmabzeichen* and *Panzerkampfabzeichen* in bronze colour were RM 1,25 retail in packets. *Ärmelschilde* were also inexpensive, though the price varied according to whether the customer required a back plate and cloth backing. In all instances the full retail price with both cloth and plate, in a packet, was RM 1,10. Medal ribbons were sold retail in 25cm and 1m lengths, the shortest and narrowest piece being RM 0,22 retail; but wholesale customers and uniform outfitters could buy ribbon in bulk lengths of anything up to 10,000m, for which the discount was 53 per cent.

Generalleutnant Karl Mauss (1898–1959) is pictured in winter uniform near Danzig, 1945. A dentist by profession, Mauss served in both world wars, winning the *Eisernes Kreuz* in both classes during World War I. By the latter part of World War II he had risen to command 7. Panzer-Division, and by early 1945 was one of a select few to be awarded the *Ritterkreuz mit Eichenlaub, Schwertern und Brillanten*. Despite sustaining very serious wounds in February 1945, he survived the war to return to dentistry. (Bundesarchiv, Bild 183-2006-0822-500, Foto: Finke)

LEFT An *Unteroffizier Anwärter* (NCO candidate) in a *Schützen* (rifle) regiment, his unit and status being shown by the 'S' and number, and the braid at the base of his *Schulterklappe*. Also clearly shown is the marksman's lanyard. This example is the design made prior to 1939, bearing a Heer eagle on a shield; new types featuring crossed swords or tanks were awarded during the war, the latter being for armoured units. There were four grades of the award, a small acorn being added to the cord for each higher grade. Artillery units added a small stylized artillery shell in the same manner.

BELOW LEFT The marksman's lanyard worn during the latter part of the war, being worn by a recipient of the *Infanterie-Sturmabzeichen*. (Roger Viollet/ Getty Images)

BELOW An aspirant officer wearing the War Service Cross ribbon, the *SA Wehrabzeichen* and a Hitlerjugend proficiency badge.

Wedding couple at Plauen, 1940.
The infantry officer wears the
optional *Geschmückte Feldbluse*
with *Feldbinde*, both classes of the
Eisernes Kreuz, an *Infanterie-
Sturmabzeichen* and other awards.

An *Oberleutnant* wearing an
Eisernes Kreuz ribbon, *Krimschild*,
Sturmabzeichen,
Verwundetenabzeichen and
Deutsches Sportabzeichen.

SELECT
BIBLIOGRAPHY

PRIMARY SOURCES

Anonymous, *Deutsche Uniformen* (Leipzig: Moritz Ruhl, 1940).

Robert Bauer, *Zellewolle Siegt* (Leipzig: Wilhelm Goldmann, 1941).

Werner von Bergen, *German Army 'Einheitstuch' Standard Cloth Field Gray*, Combined Intelligence Objectives Sub Committee Report 22, Textiles (SHAEF, June 1945).

Heinrich Doehle, *Die Auszeichen Des Großdeutsches Reichs* (Berlin: Erdender, 1943).

Hans-Joachim Feyerabend, *Unteroffizierthemen, Ein Handbuch* (Berlin: Mittler, 1943).

Heereskleiderkasse, *Preisliste der Heereskleiderkasse* (Berlin: Heereskleiderkasse, 1939).

Fritz Hiddermann, *Uniform-Maßschneidern für die Wehrmacht* (Berlin: B.G. Teubner, 1938).

Oberkommando des Heeres, *Panzerabwehr Aller Waffen*, Hdv 469/4, (Berlin: OKH, 1942).

Oberkommando des Heeres, *Taschenbuch Für den Winterkrieg* (Berlin: Erich Zander, 1942).

Oberkommando des Heeres, *Ausbildungsvorschrift für die Infanterie*, Hdv 130/2a (Berlin: OKH, 1941).

Wilhelm Reibert, *Der Dienstunterricht im Heere* (Berlin: Mittler, editions of 1940 and 1942).

Der Schneidermeister (1935–55).

Uniformen-Markt, *Uniformen-Markt: Fachzeitung der Gesamten Uniform.* Journal of the uniform trade, Dietrich, Berlin, 1934–42 (incorporated with *Deutsche Uniformen-Zeitschrift* and *Schwert und Spaten*, 1943–45).

US Field Information Agency, *General Developments in the German Staple Fibre Industry*, Report 50 (Washington, DC: Office of the Director of Intelligence, 1945).

US War Department, *Handbook on German Army Identification* (Washington, DC: US War Department, 1943).

US War Department, *Handbook on German Military Forces* (Washington, DC: US War Department, 1945).

Hauptmann A. Weber, *Unterrichtsbuch für Soldaten* (Berlin: Offene Worte, 1938).

Graf von E.-J. Westarp, *Oertzenscher. Taschenkalender Für die Offiziere des Heeres* (Grimmen: Waberg, 1940).

Major Bodo Zimmermann, *Infanteriedienst* (Berlin: Offene Worte, 1940).

Personal papers of Rudolf Dickhöfer, Hans and Franz Eichler, Georg Eiseler, Heinz Felske, Walter Gelhard, Kurt Liebeneiner, Felix Mohr, Ludwig Pöltl, the Schäfer family, Erwin Schwary, Jakob Theis and Franz Wirtz.

SECONDARY SOURCES

John R. Angolia, *For Führer and Fatherland: Military Awards of the Third Reich* (San Jose, CA: Bender, 1976).

John R. Angolia & Adolf Schlicht, *Uniforms and Traditions of The German Army 1933–1945*, three volumes (San Jose, CA: Bender, 1984–87).

Ludwig Baer, *Die Geschichte des Deutsches Stahlhelms* (Eichborn: privately published, 1977).

Ricardo R. Cardona & Antonio G. Sanchez, *German Army Uniforms* (Madrid: Accion, 2002).

Brian L. Davis, *Flags of the Third Reich* (Oxford: Osprey, 2000).

Brian L. Davis, *German Army Uniforms and Insignia 1933–1945*, second edition (London: Military Book Society, 1973).

Walther-Peer Fellgiebel, *Die Träger des Ritterkreuzes des Eisernen Kreuzes* (Wölfersheim-Berstadt: Podzun-Pallas, 2000).

Hans Dieter Götz, *German Military Rifles and Machine Pistols 1871–1945* (West Chester, PA: Schiffer, 1990).

Jill Halcomb & Wilhelm P.B.R. Saris, *Headgear of Hitler's Germany* (San Jose, CA: Bender, 1989).

Hans-Dieter Handrich, *Sturmgewehr!* (Coburg: Collector Grade, 2004).

Jörg M. Hormann, *Uniforms of the Panzer Troops* (West Chester, PA: Schiffer, 1989).

Jürgen Kraus, *Stahlhelme vom Ersten Weltkrieg bis zur Gegenwart* (Ingolstadt: Bayerisches Armeemuseum, 1984).

W. Krawczyk & B. Jansen, *The German Mountain Soldier of World War II* (Marlborough: Crowood, 2009).

Charles Lemons, *A Listing of World War II German Army Technical Manuals and Booklets* (privately published, 2011).

Daniel D. Musgrave, *German Machineguns*, revised edition (Alexandria, VA: Ironside International, 1992).

Werner Palinckx, *Camouflage Uniforms of the German Wehrmacht* (Atglen, PA: Schiffer, 2002).

Branislav Radovic, *German Steel Helmets of the Second World War*, two volumes (Atglen, PA: Schiffer, 2002).

Agustin Satz, *Deutsche Soldaten* (Philadelphia, PA: Casemate, 2008).

Albert Seaton, *The German Army 1933–1945* (New York, NY: St Martin's, 1982).

Peter R. Senich, *The German Assault Rifle 1935–1945* (Boulder, CO: Paladin, 1987).

John Walter, *German Military Letter Codes* (Hove: SARP, 1996).

John Walter, *The Luger Book* (London: Arms & Armour, 1986).

W. Darrin Weaver, *Kunststoffe: A Collector's Guide to German World War II Plastics and their Markings* (Atglen, PA: Schiffer, 2008).

Gordon Williamson, *The Iron Cross 1813–1957* (Denison: Reddick, 1994).

INDEX

References to images are in **bold**.

1936 Spanien 1939 Ärmelstreifen 234

AFRIKA medal 234
aluminium 67
ammunition pouches (*Patronentaschen*)
    78, 81, 82, **130**, **164**, **167**
annexations 222–23
Anschluss 221, 222, 223
anti-gas equipment 100, **101–2**, 103
Anti-Partisan War Badge
    (*Bandenkampfabzeichen*) 237
arm badge (*Ärmelabzeichen*) **8**, **198**
arm-of-service colours (*Waffenfarben*) 7,
    12–13, 16, 50–51, 186
arm shields (*Ärmelschilde*) 231, **232**
Armed Forces Long Service Award
    (*Wehrmacht-Dienstauszeichnung*) 222
Army Anti-Aircraft Badge (*Heeres-
    Flakabzeichen*) 236
Army chaplains (*Heeresgeistliche*) 30–31
Army clothing depots
    (*Heeresbekleidungsamt*) 28

Army clothing outlet (*Heereskleiderkasse*)
    24–25
Army Weapons Office (*Heereswaffenamt*)
    134
assault kit (*Sturmgepäck*) 78, 82
assault pistol (*Sturmpistole*) 149
Aulbach, Otto 27
Austria **8**, 33, **46**, 222, 223
    and headgear 64; and medals 221,
        229, 243; and weaponry 138
auxiliaries *see* women
awards *see* medals

backpacks (*Tornister*) 78, **80**, 81–82,
    83, 84, **85–86**, 87, **215**
badges **34–35**, 234–37
    and headgear 52, 53, 54, 67
Bäke, Oblt Franz **59**
Balkans 191, 231
Balloon Observers Badge
    (*Ballonbeobachterabzeichen*) 237
Bath and Wagawa 72

battle pistol (*Kampfpistole*) 149
Bayerlein, Genlt Fritz **226**
bayonets (*Seitengewehre*) 150, **151**
Beer Hall *Putsch* (1923) 220
belts 19, 21, **24**, 25, 29, **31**, **34**
    and brocade (*Feldbinde*) 26; and
        changes 42
Berlin-Karlsruher Industrie-Werke
    (BKIW) 132
bicycle troops **208**
binoculars **217**
blankets 81
blood group (*Blutgruppe*) **111**, 117
'Blood Order' (*Blutorden*) 220
Blue Max (*Pour le Mérite*) 220, 221
body apron 212
Böhme, Gen Franz 231
bombs 145–46, 147–48, 149
books 122
boots *see* footwear
Boss, Hugo 21–22
Brauchitsch, Gen Walther von **199**,
    234
bread bag (*Brotbeutel*) **76**, 78, **94**, 111,
    115
British Army 60, 72, 128
'brown shirts' 60
buglers (*Hornist*) **9**
Busch, GenFM Ernst **232**
butter container (*Fettbüchse*) **76**, 87,
    111

camouflage 40, 42–43, **95**, **189**,
    209–10, **211**, 212
    and mountain troops 196–97; and
        snow **200**; and steel helmets 67,
        68, 70–71; and winter **204–6**
cardigans (*Unterjacke*) 46
Carius, Lt Otto **26**
Carl Walther Waffenfabrik 134
Casberg, Paul **7**
Caucasus **195**
Chemical-Technical Reichs Institute for
    Defence Technology and Materials
    Research Berlin 72
China 65

climbing kit 198
close-combat clasp (*Nahkampfspange*)
    237
close-combat knives (*Nahkampfmesser*)
    154
clothing bag (*Bekleidungssack*) 78, **79**,
    80
coats *see* greatcoat
cockades (*Kokarden*) 50, **51**, 52, 53, 54,
    58
collars 19, 33, **34**, 35, **43**, 45
colours (*Fahnen*) 7, 16, 18–19, 33
    and issue clothing 45; and medals
        233–34; and motorized uniforms
        190–91; and peaked cap 50; and
        steel helmet 62–64, 68, 70–71; and
        tank jacket 186
    see also arm-of-service colours;
        camouflage
combat badges 234–37
combat engineers (*Pioniere*) **178**, **179**,
    216
combat pack (*Gefechtsgepäck*) 84, **85**,
    87, 92, **96**
cord chevron (*Soutache*) 54, **55**, 56, 61
cowhide 84
Crete 234
Crimea 231, **232**, **233**
cuff decorations (*Ärmelstreifen*) **11**, **23**,
    43, 192–93
currency **112**, 122
Czechoslovakia 128, 132, 138, 165,
    222

Death's head (*Totenkopf*) 52, 186, 189
decontamination 103
Demyansk 231, **232**
Dickhöfer, Rudolph **113**
Dienstrock see service tunic
Dietl, Genob Eduard **225**, 239
Dietrich, Otto 13
Doehle, Dr Heinrich 220
Drei Unteroffiziere ('Three NCOs')
    (film) **10**
dress uniform (*Waffenrock*) **10**, 16, **22**,
    23, 26–27, 29, **36**, **47**

drill jacket (*Drilljacke*) 23, **44**, 45, **184**

drill trousers (*Drillichhose*) **44**, 45

drill uniform (*Drillichanzug*) 16

Dutch Army 60

E. Reitz Uniformwerke 28

eagles 7–8, 52–53
  and belt-buckle **87**; and Iron Cross 225; and mountain cap 58; and Panzer beret 75; and peaked cap 50, 52, 53, 54; and steel helmet 63–64, 67; and tropical helmet 60; and women 213

'Eastern Dishes in the German Style' (*Östliche Speisen nach Deutscher Art*) 110

Eastern Front 65, **72**, 108, 128
  and weaponry 142, 143, 181

edged weapons *see* weaponry

'egg' grenade (*Eiergranate*) 145–46, **148**

Eichert, Robert **225**

Eichler, Franz **113**

Eisenhüttenwerke Thale 66, 67

Emaillierwerke Fulda 66

entitlement certificate (*Besitzzeugnis*) 241

Erel fibre helmet 75

Erfurter Maschinenfabrik (Erma) 140

Esiele, Georg **113**

eyewear **114**

Ezell, E.C. 134

Fabbrica d'Armi Pietro Beretta 138

Feldbluse see field blouse

Felske, Ida **113**

field blouse (*Feldbluse*) **14**, 16, 18, 19, **20**, 21, 22–23, **25**, 26
  and 1944; 40, **41**, **42**, 43; and changes 31, **32**, 33, **34**, 35, **47**; and quality 35–36, 38–40; and tropical 192–93; and women 216

field cap (*Feldmütze*) 50, 52, 54, **55**, 56
  and tropical 59, 60–61; and universal (*Einheitsfeldmütze*) 59–60

field uniform (*Feldanzug*) 16, 18, 19, 21–22, 29, **31**, **47**; and changes 33, **36**
  and wool 44–45

fighting knives (*Kampfmesser*) 150, 154

first-aid kit (*Verbandtasche*) **197**

flags 7–8, **11**

'Flower Wars' (*Blumenkriege*) medal **221**, 222–23, 243

folding spade (*Klappspaten*) **94**, 95

food 104, 108, **109**, 110–11, 115

footwear 46–47, **160**
  and boots 19, 80; and mountain troops 196, 197–98; and tank uniforms 188; and tropical uniform 193; and winter 199, **201**, **203**

footwrappings (*Fußlappen*) 47

France 108, 171, 231

Freikorps (volunteer units) 8

French Army 60, 72, 138

Fritsch, Genmaj Werner Freiherr von **8**, **44**, 64

Fry, Professor 72

fuel tablets (*Esbit Kocher*) 115

fur cap (*Pelzmützen*) 56, **57**

fur coats (*Pelzmantel*) 199

F.W. Quist Esslingen 66

gaiters (*Gamaschen*) 42, **79**

games **118**, 123

gas cape/sheet (*Gasplane*) 103

gas masks (*Gasmaske*) 100, **101–2**, 103, **191**

gauntlets **205**

Gebirgsjäger see mountain troops

Geipel, Berthold 140

Gelhard, Walter **47**

general assault badge (*Sturmabzeichen*) 236

Genschow, Fritz **10**

German Army *see* Heer

German Cross (*Deutsches Kreuz*) **238**, 239

gloves 46

Golden Party Badge (*Goldenes Parteiabzeichen*) **235**
gorgets (*Ringkragen*) **8**, **10**, **34**
'Goulash Cannon, The' (*Die Gulaschkanone*) 110
grades 23
greatcoat (*Mäntel*) 24, 78, 81, 202
    and motorcyclists (*Kradmantel*) 190; and rucksacks 88; and tropical (*Tropen Mantel*) 194; and winter 199
grenades 145–49
Guderian, Gen Heinz **214**

Halder, Genob Franz 201
Handbook on German Military Forces 208, 209, **242**
Hänsel, Dr 72
head cowl (*Kopfhaube*) 56
head protection (*Kopfschütze*) 46, 56, 58
Heer 6–7, 40
    and medals 222, 226–27; and officials (*Beamten*) **25**; and senior privates (*Gefreiter*) 19, **22**; and senior staff private (*Stabsgefrieter*) **36**; and staff sergeant (*Feldwebel*) **20**
    see also mountain troops; ranks
Heer (units):
    Deutsches Afrikakorps **48**, 61, **190**, 192–93; 44. Reichsgrenadier-Dvn *Hoch-und Deutschmeister* **8**; 97. Jäger-Dvn **131**; *Großdeutschland* Dvn **138**, **140**, **211**; Infanterie-Rgt 24 **134**; Infanterie-Rgt 67 **163**; Infanterie-Rgt 348 **20**; Panzer-Rgt 3 **187**; Weiner Infanterie-Rgt 15 **46**; Grenadier-Ersatz-Btn 414 104; Landesschützen-Btn 740 **51**
Heinrich Krieghoff & Sohn Suhl 132
helmet band (*Helmband*) 71, **73**
Himmler, Heinrich 71
Hindenburg, Paul von 50, 220
Hitchins, Capt 174, 181
Hitler, Adolf 7, 108, 202, 228

and medals 220, 224, 226, 233, 237, 239, 241
Hitler Youth (*Hitlerjugend*) 7, **11**, **245**
Honour Cross (*Ehrenkreuz*) **17**, 220, **221**
horses **191**, **208**

ice axes 197
identification tab (*Erkennungsmarke*) **111**, 117, 120
IG Farben 19, 36
Imperial German Army 6, 52, 132
Infantry Assault Badge (*Infanterie-Sturmabzeichen*) **218**, 234–35, **236**, 244
insignia 16, **36**, 40, **41**, 45
    and camouflage **207**; and rank (*Dienstgradabzeichen*) **21**, **22**; and tank jacket 186; and tropical uniform 192; and women 216
    see also badges; eagles; oak-leaf wreath; swastikas
Iron Cross (*Eisernes Kreuz*) 220, 221, 224–25, **227**, **229**, **232**, **240**
    and ribbons 243–44, **246**
issue clothing 44–47, **121**
Italy 70, 138, 193

Keitel, Gen Wilhelm **230**
Kholm 231, **232**
kitchens **104**, 110–11
Klein, Richard 223
Knesebeck, Amelie Banfield von dem 72
Knight's Cross of the Iron Cross (*Ritterkreuz des Eisernen Kreuzes*) **57**, **59**, 225–27, **232**, **233**, 238–39
Knight's Cross of the War Merit Cross (*Ritterkreuz des Kriegsverdienstkreuzes*) 228
Konopka, Maj Gerhard **138**
Krause, Ernst 233
KRETA medal 234
Kriegsmarine (German Navy) 6, 40, 222, 226

Kuban 231, **232**
KURLAND medal 234

Landemarck medal (*Langemarck-Kreuz*)
  220
Langweiler, Dr Heinrich 174
large medal bar (*große Ordenschnalle*)
  222
Latvia 234
LDO (Guild of German Orders
  Manufacturers) 239, 241
leisure items **118**, 122–23
Leven, Hugo 72
Liebeneiner, Oblt Kurt **26**, 27, 104,
  113
Lithuania 222
Low Countries 231
Lubstein, Robert 75
Luftwaffe (German Air Force) 6, 40,
  222, 226
Luger, Georg 132

machine-gunners **69**, **73**, **96**
Manstein, GenFM Erich von **232**
maps **116**
marksman's lanyard **245**
Martin, Maj 174, 181
materials 24, 35–36, 38–40, 46, 51–52
  and bags 78, 80, 81, 84
Mauss, Genlt Karl **244**
Medal to Commemorate 9 November
  1923 (*Medaille zur Erinnerung an den
  9. November 1923*) 220
medals 7, 220–28, **245**
  and campaigns 231, **232**, 233–34;
    and manufacture 239, 241,
    243–44; and senior grades 238–39
  see also badges
medics **198**
Memel 221–22, 223, 224
mess tin (*Kochgeschirr*) 78, 81, 84, **94**,
  96, **105**
metal backpack carriers (*Essenbehälter*)
  111
Metallwarenfabrik Spreewerke Spandau
  134

Metzger, Herman **21**
military administration **112**
military bands (*Musikkorps*) **10**
Military Merit Order
  (*Militärverdienstorden*) 221
Military Order of Maria Theresa
  (*Militär-Maria-Theresien-Orden*) 221
Military Order of Max Joseph (*Militär-
  Max-Joseph-Orden*) 221
mines 182, **183**
Mohr, Felix 23
motorcyclists 189–91
mountain cap (*Bergmütze*) 54, 56,
  58–59
mountain troops (*Gebirgsjäger*) 16, 46,
  53, 58, 88, 194–98
Mrousek, S Sgt Ewald **227**
Mühlenbeck, Wilhelm **112**

Narvik (*Narvikschild*) 231
Nazi Party 6–7, 8, 220–23
NCOs **8**, 19, 26, **138**
Neckermann, Joseph 202
Netherlands, the 108
nets **69**, 71, **72**, 212
nightwear 25, 47
Nitpolit bomb 149
North Africa 60, 70, 71, 92, 231
  and medals 234; and tropical
  uniforms 191, 192–94; and
  weaponry 146
Norway 87–88, 138, 231, 239

oak-leaf wreath 26, **35**, 50, 52, 54, 75
  and Iron Cross 225
officers' dress 24–27
open collars 33, 35
Operation *Barbarossa* (1941) 108, 110,
  162
overcoats (*Übermäntel*) 199

Panzer beret (*Schutzmütze*) **74**, 75
parade helmets 74–75
pay book (*Soldbuch*) 44, 45–46, 47,
  120
peaked cap (*Schirmmütze*) **25**, 50–54

Peekhaus, Wilhelm Ernst 236
personal equipment 78, **79**, 80–82, **83**, 84, **85–86**, 87, **94**
  and anti-gas 100, **101–2**, 103; and digging tools 93, **94**, 95, **97**; and food and drink 104, **105–7**, 108, **109**, 110–11, 115; and pocket items **112**, **116**, 117, **118**, 120, 122–23; and rucksacks 87–88, **89–90**, 91–92; and tents **96**, 99
photography 123
Pocket Book for Winter Warfare (*Taschenbuch Für Den Winterkrieg*) 202
pocket calendar (*Taschenkalendar*) 29, 31, 80, 81
poison gas 100
Poland 138, 140, 224, 231
postal system (*Feldpost*) 123
Prechel, Richard 23
Preß, Joachim 234
prisoners of war (POWs) 42, 110
Prussia 6, **11**, 220, 221
pullovers (*Schlupfjacke*) 46
pyjamas 25, 27, 47

radio **214**
ranks 16, **21**, 22, **24**, 25, 26, **35**
  and order of dress 29–30
rayon 35–36, 38, 46, 52
RB code numbers (*Reichsbetriebsnummer*) 28
Red Army 142
Reibert, Wilhelm: *Dienstunterricht im Heere, Der* ('Service Instruction in the Army') 29
Reichsheer (National Army) 6, 220
Reitz, Erich 28
Rettemeir, Joseph **233**
Rheinmetall-Borsig 158, 162
ribbons 243–44, **246**
riding breeches (*Reithose*) **43**
riding jackets (*Reitjacken*) **44**
rifle-cleaning kit **76**
Rommel, GenFM Erwin **226**
rucksacks 87–88, **89–90**, 91–92

Rudel, Hans-Ulrich 239
Russia *see* Soviet Union

sabres (*Säbel*) 150, 152–54
Sächsische Emaillier-und Stanzwerke Lauter 66
saddle bags **191**
Schäfer, Edward **113**
Schäfer, Konrad **113**
Schick, Johann 71
Schielicke, Richard: 'Meatless and Reduced-meat Field-kitchen Dishes' 110
Schmidt, Franz 72
Schumm, Erich 115
Schutzstaffel (SS) 66
seamstresses 22
service cap (*Dienst-mütze*) 50
service shirt (*Diensthemd*) 25
service tunic (*Dienstrock*) 16, **17**, 40
shelter-quarter (*Zeltbahn*) 78, 81, 84, **94**, **96**, **98**
  and camouflage **95**, 99, 209; and rucksacks 88, **89–90**, 91
shirts 45, **79**; *see also* field blouse
shorts (*Kurze Hose*) 193
shoulder boards (*Schulterstücke*) **21**, 25, 26, **30**
shoulder straps (*Schulterklappen*) 16, **17**, 19, **20**
  and 1944 40, **42**
  and ranks **38**, **39**, **46**
  and tank jacket 186
signallers **214–15**
Simson & Co Suhl 132
sizings 28–29, 46, 65
skin-decontamination tablets (*Losantin*) 103
skis 198, **201**
small arms *see* weaponry
small entrenching tool (*kleines Schanzzeug*) 93, 95
smocks **189**, 196–97, 209–10
Smolensk **170**
Sniper ('Sharpshooter') Badge (*Scharfshützenabzeichen*) 237

snipers **126**, **131**
socks 46–47, 193
Solingen 150, 154
songbooks (*Liederbuchen*) **118**, 122
Soviet Union 42, 54, 56, 110,
201–2
and medals 233–34; and weaponry
138, 162; *see also* Eastern Front
Spanish Civil War (1936–39) 140, 158,
223, 228
Special Badge for the Single-Handed
Destruction of a Tank
(*Sonderabzeichen für das
Niederkämpfen von Panzerkampfwagen
durch Einzelkämpfer*) 237
special clothing:
and camouflage 209–10, **211**, 212;
motorized uniforms 189–91; and
mountain uniforms 194–98; tank
uniforms **155**, 186, **187**, 188–89;
tropical uniforms **190**, 191–94;
and winter 199, **200**, 201–2,
203–6, 207–9
special weapons *see* weaponry
sports badges (*Deutsches Sportabzeichen*)
240, 241, 243
sports kit **217**
Stalin, Joseph 110
Stalingrad **94**, **161**, 208
standards (*Standarten*) 7
Stange, Louis 158
steel helmets (*Stahhelm*) **9**, **16**, **18**,
62–68, **69**, 70–72, **73**, 74
Stelmasik, Ob Rudi **235**
stick hand grenade (*Steilhandgranate*)
145–46
Sudetenland 222, 223, **240**
support straps (*Koppeltragegestell mit
Hilfestragerriemen*) 82, **83**, 84, 91,
119
support weapons *see* weaponry
Süweda company 27
swastikas 7, 8, **87**
and headgear 50, 54, 58, 60, 63–64,
75; and Iron Cross 224–25; and
medals **240**, 244

tailors 22
Tank Combat Badge
(*Panzerkampfabzeichen*) 235, 236
tanks 75, 103, 149–50, **155**, 176, **178**
and badges 235, 236–37
Tiger I **188**
tents **96**, 99
Theis, Jakob **113**
torches **79**
tropical headgear **48**, 59, 60–61
Tropical Institute (*Tropeninstitut*) 191
trousers (*Hose*) 16, 19, **38**, 40, 42
and mountain uniform (*Berghose*)
195; and tank uniforms 188; and
tropical uniform 193; and winter
206
Tunisia **194**

underpants (*Unterhose*) 25, 47
uniform trade 8, 13, 22, **25**, 27–18
Uniformen-Markt (journal) 13, 22
uniforms 16–24, 25–27, 40–44
and changes 31–40; and markings
27–29; and orders of dress 29–31;
and women 212–13, 216
universal cap (*Einheitsmütze*) 50
universal cloth (*Einheitstuch*) 40, 44
US Army 120, 128
Handbook on German Military Forces
208, 209, **242**

Vereinigte Deutsche Nickelwerke
Schwerte 66
Vereinigte Glanzstoff-Fabriken 36
Versailles, Treaty of (1919) 139, 186,
222
Vogt, Oblt Adolf **226**
Volkssturm (people's militia) 7
Vollmer, Heinrich 139, 140

Waffen-SS 40
Waffenrock see dress uniform
walking-out dress (*Ausgehenanzug*)
16
War Commemorative Cross
(*Kriegserinnerungsskreuz*) 220, **230**

War Merit Cross (*Kriegsverdienstkreuz*) 227–28, **230**, **240**

War Merit Medal (*Kriegsverdienstmedaille*) 228

War Service Cross ribbon **245**

watch coats (*Wachtmäntel*) 199

"Watch in the East" (*Wacht im Osten*) (Dielmann) **200**

water bottle (*Feldflasche*) 78, **94**, **105–7**, 115, **197**

weaponry 65, 72
  anti-tank (*Panzerfaust/schreck*) 171–72, **173**, 174, **175**, 176, **177**, 178, **179–80**, 181–82, **183**; automatic and semi-automatic rifles 142–45; edged 150, **151**, 152–54, **155**; machine guns 158, **159–60**, 161–62, **163–64**, 165–66, **167**, 168; mortars **156**, 168, **169–70**, 171; officers' daggers (*Dolche*) **26**, 27, 150, 154; pistols 132, **133**, 134, **135–37**, 138, 149; rifles **124**, 126, **127**, 128, **129–31**, 132, 171–72; submachine guns 139–42, **147**

Wehrmacht (German armed forces) 6

Weimar Republic (1918–33) 6

Welte, Josef 72

'West Wall Medal' (*Deutsches*

Schutzwall-Ehrenzeichen) 223–24, **235**, **240**

Westfälisch-Anhaltische-Sprengstoff AG (WASAG) 149

white tunic (*Weisser Rock*) **26**, **44**

wind jacket (*Windjacke*) 195

Winter Battle in the East 1941/42 (*Winterschlacht im Osten 1941/42*) 233–34, **240**, **243**

winter clothing 199, **200**, 201–2, **203–6**, 207–9

winter relief organization (*Winterhilfswerk*) 202

winter suit (*Winteranzug*) 202, **203**, 207–9

Wirtz, Franz 23, 87, **112**, 120

women **56**, 212–13, 216

wool 35, 36, 38–39, 44–45, 46

World War I (1914–18) 16, 40, 50, 100
  and headgear 60, 62, **63**, 64; and medals 220, **221**, 224, 228, 243; and mountain troops 58, 194; and personal equipment 78; and weaponry 132, 139, 142, 145, 161–62, 168; and women 212

Wound Badge (*Verwundetenabzeichen*) **17**, 228, **229**, **235**, **236**, 241, **243**, 244